By *Robert L. Heilbroner*

THE
WORLDLY
PHILOSOPHERS

The Lives, Times, and Ideas
of the Great Economic Thinkers

REVISED SEVENTH EDITION

Robert L. Heilbroner

A TOUCHSTONE BOOK
PUBLISHED BY SIMON & SCHUSTER

TOUCHSTONE
Rockefeller Center
1230 Avenue of the Americas
New York, NY 10020

Updated Seventh Edition

TOUCHSTONE and colophon are registered trademarks
of Simon & Schuster Inc.

Manufactured in the United States of America

13 15 17 19 20 18 16 14

Library of Congress Cataloging-in-Publication Data
Heilbroner, Robert L.
The worldly philosophers : the lives, times, and ideas of the
great economic thinkers / Robert L. Heilbroner. —Rev. 7th ed.
p.   cm.
"A Touchstone book."
Includes bibliographical references and index.
1. Economists—Biography. 2. Economics—History.
I. Title.
HB76.H4   1999
330'.092'2—dc21

[b]
                                                      99-14050
                                                           CIP

ISBN 0-684-86214-X

To my teachers

Preface to
the Seventh Edition

This is the seventh revision of a book I wrote some forty-six years ago, making *The Worldly Philosophers* today a good deal older than I was when I wrote it. The altogether unforeseen life span of this venture, undertaken when I was still a graduate student, serves as an excuse briefly to tell its story, before saying a word with respect to important changes that have been made in this latest, and, I expect, last edition.

While pursuing my graduate studies in the early 1950s, I earned my living as a free-lance writer, ranging very far from economics when the need or the occasion presented itself. As a consequence of one or another such piece, Joseph Barnes, a senior editor at Simon & Schuster, asked me to lunch to explore various book ideas. None of them seemed quite right, and a pall fell as the salad arrived and I realized that my first publisher's lunch was not likely to result in a book contract. Barnes, however, was not so easily discouraged. He began asking me about my graduate studies at the New School for Social Research and I found myself talking with enthusiasm about a particularly fascinating seminar on Adam Smith that I was taking under the inspired teaching of Adolph Lowe, of whom the reader will learn more later in this book. Before dessert had arrived we both knew that I had found my subject. After my next class I hastened to tell Professor Lowe of my determination to write a history of the evolution of economic thought.

The very exemplar of German scholarship at its formidable best, Lowe was aghast. "That you cannot do!" he declared with magisterial finality. But I had the strong conviction that I *could* do it—born, as I have written elsewhere, of the necessary combination of confidence and ignorance that only a graduate student could have possessed. Between free-lance assignments and further studies, I produced the first three chapters and with some trepidation showed them to Professor Lowe. It is a measure of that remarkable man (who remained, until his death at 102, my warmest and severest critic) that after he read the pages he said, "That you *must* do!" With his help, that is what I did.

The book written, it was necessary to find a title. I was aware that the word "economics" was death at the box office, and I racked my brains for a substitute. A second crucial lunch then took place with Frederick Lewis Allen, editor of *Harper's* magazine, for whom I had done a number of pieces, and who had been extraordinarily kind and helpful to me. I told him about my title difficulties, and said that I was thinking of calling the book *The Money Philosophers,* although I knew "money" wasn't quite right. "You mean 'worldly,'" he said. I said, "I'll buy lunch."

My publishers were not as pleased with the title as I was, and after the book to everyone's surprise began to sell, they suggested retitling it *The Great Economists.* Fortunately nothing came of this. Perhaps they anticipated that the public would not be able to master "worldly," which has indeed been misspelled "wordly" on a thousand students' papers, or perhaps they foresaw difficulties such as one about which I heard many years later. A student inquired at his college bookstore about a book whose author's name he could not remember, but whose queer title was, to the best of his recollection, "A World Full of Lobsters."

Over the years *The Worldly Philosophers* has sold more copies than I could have imagined possible, and has lured, I am told, tens of thousands of unsuspecting victims into a course on economics. I cannot answer for the pains that may have been experienced as a consequence, but I have had the pleasure of hearing from a number of economists that their interest was first aroused by the vision of economics conveyed by the book.

This edition differs from previous editions in two respects. The first is that, as before, a fresh look at its pages enables me to rectify the errors that inevitably creep into manuscripts or that are revealed by research after publication. It is a chance, as well, to alter emphases and interpretations that reflect my own evolving views. These changes are small, noticeable perhaps only to scholars in the field, and not of sufficient significance in themselves to warrant a new edition.

A second change is more important. For some time I had been considering whether there might not be an important thread missing from my book—a thread that would tie together its chapters more firmly than a mere chronology of remarkable men with interesting ideas. Then, a few years ago, I became convinced that precisely such a thread existed in the changing concepts—the "visions"—that lay behind all social analysis. That idea was broached in the 1950s by Josef Schumpeter, one of the most imaginative of the worldly philosophers. Insofar as Schumpeter himself did not apply his insight to the history of economic thought, I hope I may be forgiven for having missed it myself for so many years.

In this preface I do not want to discuss further this new view of the evolution of the worldly philosophy—that would be like announcing the plot of a mystery novel before the action had even begun. Hence, although the role of social vision will be mentioned many times as we go along, not until we reach our last chapter will we stop to consider its relevance for our own time.

That leads to a final remark. A reader who has already turned this page may have noted that that concluding chapter has a strange title: "The End of the Worldly Philosophy?" The question mark makes clear that this is not a pronouncement of doom, but it certainly implies a change in the character of our subject. As to what that change may be, we will have to wait until the very end of the book, not to tease the reader, but because only at the end—which is to say, today— does that change challenge the nature and significance of economic thought itself.

But all that remains to be demonstrated. Let me conclude this very personal salutation by thanking my readers,
especially students and instructors, who have been thoughtful enough to send me notes of correction, disagreement, or
approval, all equally welcomed, and to express my hope that
The Worldly Philosophers will continue to open the vista of
economics to readers who go on to become lobster fishermen
or publishers, as well as to those braver souls who decide to
become economists.

ROBERT L. HEILBRONER
New York, N.Y.
July, 1998

Contents

11

i

Introduction

This is a book about a handful of men with a curious claim to fame. By all the rules of schoolboy history books, they were nonentities: they commanded no armies, sent no men to their deaths, ruled no empires, took little part in history-making decisions. A few of them achieved renown, but none was ever a national hero; a few were roundly abused, but none was ever quite a national villain. Yet what they did was more decisive for history than many acts of statesmen who basked in brighter glory, often more profoundly disturbing than the shuttling of armies back and forth across frontiers, more powerful for good and bad than the edicts of kings and legislatures. It was this: they shaped and swayed men's minds.

And because he who enlists a man's mind wields a power even greater than the sword or the scepter, these men shaped and swayed the world. Few of them ever lifted a finger in action; they worked, in the main, as scholars—quietly, inconspicuously, and without much regard for what the world had to say about them. But they left in their train shattered empires and exploded continents; they buttressed and undermined political regimes; they set class against class and even nation against nation—not because they plotted mischief, but because of the extraordinary power of their ideas.

Who were these men? We know them as the Great

Economists. But what is strange is how little we know about them. One would think that in a world torn by economic problems, a world that constantly worries about economic affairs and talks of economic issues, the great economists would be as familiar as the great philosophers or statesmen. Instead they are only shadowy figures of the past, and the matters they so passionately debated are regarded with a kind of distant awe. Economics, it is said, is undeniably important, but it is cold and difficult, and best left to those who are at home in abstruse realms of thought.

Nothing could be further from the truth. A man who thinks that economics is only a matter for professors forgets that this is the science that has sent men to the barricades. A man who has looked into an economics textbook and concluded that economics is boring is like a man who has read a primer on logistics and decided that the study of warfare must be dull.

No, the great economists pursued an inquiry as exciting—and as dangerous—as any the world has ever known. The ideas they dealt with, unlike the ideas of the great philosophers, did not make little difference to our daily working lives; the experiments they urged could not, like the scientists', be carried out in the isolation of a laboratory. The notions of the great economists were world-shaking, and their mistakes nothing short of calamitous.

"The ideas of economists and political philosophers," wrote Lord Keynes, himself a great economist, "both when they are right and when they are wrong, are more powerful than is commonly understood. Indeed the world is ruled by little else. Practical men, who believe themselves to be quite exempt from any intellectual influences, are usually the slaves of some defunct economist. Madmen in authority, who hear voices in the air, are distilling their frenzy from some academic scribbler of a few years back. I am sure that the power of vested interests is vastly exaggerated compared with the gradual encroachment of ideas."

To be sure, not all the economists were such titans. Thousands of them wrote texts; some of them monuments of dullness, and explored minutiae with all the zeal of medieval scholars. If economics today has little glamour, if its sense of great adventure is often lacking, it has no one to blame but its own practitioners. For the great economists were no mere intellectual fusspots. They took the whole world as their subject and portrayed that world in a dozen bold attitudes—angry, desperate, hopeful. The evolution of their heretical opinions into common sense, and their exposure of common sense as superstition, constitute nothing less than the gradual construction of the intellectual architecture of much of contemporary life.

An odder group of men—one less apparently destined to remake the world—could scarcely be imagined.

There were among them a philosopher and a madman, a cleric and a stockbroker, a revolutionary and a nobleman, an aesthete, a skeptic, and a tramp. They were of every nationality, of every walk of life, of every turn of temperament. Some were brilliant, some were bores; some ingratiating, some impossible. At least three made their own fortunes, but as many could never master the elementary economics of their personal finances. Two were eminent businessmen, one was never much more than a traveling salesman, another frittered away his fortune.

Their viewpoints toward the world were as varied as their fortunes—there was never such a quarrelsome group of thinkers. One was a lifelong advocate of women's rights; another insisted that women were demonstrably inferior to men. One held that "gentlemen" were only barbarians in disguise, whereas another maintained that nongentlemen were savages. One of them—who was very rich—urged the abolition of riches; another—quite poor—disapproved of charity. Several of them claimed that with all its shortcomings, this was the best of all possible worlds; several others devoted their lives to proving that it wasn't.

All of them wrote books, but a more varied library has never been seen. One or two wrote best-sellers that reached to the mud huts of Asia; others had to pay to have their obscure works published and never touched an audience beyond the most restricted circles. A few wrote in language that stirred the pulse of millions; others—no less important to the world—wrote in a prose that fogs the brain.

Thus it was neither their personalities, their careers, their biases, nor even their ideas that bound them together. Their common denominator was something else: a common curiosity. They were all fascinated by the world about them, by its complexity and its seeming disorder, by the cruelty that it so often masked in sanctimony and the success of which it was equally often unaware. They were all of them absorbed in the behavior of their fellow man, first as he created material wealth, and then as he trod on the toes of his neighbor to gain a share of it.

Hence they can be called worldly philosophers, for they sought to embrace in a scheme of philosophy the most worldly of all of man's activities—his drive for wealth. It is not, perhaps, the most elegant kind of philosophy, but there is no more intriguing or more important one. Who would think to look for Order and Design in a pauper family and a speculator breathlessly awaiting ruin, or seek Consistent Laws and Principles in a mob marching in a street and a greengrocer smiling at his customers? Yet it was the faith of the great economists that just such seemingly unrelated threads could be woven into a single tapestry, that at a sufficient distance the milling world could be seen as an orderly progression, and the tumult resolved into a chord.

A large order of faith, indeed! And yet, astonishingly enough, it turned out to be justified. Once the economists had unfolded their patterns before the eyes of their generations, the pauper and the speculator, the greengrocer and the mob were no longer incongruous actors inexplicably thrown together on a stage; but each was understood to play a role, happy or otherwise, that was essential for the advancement of the human drama itself. When the economists were done, what had been only a humdrum or a chaotic world, became an ordered society with a meaningful life history of its own.

It is this search for the order and meaning of social history that lies at the heart of economics. Hence it is the central theme of this book. We are embarked not on a lecture tour of principles, but on a journey through history-shaping ideas. We will meet not only ~~pedagogues~~ *teachers* on our way, but many paupers, many speculators, both ruined and triumphant, many mobs, even here and there a grocer. We shall be going back to rediscover the roots of our own society in the welter of social patterns that the great economists discerned, and in so doing we shall come to know the great economists themselves—not merely because their personalities were often colorful, but because their ideas bore the stamp of their originators.

It would be convenient if we could begin straight off with the first of the great economists—Adam Smith himself. But Adam Smith lived at the time of the American Revolution, and we must account for the perplexing fact that six thousand years of recorded history had rolled by and no *worldly* philosopher had yet come to dominate the scene. An odd fact: Man had struggled with the economic problem since long before the time of the Pharaohs, and in these centuries he had produced philosophers by the score, scientists, political thinkers, historians, artists by the gross, statesmen by the hundred dozen. Why, then, were there no economists?

It will take us a chapter to find out. Until we have probed the nature of an earlier and far longer-lasting world than our own—a world in which an economist would have been not only unnecessary, but impossible—we cannot set the stage on which the great economists may take their places. Our main concern will be with the handful of men who lived in the last three centuries. First, however, we must understand the world that preceded their entrance and we must watch that earlier world give birth to the modern age— the age of the economists—amid all the upheaval and agony of a major revolution.

ii

The Economic Revolution

Since he came down from the trees, man has faced the problem of survival, not as an individual but as a member of a social group. His continued existence is testimony to the fact that he has succeeded in solving the problem; but the continued existence of want and misery, even in the richest of nations, is evidence that his solution has been, at best, a partial one.

Yet man is not to be too severely censured for his failure to achieve a paradise on earth. It is hard to wring a livelihood from the surface of this planet. It staggers the imagination to think of the endless efforts that must have been expended in the first domestication of animals, in the discovery of planting seed, in the first working of surface ores. It is only because man is a socially cooperative creature that he has succeeded in perpetuating himself at all.

But the very fact that he has had to depend on his fellow man has made the problem of survival extraordinarily difficult. Man is not an ant, conveniently equipped with an inborn pattern of social instincts. On the contrary, he seems to be strongly endowed with a self-centered nature. If his relatively weak physique forces him to seek cooperation, his inner drives constantly threaten to disrupt his social working partnerships.

In primitive society, the struggle between self-centered-ness and cooperation is taken care of by the environment; when the specter of starvation can look a community in the face—as with the Eskimos—the pure need to secure its own existence pushes society to the cooperative completion of its daily labors. Under less stringent conditions, anthropologists tell us, men and women perform their regular tasks under the powerful guidance of universally accepted norms of kinship and reciprocity: in her marvelous book on the African Bushmen, Elizabeth Marshall Thomas describes how a gemsbok is divided among relatives and relatives' relatives, until in the end "no person eats more than any other." But in an advanced community this tangible pressure of the environment, or this web of social obligations, is lacking. When men and women no longer work shoulder to shoulder in tasks directly related to survival—indeed when two-thirds of the population never touches the earth, enters the mines, builds with its hands, or even enters a factory—or when the claims of kinship have all but disappeared, the perpetuation of the human animal becomes a remarkable social feat.

So remarkable, in fact, that society's existence hangs by a hair. A modern community is at the mercy of a thousand dangers: if its farmers should fail to plant enough crops; if its railroad men should take it into their heads to become bookkeepers or its bookkeepers should decide to become railroad men; if too few should offer their services as miners, puddlers of steel, candidates for engineering degrees—in a word, if any of a thousand intertwined tasks of society should fail to get done—industrial life would soon become hopelessly disorganized. Every day the community faces the possibility of breakdown—not from the forces of nature, but from sheer human unpredictability.

Over the centuries man has found only three ways of guarding against this calamity.

He has ensured his continuity by organizing his society around tradition, by handing down the varied and necessary tasks from generation to generation according to custom and usage: son follows father, and a pattern is preserved. In ancient Egypt, says Adam Smith, "every man was bound by a principle of religion to follow the occupation of his father, and was supposed to commit the most horrible sacrilege if he changed it for another." Similarly, in India, until recently, certain occupations were traditionally assigned by caste; in fact, in much of the unindustrialized world one is still born to one's social task.

Or society can solve the problem differently. It can use the whip of authoritarian rule to see that its tasks get done. The pyramids of ancient Egypt did not get built because some enterprising contractor took it into his head to build them, nor did the Five Year Plans of the Soviet Union get carried out because they happened to accord with hand-me-down custom or individual self-interest. Both Russia and Egypt were Command societies; politics aside, they ensured their *economic* survival by the edicts of one authority and by the penalties that supreme authority saw fit to issue.

For countless centuries man dealt with the problem of survival according to one or the other of these solutions. And as long as the problem was handled by tradition or command, it never gave rise to that special field of study called "economics." Although the societies of history have shown the most astonishing economic diversity, although they have exalted kings and commissars, used dried codfish and immovable stones for money, distributed their goods in the simplest communistic patterns or in the most highly ritualistic fashion, so long as they ran by custom or command, they needed no economists to make them comprehensible. Theologians, political theorists, statesmen, philosophers, historians, yes—but, strange as it may seem, economists, no.

For the economists waited upon the invention of a third solution to the problem of survival. They waited upon the development of an astonishing arrangement in which society assured its own continuance by allowing each individual to do exactly as he saw fit—provided he followed a central guiding rule. The arrangement was called the "market system," and the rule was deceptively simple: each should do what was to his best monetary advantage. In the market system the lure of gain, not the pull of tradition or the whip of authority, steered the great majority to his (or her) task. And yet, although each was free to go wherever his acquisitive nose directed him, the interplay of one person against another resulted in the necessary tasks of society getting done.

It was this paradoxical, subtle, and difficult solution to the problem of survival that called forth the economists. For unlike the simplicity of custom and command, it was not at all obvious that with each person out only for his own gain, society could in fact endure. It was by no means clear that all the jobs of society—the dirty ones as well as the plush ones— would be done if custom and command no longer ran the world. When society no longer obeyed a ruler's dictates, who was to say where it would end?

It was the economists who undertook to explain this puzzle. But until the idea of the market system itself had gained acceptance, there was no puzzle to explain. And until a very few centuries ago, men were not at all sure that the market system was to be viewed without suspicion, distaste, and distrust. The world had gotten along for centuries in the comfortable rut of tradition and command; to abandon this security for the dubious and perplexing workings of the market system, nothing short of a revolution was required.

It was the most important revolution, from the point of view of shaping modern society, that ever took place—fundamentally more disturbing by far than the French, the American, or even the Russian Revolution. To appreciate its magnitude, to understand the wrenching that it gave society, we must immerse ourselves in that earlier and long-forgotten world from which our own society finally sprang. Only then will it be clear why the economists had so long to wait.

First stop: France. The year, 1305.

It is a fair we visit. The traveling merchants have arrived this morning with their armed guard, have set up their gaily striped tents, and are trading among themselves and with the local population. A variety of exotic goods is for sale: silks and taffetas, spices and perfumes, hides and furs. Some have been transported from the Levant, some from Scandinavia, some from only a few hundred miles away. Along with the common people, local lords and ladies frequent the stalls, eager to relieve the tedium of their boring, drafty, manorial lives; they are eagerly acquiring, along with the strange goods from Araby, new words from that incredibly distant land: divan, syrup, tariff, artichoke, spinach, jar.

But inside the tents, we meet with a strange sight. Books of business, open on the table, are sometimes no more than notebooks of transactions; a sample extract from one merchant reads: "Owed ten gulden by a man since Whitsuntide. I forgot his name." Calculations are made largely in Roman numerals, and sums are often wrong; long division is reckoned as something of a mystery, and the use of zero is not clearly understood. And for all the gaudiness of the display and the excitement of the people, the fair is a small thing. The total amount of goods which comes into France in a year over the Saint Gothard pass (on the first suspension bridge in history) would not fill a modern freight train; the total amount of merchandise carried in the great Venetian fleet would not fill one modern steel freighter.

Next stop: Germany. The year, 1550 odd.

Andreas Ryff, a merchant, bearded and fur-coated, is coming back to his home in Baden; he writes in a letter to his wife that he has visited thirty markets and is troubled with saddle burn. He is even more troubled by the nuisances of the times; as he travels he is stopped approximately once every ten miles to pay a customs toll; between Basle and Cologne he pays thirty-one levies.

And that is not all. Each community he visits has its own money, its own rules and regulations, its own law and order. In the area around Baden alone there are 112 different measures of length, 92 different square measures, 65 different dry measures, 163 different measures for cereals and 123 for liquids, 63 special measures for liquor, and 80 different pound weights

We move on: we are in Boston in the year 1639.

A trial is in progress; one Robert Keayne, "an ancient professor of the gospel, a man of eminent parts, wealthy and having but one child, and having come over for conscience' sake and for the advancement of the gospel," is charged with a heinous crime: he has made over sixpence profit on the shilling, an outrageous gain. The court is debating whether to excommunicate him for his sin, but in view of his spotless past it finally relents and dismisses him with a fine of two hundred pounds. But poor Mr. Keayne is so upset that before the elders of the Church he does "with tears acknowledge his covetous and corrupt heart." The minister of Boston cannot resist this golden opportunity to profit from the living example of a wayward sinner, and he uses the example of Keayne's avarice to thunder forth in his Sunday sermon on some false principles of trade. Among them are these:

I. That a man might sell as dear as he can, and buy as cheap as he can.

II. If a man lose by casualty of sea, etc., in some of his commodities, he may raise the price of the rest.

III. That he may sell as he bought, though he paid too dear . . .

All false, false, false, cries the minister; to seek riches for riches' sake is to fall into the sin of avarice. ➔ capitalism

We turn back to England and France.

In England a great trading organization, The Merchant Adventurers Company, has drawn up its articles of incorporation; among them are these rules for the participating merchants: no indecent language, no quarrels among the brethren, no card playing, no keeping of hunting dogs. No one is to carry unsightly bundles in the streets. This is indeed an odd business firm; it sounds more nearly like a fraternal lodge.

In France there has been entirely too much initiative displayed of late by the weaving industry, and a *règlement* has been promulgated by Colbert in 1666 to get away from this dangerous and disruptive tendency. Henceforth the fabrics of Dijon and Selangey are to contain 1,408 threads including selvages, neither more nor less. At Auxerre, Avallon, and two other manufacturing towns, the threads are to number 1,376; at Châtillon, 1,216. Any cloth found to be objectionable is to be pilloried. If it is found three times to be objectionable, the merchant is to be pilloried instead.

There is something common to all these scattered fragments of bygone worlds. It is this: first, the idea of the propriety (not to say the necessity) of a system organized on the basis of *personal gain* has not yet taken root. Second, a separate, self-contained economic world has not yet lifted itself from its social context. The world of practical affairs is inextricably mixed up with the world of political, social, and religious life. Until the two worlds separate, there will be nothing that resembles the tempo and the feeling of modern life. And for the two to separate, a long and bitter struggle must take place.

It may strike us as odd that the idea of gain is a relatively modern one; we are schooled to believe that man is essentially an acquisitive creature and that left to himself he will behave as any self-respecting businessman would. The profit motive, we are constantly being told, is as old as man himself.

But it is not. The profit motive as we know it is only as old as "modern man." Even today the notion of gain for gain's sake is foreign to a large portion of the world's population, and it has been conspicuous by its absence over most of recorded history. Sir William Petty, an astonishing seventeenth-century character (who was in his lifetime cabin boy, hawker, clothier, physician, professor of music, and founder of a school named Political Arithmetick), claimed that when wages were good, labor was "scarce to be had at all, so licentious are they who labor only to eat, or rather to drink." And Sir William was not merely venting the bourgeois prejudices of his day. He was observing a fact that can still be remarked among the unindustrialized peoples of the world: a raw working force, unused to wagework, uncomfortable in factory life, unschooled to the idea of an ever-rising standard of living, will not work harder if wages rise; it will simply take more time off. The idea of gain, the idea that each working person not only may, but should, constantly strive to better his or her material lot, is an idea that was quite foreign to the great lower and middle strata of Egyptian, Greek, Roman, and medieval cultures, only scattered throughout Renaissance and Reformation times; and largely absent in the majority of

Eastern civilizations. As a ubiquitous characteristic of society, it is as modern an invention as printing.

Not only is the idea of gain by no means as universal as we sometimes suppose, but the social sanction of gain is an even more modern and restricted development. In the Middle Ages the Church taught that no Christian ought to be a merchant, and behind that teaching lay the thought that merchants were a disturbing yeast in the leaven of society. In Shakespeare's time the object of life for the ordinary citizen, for everybody, in fact, except the gentility, was not to advance his station in life, but to maintain it. Even to our Pilgrim forefathers, the idea that gain might be a tolerable—even a useful—goal in life would have appeared as nothing short of a doctrine of the devil. but w/ religion seperate from the raffain's now.

Wealth, of course, there has always been, and covetousness is at least as old as the Biblical tales. But there is a vast deal of difference between the envy inspired by the wealth of a few mighty personages and a general struggle for wealth diffused throughout society. Merchant adventurers have existed as far back as the Phoenician sailors, and can be seen all through history, in the speculators of Rome, the trading Venetians, the Hanseatic League, and the great Portuguese and Spanish voyagers who sought a route to the Indies and to their personal fortunes. But the adventures of a few are a far different thing from an entire society moved by the venture spirit.

Take, for example, the extraordinary family of the Fuggers, the great German bankers of the sixteenth century. At their height, the Fuggers owned gold and silver mines, trade concessions, and even the right to coin their own money; their credit was far greater than the wealth of the kings and emperors whose wars (and household expenses) they financed. But when old Anton Fugger died, his eldest nephew, Hans Jacob, refused to take over the banking empire on the ground that the business of the city and his own affairs gave him too much to do; Hans Jacob's brother, George, said he would rather live in peace; a third nephew, Christopher, was equally uninterested. None of the potential heirs to a kingdom of wealth apparently thought it was worth the bother.

Apart from kings (those that were solvent) and a scatter-
ing of families like the Fuggers, the early capitalists were not
the pillars of society, but often its outcasts and *déracinés*.
Here and there an enterprising lad like Saint Godric of Fin-
chale would start as a beachcomber, gather enough wares
from the wrecks of ships to become a merchant, and, after
making his fortune, retire in sanctity as a hermit. But such
men were few. As long as the paramount idea was that life on
earth was only a trying preamble to Life Eternal, the business
spirit neither was encouraged nor found spontaneous nour-
ishment. Kings wanted treasure, and for that they fought
wars; the nobility wanted land, and since no self-respecting
nobleman would willingly sell his ancestral estates, that entailed conquest, too. But most people—serfs, village crafts-
men, even the masters of the manufacturing guilds—wanted
to be left alone to live as their fathers had lived and as their
sons would live in turn.

The absence of the idea of gain as a normal guide for
daily life—in fact the positive disrepute in which the idea was
held by the Church—constituted one enormous difference
between the strange world of the tenth to sixteenth centuries
and the world that began, a century or two before Adam
Smith, to resemble our own. But there was an even more
fundamental difference. The idea of "making a living" had
not yet come into being. Economic life and social life were
one and the same thing. Work was not yet a means to an
end—the end being money and the things it buys. Work was
an end in itself, encompassing, of course, money and commodities, but engaged in as a part of a tradition, as a natural
way of life. In a word, the great social invention of "the market" had not yet been made.

Markets have existed as far back as history goes. The
Tablets of Tell-el-Amarna tell of lively trade between the
Pharaohs and the Levantine kings in 1400 B.C.: gold and war
chariots were swapped for slaves and horses. But while the
idea of exchange must be very nearly as old as man, as with
the idea of gain, we must not make the mistake of assuming
that all the world has the bargaining propensities of a mod-

ern-day American schoolboy. Purely by way of curious illustration, it is reported that among the New Zealand Maoris you cannot ask how much food a bonito hook is worth, for such a trade is never made and the question would be regarded as ridiculous. By way of turnabout, however, in some African communities it is perfectly legitimate to inquire how many oxen a woman is worth—an exchange which we look upon as the Maoris look upon swapping food and fishhooks (although where dowries still exist, they narrow the gap between ourselves and these Africans).

But markets, whether they be exchanges between primitive tribes where objects are casually dropped on the ground or the exciting traveling fairs of the Middle Ages, are not the same as the market system. For the market system is not just a means of exchanging goods; *it is a mechanism for sustaining and maintaining an entire society.*

And that mechanism was far from clear to the minds of the medieval world. The concept of widespread gain was blasphemous enough, as we have seen. The broader notion that a general struggle for gain might actually bind together a community would have been held as little short of madness.

There was a reason for this blindness. The Middle Ages, the Renaissance, the Reformation—indeed the whole world until the sixteenth or seventeenth century—could not envisage the market system for the thoroughly sound reason that Land, Labor, and Capital—the basic agents of production which the market system allocates—did not yet exist. Land, labor, and capital in the sense of soil, human beings, and tools are of course coexistent with society itself. But the idea of abstract land or abstract labor did not immediately suggest itself to the human mind any more than did the idea of abstract energy or matter. Land, labor, and capital as "agents of production, as impersonal, dehumanized economic entities, are as much modern conceptions as the calculus. Indeed, they are not much older.

Take, for example, land. As late as the fourteenth or fifteenth century there was no such thing as land in the sense of freely salable, rent-producing property. There were lands, of course—estates, manors, and principalities—but these were emphatically not real estate to be bought and sold as the occasion warranted. Such lands formed the core of social life, provided the basis for prestige and status, and constituted the foundation for the military, judicial, and administrative organization of society. Although land was salable under certain conditions (with many strings attached), it was not generally *for sale*. A medieval nobleman in good standing would no more have thought of selling his land than the governor of Connecticut would think of selling a few counties to the governor of Rhode Island.

The same lack of salability was true for labor. When we talk of the labor market today, we mean the great network of job-seeking in which individuals sell their services to the highest bidder. There simply was no such network in the precapitalist world. There was a vast hodgepodge of serfs, apprentices, and journeymen who labored, but most of this labor never entered a market to be bought and sold. In the country, the peasant lived tied to his lord's estate; he baked at the lord's oven and ground at the lord's mill, tilled the lord's fields and served his lord in war, but he was rarely if ever paid for any of his services: these were his duties as a serf, not the "labor" of a freely contracting agent. In the towns the apprentice entered the service of a master; the length of his apprenticeship, the number of his colleagues, his rate of pay, his hours of work, the very methods he used, were all regulated by a guild. There was little or no bargaining between servant and master except for sporadic strikes when conditions became intolerable. This was no more of a labor market than is provided by interns in a hospital.

Or take capital. Certainly capital existed in the precapitalist world, in the sense of private wealth. But although the funds existed, there was no impetus to put them to new and aggressive use. Instead of risk and change, the motto was "Safety first." Not the shortest and most efficient, but the longest and most labor-consuming process was the preferred technique of production. Advertising was forbidden, and the idea that one master guildsman might produce a better product than his colleagues was regarded as treasonable. In sixteenth-century England, when mass production in the weaving trade first reared its ugly head, the guilds protested to the king. The "wonderworkshop"—reputedly containing two hundred looms and a service staff including butchers and bakers to take care of the working force—was thereupon outlawed by His Majesty: such efficiency and concentration of wealth would set a bad precedent. *why?*

Hence the fact that the medieval world could not conceive the market system rested on the good and sufficient reason that it had not yet conceived the abstract elements of production itself. Lacking land, labor, and capital, the Middle Ages lacked the market; and lacking the market (despite its colorful local marts and traveling fairs), society ran by local command and tradition. The lords gave orders, and production waxed and waned accordingly. Where no orders were given, life went on in its established groove. Had Adam Smith lived in the years before 1400 he would have felt no need to construct a theory of political economy. There was no mystery to penetrate in understanding what made the Middle Ages hang together and no veil to pierce to discover both order and design. Ethics and politics, yes; there was much to be explained and rationalized in the relations of lower lords to higher lords and higher lords to kings, and a great deal to be puzzled over in the conflict between the teachings of the Church and the incorrigible tendencies of the merchant class. But economics, no. Who would look for abstract laws of supply and demand, or cost, or value, when the explanation of the world lay like an open book in the laws of the manor and the Church and the city, along with the customs of a lifetime? Adam Smith might have been a great moral philosopher in that earlier age, but he could never have been a great economist; there would have been nothing for him to do.

There would be nothing for any economist to do for several centuries—until this great self-reproducing, self-sufficient world erupted into the bustling, scurrying, free-for-all of the eighteenth century. "Erupted" is perhaps too dramatic a word, for the change would take place over centuries rather than in a single violent spasm. But the change, long drawn out though it was, was not a peaceful evolution; it was an agonized convulsion of society, a revolution.

Just to commercialize the land—to convert the hierarchy of social relationships into so many vacant lots and advantageous sites—required nothing less than the uprooting of an entrenched feudal way of life. To make "workers" out of the sheltered serfs and apprentices—no matter how exploitative the cloak of paternalism might have been—required the creation of a frightened disoriented class called the proletariat. To make capitalists out of guild masters meant that the laws of the jungle had to be taught to the timid denizens of the barnyard.

Hardly a peaceful prospect, any of this. Nobody *wanted* this commercialization of life. How bitterly it was resisted can be appreciated only if we take one last journey back to watch the economic revolution taking place.

We are back in France; the year, 1666.

The capitalists of the day face a disturbing challenge that the widening market mechanism has inevitably brought in its wake: change.

The question has come up whether a guild master of the weaving industry should be allowed to try an innovation in his product. The verdict: "If a cloth weaver intends to process a piece according to his own invention, he must not set it on the loom, but should obtain permission from the judges of the town to employ the number and length of threads that he desires, after the question has been considered by four of the oldest merchants and four of the oldest weavers of the guild." One can imagine how many suggestions for change were proposed.

Shortly after the matter of cloth weaving has been disposed of, the button makers guild raises a cry of outrage; the tailors are beginning to make buttons out of cloth, an unheard-of thing. The government, indignant that an innovation should threaten a settled industry, imposes a fine on the cloth-button makers. But the wardens of the button guild are not yet satisfied. They demand the right to search people's homes and wardrobes and fine and even arrest them on the streets if they are seen wearing these subversive goods.

And this dread of change and innovation is not just the comic resistance of a few frightened merchants. Capital is fighting in earnest against change, and no holds are barred. In England some years earlier, a revolutionary patent for a stocking frame not only was denied, but the Privy Council ordered the dangerous contraption abolished. In France the importation of printed calicoes now threatens to undermine the clothing industry. It is met with measures that cost the lives of 16,000 people! In Valence alone on one occasion 77 persons are sentenced to be hanged, 58 broken on the wheel, 631 sent to the galleys, and one lone and lucky individual is set free, for the crime of dealing in forbidden calico wares.

But capital is not the only agent of production that is frantically seeking to avoid the dangers of the market way of life. What is happening to labor is still more desperate.

Let us turn back to England.

It is the end of the sixteenth century, the great era of English expansion and adventure. Queen Elizabeth has made a triumphal tour of her kingdom. But she returns with a strange plaint. "Paupers are everywhere!" she cries. This is a strange observation, for only a hundred years before, the English countryside consisted in large part of peasant proprietors tilling their own lands, the yeomen, the pride of England, the largest body of independent, free, and prosperous citizens in the world. Now, "Paupers are everywhere!" What has happened in the interim?

What has happened has been an enormous movement of expropriation—or, rather, the beginning of such a movement, for it was then only in its inception. Wool has become a new, profitable commodity, and wool demands grazing pastures for the wool producer. The pastures are made by enclosing the common land; the patchwork crazy quilt of small scattered holdings (unfenced and recognizable only by a tree here and a rock there, dividing one man's land from another) and the common lands on which all might graze their cattle or gather peat are suddenly declared to be all the property of the lord of the manor and no longer available to the whole parish. Where before was a kind of communality of ownership, now there is private property. Where there were yeomen, now there are sheep. One John Hales wrote in

1549: ". . . where XL persons had their lyvings, now one man and his shepherd hath all. . . . Yes, those shepe is the cause of all theise meschieves, for they have driven husbandrie out of the countries, by the which was encreased before all kynde of victuall, and now altogether shepe, shepe."

It is almost impossible to imagine the scope and impact of the process of enclosure. As early as the middle of the sixteenth century, riots had broken out against it; in one such uprising, 3,500 people were killed. In the mid-eighteenth century, the process was still in full swing; not until the mid-nineteenth would it have run its terrible historic course. Thus, in 1820, nearly fifty years after the American Revolution, the Duchess of Sutherland dispossessed 15,000 tenants from 794,000 acres of land, replaced them with 131,000 sheep, and by way of compensation rented her evicted families an average of two acres of submarginal land each.

But it was not merely the wholesale land-grabbing that warrants attention. The tragedy is what happened to the peasant. Deprived of the right to use the common land, he could no longer maintain himself as a "farmer." Since no factories were available, he could not—even if he had wanted to—metamorphose into a factory worker. Instead, he became that most miserable of all social classes, an agricultural proletarian, and where agricultural work was lacking, a beggar, sometimes a robber, usually a pauper. Terrified at the alarming increase in pauperism throughout the country, the English Parliament tried to deal with the problem by localizing it. It tied paupers to their parishes for a pittance of relief and dealt with wanderers by whipping, branding, and mutilation. A clergyman at the time of Adam Smith seriously described the parochial workhouses in which the poor were kept as "Houses of Terror." But what was worst of all was that the very measures that the country took to protect itself from the pauper—tying him to his local parish where he could be kept alive on poor relief—prevented the only possible solution to the problem. It was not that the English ruling classes were utterly heartless and cruel. Rather, they failed to understand the concept of a fluid, mobile labor force that would seek work wherever work was to be found according to the dictates of the market. At every step, the commercialization of labor, like the commercialization of capital, was misconceived, feared, and fought.

The market system with its essential components of land, labor, and capital was thus born in agony—an agony that began in the thirteenth century and had not run its course until well into the nineteenth. Never was a revolution less well understood, less welcomed, less planned. But the great market-making forces would not be denied. Insidiously they ripped apart the mold of custom; insolently they tore away the usages of tradition. For all the clamor of the button makers, cloth buttons won the day. For all the action of the Privy Council, the stocking frame became so valuable that in another seventy years the same Privy Council would forbid its exportation. For all the breakings on the wheel, the trade in calicoes increased apace. Over last-ditch opposition from the Old Guard, economic land was created out of ancestral estates, and over the wails of protest from employees and masters alike, economic labor was ground out of unemployed apprentices and dispossessed farm laborers.

The great chariot of society, which for so long had run down the gentle slope of tradition, now found itself powered by an internal combustion machine. Transactions, transactions, transactions and gain, gain, gain provided a new and startlingly powerful motive force.

What forces could have been sufficiently powerful to smash a comfortable and established world and institute in its place this new unwanted society?

There was no single massive cause. The new way of life grew inside the old, like a butterfly inside a chrysalis, and when the stir of life was strong enough it burst the old structure asunder. It was not great events, single adventures, individual laws, or powerful personalities that brought about the economic revolution. It was a process of spontaneous, many-sided change.

First, there was the gradual emergence of national political units in Europe. Under the blows of peasant wars and kingly conquest, the isolated existence of early feudalism gave way to centralized monarchies. And with monarchies came the growth of the national spirit; in turn this meant royal patronage for favored industries, such as the great French tapestry works, and the development of armadas and armies with all their necessary satellite industries. The infinity of rules and regulations which plagued Andreas Ryff and his fellow sixteenth-century traveling merchants gave way to national laws, common measurements, and more or less standardized currencies.

An aspect of the political change that was revolutionizing Europe was the encouragement of foreign adventure and exploration. In the thirteenth century, the brothers Polo went as unprotected merchants on their daring journey into the land of the great Khan; in the fifteenth century Columbus sailed for what he hoped would be the same destination under the royal auspices of Isabella. The change from private to national exploration was part and parcel of the change from private to national life. And in turn the great national adventures of the English and Spanish and Portuguese sailor-capitalists brought a flood of treasure and treasure-consciousness back to Europe. "He who has gold," Christopher Columbus said, "makes and accomplishes whatever he wishes in the world and finally uses it to send souls into paradise." The sentiments of Christopher Columbus were the sentiments of an age, and hastened the advent of a society oriented toward gain and chance and activated by the chase after money. Be it noted, in passing, that the treasures of the East were truly fabulous. With the share received as a stockholder in Sir Francis Drake's voyage of the *Golden Hynd,* Queen Elizabeth paid off all England's foreign debts, balanced its budget, and invested abroad a sum large enough, at compound interest, to account for Britain's entire overseas wealth in 1930!

A second great current of change was to be found in the slow decay of the religious spirit under the impact of the skeptical, inquiring, humanist views of the Italian Renaissance. The world of Today elbowed aside the world of Tomorrow, and as life on earth became more important, so did the notion of material standards and ordinary comforts. Behind the change in religious tolerance was the rise of Protestantism, which hastened a new attitude toward work and wealth. The Church of Rome had always regarded the merchant with a dubious eye and had not hesitated to call usury a sin. But now that this merchant was every day climbing in society, now that he was no longer a mere useful appendage but an integral part of a new kind of world, some reevaluation of his function became necessary. The Protestant leaders paved the way for an amalgamation of spiritual and temporal life. Far from eulogizing the life of poverty and spiritual contemplation, as separate from worldly life, they preached that it was pious to make the most of one's God-given talents in daily business. Acquisitiveness became a recognized virtue—not immediately for one's private enjoyment, but for the greater glory of God. From here it was only a step to the identification of riches with spiritual excellence, and of rich men with saintly ones.

A local folk tale from the twelfth century tells of a usurer who was crushed by a falling statue as he was entering a church to be married. On examination, the statue was found to be that of another usurer, thus revealing God's displeasure with dealers in money. Even in the mid-1600s, as we may remember, poor Robert Keayne collided head on with the Puritan religious authorities because of his business practices. In such an atmosphere of hostility, it was not easy for the market system to expand. Hence the gradual acceptance by the spiritual leaders of the innocuousness, indeed the benefits, of the market way was essential for the full growth of the system.   *Inoffensive*

Still another deep current lies in the material changes that eventually made the market system possible. We are accustomed to thinking of the Middle Ages as a time of stagnation and lack of progress. Yet in five hundred years, the feudal age fathered one thousand towns (an immense achievement), connected them with rudimentary but usable roads, and maintained their populations with food brought from the countryside. All this developed the familiarity with money and markets and the buying and selling way of life. In the course of this change, power naturally began to gravitate into the hands of those who understood money matters—the merchants—and away from the disdainful nobility, who did not.

Progress was not only a matter of this slow monetization. There was technical progress too, of a vastly important sort. The commercial revolution could not begin until some form of rational money accounting had developed: although the Venetians of the twelfth century were already using sophisticated accounting devices, the merchants in Europe were little better than schoolboys in their accounting ignorance. It took time for a recognition of the need for bookkeeping to spread; not until the seventeenth century was double entry a standard practice. And not until money was rationally accounted for could large-scale business operations run successfully.

Perhaps the most important change of all in the pervasiveness of its effect was a rise in scientific curiosity. Although the world would wait until after the age of Adam Smith for its pyrotechnic burst of technology, the Industrial Revolution could not have taken place had not the ground been prepared by a succession of basic subindustrial discoveries. The precapitalist era saw the birth of the printing press, the paper mill, the windmill, the mechanical clock, the map, and a host of other inventions. The idea of invention itself took hold; experimentation and innovation were looked on for the first time with a friendly eye.

No single one of these currents, acting by itself, could have turned society upside down. Indeed, many of them might have been as much the effects as the causes of a great convulsion in human organization. History takes no sharp corners, and the whole vast upheaval sprawled out over time. Evidences of the market way of life sprang up side by side with older traditional ways, and remnants of the former day persisted long after the market had for all practical purposes taken over as the guiding principle of economic organization. Thus, guilds and feudal privileges were not finally abolished in France until 1790, and the Statute of Artificers which regulated guild practices in England was not repealed until 1813.

But by the year 1700, twenty-three years before Adam Smith was born, the world that had tried Robert Keayne, prohibited merchants from carrying unsightly bundles, worried over "just" prices, and fought for the privilege of carrying on in its fathers' footsteps was on the wane. In its place society has begun to heed a new set of "self-evident" dicta. Some of them are:

"Every man is naturally covetous of lucre."

"No laws are prevalent against gaine."

"Gaine is the Centre of the Circle of Commerce."

A new idea had come into being: "economic man"—a pale wraith of a creature who followed his adding-machine brain wherever it led him. The textbooks would soon come to talk of Robinson Crusoes on desert isles who organized their affairs as if they were so many penny-pinching accountants.

In the world of affairs a new fever of wealth and speculation had gripped Europe. In France in 1718 a Scottish adventurer named John Law organized a wild blue-sky venture known as the Mississippi Company, selling shares in an enterprise that would mine the mountains of gold in America. Men and women fought in the streets for the privilege of winning shares, murders were committed, fortunes made overnight. One hotel waiter netted thirty million *livres*. When the company was about to topple with frightful losses for all investors, the government sought to stave off disaster by rounding up a thousand beggars, arming them with picks and shovels, and marching them through the streets of Paris as a band of miners off for the Land of Eldorado. Of course, the structure collapsed. But what a change from the timid capitalists of a hundred years before to the get-rich-quick mobs jostling in the Rue de Quincampoix; what a money-hungry public this must have been to swallow such a bare-faced fraud!

No mistake about it, the travail was over and the market system had been born. The problem of survival was henceforth to be solved neither by custom nor by command, but by the free action of profit-seeking men bound together only by the market itself. The system was to be called capitalism, although the word would not be widely used until the late nineteenth century! And the idea of gain which underlay it was to become so firmly rooted that men would soon vigorously affirm that it was an eternal and omnipresent part of human nature.

The idea needed a philosophy.

The human animal, it is repeatedly said, is distinguished above all by his self-consciousness. This seems to mean that, having set up his society, he is not content to let things be; he must tell himself that the particular society in which he lives is the best of all possible societies, and that the arrangements within it mirror in their own small way the arrangements that providence has made outside. Hence every age breeds its philosophers, apologists, critics, and reformers.

But the questions with which the earliest social philosophers concerned themselves were focused on the political rather than the economic side of life. As long as custom and command ruled the world, the problem of riches and poverty hardly struck the earlier philosophers at all, other than to be accepted with a sigh or railed at as another sign of man's inner worthlessness. As long as men, like bees, were born to be drones, no one much worried over the rationale of the laboring poor—the vagaries of queens were infinitely more elevating and exciting.

"From the hour of their birth," wrote Aristotle, "some are marked out for subjection, others for rule," and in that comment was summed up not so much the contempt as the indifference with which the early philosophers looked at the workaday world. The existence of a vast laboring substratum was simply taken for granted, and money and market matters were not only too sweaty but too vulgar to engage the consideration of a gentleman and a scholar. It was the rights of kings, divine and otherwise, and the great questions of power temporal and power spiritual which provided the arena for the contest of ideas—not the pretensions of pushy merchants. Although personal riches had their role to play in making the world go round, until the struggle for riches became general, ubiquitous, and patently vital to society, there was no need for a general philosophy of riches.

But one might ignore the nasty struggling aspect of the marketplace world for just so long; then one might fulminate

against it. Finally when it penetrated to the very sanctums of
the philosophers themselves, it was better to ask whether
even here the evidences of some master pattern might not
yet be seen. To this end, for two hundred years before Adam
Smith, the philosophers spun their theories of daily life.

But into what a strange succession of molds they cast the
world as they sought to reveal its underlying purposes!

At first the wretched struggle for existence found its be-
all and end-all in the accumulation of gold. Christopher
Columbus, Cortés, and Francis Drake were not only state adventurers; they were thought to be the agents of *economic
progress* as well. To the Mercantilists (as we call the group of
pamphleteers and essayists who wrote on trade), it was evident that national power was the natural object of economic
endeavor, and that the most important ingredient in national
power was gold. Theirs was thus a philosophy of great armadas and adventures, kingly wealth and national stinginess,
and an overriding belief that if all went well in the search for
treasure, a nation could scarcely fail to prosper.

Was there a unifying concept behind these ideas? Here
we confront for the first time the notion mentioned at the
end of our preface—the idea that "visions" underlie and pre-
cede practice. There is, in fact, a realization of such a vision
in the frontispiece to *Leviathan*, the influential tract published in 1651 by the English philosopher and political theo-
rist Thomas Hobbes. The etching shows an immense figure
towering over and protecting a placid countryside below. It is
a king—sword in one hand, royal sceptre in the other—
whose suit of armor, on close inspection, reveals that each of
its platelets depicts the head of a human being.

Note that this is a political, not an economic vision. The
central argument of *Leviathan* is that an all-powerful state is
necessary to prevent human beings from falling into a condition described by Hobbes as "solitary, poore, nasty, brutish,
and short." Although mercantile activities played an important role, they threatened to disturb, as well as to support the
all-important State. Thus, for all their interest in accumulating bullion, a common concern of all royal houses was that
merchant ships would bring gold to foreign countries where

it would be spent for silks and other luxuries, to the loss of the royal treasury.

Yet, even here, the vision serves as the basis for the first efforts to formulate what we would call economic analysis. Even before *Leviathan* appeared, spokesmen for the world of commerce were publishing pamphlets whose purpose was to show that the merchant ships sailing down the Thames were an asset, not a threat, to the sovereign. True, some of the gold they carried abroad might be spent for foreign goods, but the British goods they also carried would be sold for even more gold. Indeed, as Thomas Mun, director of the East India company, explained in *England's Treasure by Forraign Trade*, the "ordinary means" by which a nation increased its wealth and treasure was by trade, "wherein wee must ever observe this rule; to sell more to strangers yearly than wee consume of theirs in Value."

By the eighteenth century the initial emphasis on gold was beginning to look a trifle naïve. New schools of thought were growing up which more and more emphasized *commerce* as the great source of national vitality. Hence the philosophical question to which they addressed themselves was not how to corner the gold market but how to create ever more and more wealth by assisting the rising merchant class in the furtherance of its tasks.

The new philosophy brought with it a new social problem: how to keep the poor poor. It was generally admitted that unless the poor were poor, they could not be counted upon to do an honest day's toil without asking for exorbitant wages. "To make the Society Happy. . . , it is requisite that great numbers should be Ignorant as well as Poor," wrote Bernard Mandeville, the shrewdest and wickedest social commentator of the early eighteenth century. So the Mercantilist writers looked on the cheap agricultural and industrial labor of England and gravely nodded approval.

Gold and commerce were by no means the only ideas that superimposed some kind of order over the chaos of daily life. There were countless pamphleteers, parsons, cranks, and bigots who sought justification—or damnation—for society in a dozen different explanations. But the trouble was, all the models were so unsatisfactory. One man said a nation obviously must not buy more than it sells, while another as stoutly maintained that a nation was quite obviously better off if it took in more than it gave in exchange. Some insisted it was trade that made a nation rich, and exalted the trader; others argued that trade was only a parasitical growth on the strong body of the farmer. Some said the poor were meant by God to be poor and even if they weren't, their poverty was essential to the wealth of the nation; others saw in pauperism a social evil and could not see how poverty could create wealth.

Out of the *mêlée* of contradictory rationalizations one thing alone stood clear: man insisted on some sort of intellectual ordering to help him understand the world in which he lived. The harsh and disconcerting economic world loomed ever more important. No wonder Dr. Samuel Johnson himself said, "There is nothing which requires more to be illustrated by philosophy than trade does." In a word, the time for the economists had arrived.

Out of the *mêlée* came also a philosopher of astonishing scope. Adam Smith published his *Inquiry into the Nature and Causes of the Wealth of Nations* in 1776, thereby adding a second revolutionary event to that fateful year. A political democracy was born on one side of the ocean; an economic blueprint was unfolded on the other. But while not all Europe followed America's political lead, after Smith had displayed the first true tableau of modern society, all the Western world became the world of Adam Smith: his vision became the prescription for the spectacles of generations. Adam Smith would never have thought of himself as a revolutionist; he was only explaining what to him was very clear, sensible, and conservative. But he gave the world the image of itself for which it had been searching. After *The Wealth of Nations*, men began to see the world about themselves with new eyes; they saw how the tasks they did fitted into the whole of society, and they saw that society as a whole was proceeding at a majestic pace toward a distant but clearly visible goal. In a word, a new vision had come into being.

The Wonderful World of Adam Smith

— positive
— capitalism solves all the problems

What was that new vision? As we might expect, it was not a State but a System—more precisely, a System of Perfect Liberty. But it would be a mistake to plunge into its extraordinary conception until we had made the acquaintance of its no less extraordinary—certainly unusual—author.

A visitor to England in the 1760s would quite probably have learned of a certain Adam Smith of the University of Glasgow. Dr. Smith was a well-known, if not a famous, man; Voltaire had heard of him, David Hume was his intimate, students had traveled all the way from Russia to hear his labored but enthusiastic discourse. In addition to being renowned for his scholastic accomplishments, Dr. Smith was known as a remarkable personality. He was, for example, notoriously absentminded: once, walking along in earnest disquisition with a friend, he fell into a tanning pit, and it was said that he had brewed himself a beverage of bread and butter and pronounced it the worst cup of tea he had ever tasted. But his personal quirks, which were many, did not interfere with his intellectual abilities. Adam Smith was among the foremost philosophers of his age.

At Glasgow, Adam Smith lectured on problems of Moral Philosophy, a discipline a great deal more broadly conceived in that day than in ours. Moral Philosophy covered Natural Theology, Ethics, Jurisprudence, and Political Economy: it thus ranged all the way from man's sublimest impulses toward order and harmony to his somewhat less orderly and harmonious activities in the grimmer business of gouging out a living for himself.

Natural theology—the search for design in the confusion of the cosmos—had been an object of the human rationalizing impulse from earliest times; our traveler would have felt quite at ease as Dr. Smith expounded the natural laws that underlay the seeming chaos of the universe. But when it came to the other end of the spectrum—the search for a grand architecture beneath the hurly-burly of daily life—our traveler might have felt that the good doctor was really stretching philosophy beyond its proper limits.

For if the English social scene of the late eighteenth century suggested anything, it was most emphatically not rational order or moral purpose. As soon as one looked away from the elegant lives of the leisure classes, society presented itself as a brute struggle for existence in its meanest form. Outside the drawing rooms of London or the pleasant rich estates of the counties, all that one saw was rapacity, cruelty, and degradation mingled with the most irrational and bewildering customs and traditions of some still earlier and already anachronistic day. Rather than a carefully engineered machine where each part could be seen to contribute to the whole, the body social resembled one of James Watt's strange steam machines: black, noisy, inefficient, dangerous. How curious that Dr. Smith should have professed to see order, design, and purpose in all of this!

Suppose, for example, our visitor had gone to see the tin mines of Cornwall. There he would have watched miners lower themselves down the black shafts, and on reaching bottom draw a candle from their belts and stretch out for a sleep until the candle guttered. Then for two or three hours they would work the ore until the next traditional break, this time for as long as it took to smoke a pipe. A full half-day was spent in lounging, half in picking at the seams. But had our visitor traveled up north and nerved himself against a descent into the pits of Durham or Northumberland, he would have seen something quite different. Here men and women worked together, stripped to the waist, and sometimes reduced from pure fatigue to a whimpering half-human state. The wildest and most brutish customs were practiced; sexual appetites aroused at a glance were gratified down some deserted shaftway; children of seven or ten who never saw daylight during the winter months were used and abused and paid a pittance by the miners to help drag away their tubs of coal; pregnant women drew coal cars like horses and even gave birth in the dark black caverns.

But it was not just in the mines that life appeared colorful, traditional, or ferocious. On the land, too, an observant traveler would have seen sights hardly more suggestive of order, harmony, and design. In many parts of the country bands of agricultural poor roamed in search of work. From the Welsh highlands, Companies of Ancient Britons (as they styled themselves) would come trooping down at harvest time; sometimes they had one horse, unsaddled and unbridled, for the entire company; sometimes they all simply walked. Not infrequently there would be only one of the lot who spoke English and so could serve as intermediary between the band and the gentlemen farmers whose lands they asked permission to aid in harvesting. It is not surprising that wages were as low as sixpence a day.

And finally, had our visitor stopped at a manufacturing town, he would have seen still other remarkable sights—but again, not such as to betoken order to the uneducated eye. He might have marveled at the factory built by the brothers Lombe in 1742. It was a huge building for those days, five hundred feet long and six stories high, and inside were machines described by Daniel Defoe as consisting of "26,586 Wheels and 97,746 Movements, which work 73,726 Yards of Silk-Thread every time the Water-Wheel goes round, which is three times in one minute." Equally worthy of note were the children who tended the machines round the clock for twelve or fourteen hours at a turn, cooked their meals on the grimy black boilers, and were boarded in shifts in barracks where, it was said, the beds were always warm.

A strange, cruel, haphazard world this must have appeared to eighteenth-century as well as to our modern eyes.

All the more remarkable, then, to find that it could be reconciled with a scheme of Moral Philosophy envisioned by Dr. Smith, and that that learned man actually claimed to fathom within it the clear-cut outlines of great purposeful laws fitting an overarching and meaningful whole.

What sort of man was this urbane philosopher?

"I am a beau in nothing but my books," was the way Adam Smith once described himself, proudly showing off his treasured library to a friend. He was certainly not a handsome man. A medallion profile shows us a protruding lower lip thrust up to meet a large aquiline nose and heavy bulging eyes looking out from heavy lids. All his life Smith was troubled with a nervous affliction; his head shook, and he had an odd and stumbling manner of speech.

In addition, there was his notorious absentmindedness. In the 1780s, when Smith was in his late fifties, the inhabitants of Edinburgh were regularly treated to the amusing spectacle of their most illustrious citizen, attired in a light-colored coat, knee breeches, white silk stockings, buckle shoes, flat broad-brimmed beaver hat, and cane, walking down the cobbled streets with his eyes fixed on infinity and his lips moving in silent discourse. Every pace or two he would hesitate as if to change his direction or even reverse it; his gait was described by a friend as "vermicular." *resembling a worm in form & motion*

Accounts of his absence of mind were common. On one occasion he descended into his garden clad only in a dressing gown and, falling into a reverie, walked fifteen miles before coming to. Another time while Smith was walking with an eminent friend in Edinburgh, a guard presented his pike in salute. Smith, who had been thus honored on countless occasions, was suddenly hypnotized by the saluting soldier. He returned the honor with his cane and then further astonished his guest by following exactly in the guard's footsteps, duplicating with his cane every motion of the pike. When the spell was broken, Smith was standing at the head of a long flight of steps, cane held at the ready. Having no idea that he had done anything out of the ordinary, he grounded his stick and took up his conversation where he had left off.

This absent-minded professor was born in 1723 in the town of Kirkcaldy, County Fife, Scotland. Kirkcaldy boasted a population of fifteen hundred; at the time of Smith's birth, nails were still used as money by some of the local townspeople. When he was four years old, a most curious incident took place. Smith was kidnaped by a band of passing gypsies. Through the efforts of his uncle (his father had died before his birth), the gypsies were traced and pursued, and in their flight they abandoned young Adam by the roadside. "He would have made, I fear, a poor gypsy," says one of his early biographers.

From his earliest days, Smith was an apt pupil, although even as a child given to fits of abstraction. He was obviously destined for teaching, and so at seventeen he went to Oxford on a scholarship—making the journey on horseback—and there he remained for six years. But Oxford was not then the citadel of learning which it later became. Most of the public professors had long ago given up even a pretense of teaching. A foreign traveler recounts his astonishment over a public debate there in 1788. All four participants passed the allotted time in profound silence, each absorbed in reading a popular novel of the day. Since instruction was the exception rather than the rule, Smith spent the years largely untutored and untaught, reading as he saw fit. In fact he was once nearly expelled from the university because a copy of David Hume's *A Treatise of Human Nature* was found in his rooms—Hume was no fit reading matter, even for a would-be philosopher.

In 1751—he was not yet twenty-eight—Smith was offered the Chair of Logic at the University of Glasgow, and shortly thereafter he was given the Chair of Moral Philosophy. Unlike Oxford, Glasgow was a serious center of what has come to be called the Scottish Enlightenment, and it boasted a galaxy of talent. But it still differed considerably from the modern conception of a university. The prim professorial group did not entirely appreciate a certain levity and enthusiasm in Smith's manner. He was accused of sometimes smiling during religious services (no doubt during a reverie), of being a firm friend of that outrageous Hume, of not holding Sunday classes on Christian evidences, of petitioning the

Senatus Academicus for permission to dispense with prayers on the opening of class, and of delivering prayers that smacked of a certain "natural religion." Perhaps this all fits into better perspective if we remember that Smith's own teacher, Francis Hutcheson, broke new ground at Glasgow by refusing to lecture to his students in Latin!

The disapproval could not have been too severe, for smith rose to be dean in 1758. Unquestionably he was happy at Glasgow. In the evenings he played whist—his absent-mindedness made him a somewhat undependable player—attended learned societies, and lived a quiet life. He was beloved of his students, noted as a lecturer—even Boswell came to hear him—and his odd gait and manner of speech gained the homage of imitation. Little busts of him even appeared in booksellers' windows.

It was not merely his eccentric personality that gave him prestige. In 1759 he published a book that made an instant sensation. It was entitled *The Theory of Moral Sentiments*, and it catapulted Smith immediately into the forefront of English philosophers. *Theory* was an inquiry into the origin of moral approbation and disapproval. How does it happen that man, who is a creature of self-interest, can form moral judgments in which self-interest seems to be held in abeyance or transmuted to a higher plane? Smith held that the answer lay in our ability to put ourselves in the position of a third person, an impartial observer, and in this way to form a sympathetic notion of the objective (as opposed to the selfish) merits of a case.

The book and its problems attracted widespread interest. In Germany *das Adam Smith Problem* became a favorite subject for debate. More importantly, from our point of view, the treatise met with the favor of an intriguing man named Charles Townshend.

Townshend is one of those wonderful figures with which the eighteenth century seems to abound. A witty and even learned man, Townshend was, in the words of Horace Walpole, "a man endowed with every great talent, who must have been the greatest man of his age, if only he had common sincerity, common steadiness, and common sense." Townshend's fickleness was notorious; a quip of the times put it that Mr. Townshend was ill of a pain in his side, but declined to specify which side. As evidence of his lack of common sense, it was Townshend, as Chancellor of the Exchequer, who helped precipitate the American Revolution, first by refusing the colonists the right to elect their own judges and then by imposing a heavy duty on American tea.

But his political shortsightedness notwithstanding, Townshend was a sincere student of philosophy and politics, and as such a devotee of Adam Smith. What is more important, he was in a position to make him an unusual offer. In 1754, Townshend had made a brilliant and lucrative marriage to the Countess of Dalkeith, the widow of the Duke of Buccleuch, and he now found himself casting about for a tutor for his wife's son. Education for a young man of the upper classes consisted largely of the Grand Tour, a stay in Europe where one might acquire that polish so highly praised by Lord Chesterfield. Dr. Adam Smith would be an ideal companion for the young duke, thought Townshend, and accordingly he offered him five hundred pounds a year plus expenses and a pension of five hundred pounds a year for life. It was too good an offer to be declined. At best Smith never realized more than one hundred seventy pounds from the fees which, in those days, professors collected directly from their students. It is pleasant to note that his pupils refused to accept a refund from Dr. Smith when he left, saying that they had already been more than recompensed.

The tutor and His young Grace left for France in 1764. For eighteen months they stayed in Toulouse, where a combination of abominably boring company and Smith's execrable French made his sedate life at Glasgow look like dissipation. Then they moved on to the south of France (where he met and worshiped Voltaire and repulsed the attentions of an amorous marquise), thence to Geneva, and finally to Paris. To relieve the tedium of the provinces, Smith began work on a treatise of political economy, a subject on which he had lectured at Glasgow, debated many evenings at the Select Society in Edinburgh, and discussed at length with his beloved friend David Hume. The book was to be *The Wealth of Nations,* but it would be twelve years before it was finished.

Paris was better going. By this time Smith's French, although dreadful, was good enough to enable him to talk at length with the foremost economic thinker in France. This was François Quesnay, a physician in the court of Louis XV and personal doctor to Mme. Pompadour. Quesnay had propounded a school of economics known as Physiocracy and devised a chart of the economy called a *tableau économique.* The *tableau* was truly a physician's insight: in contradistinction to the ideas of the day, which still held that wealth was the solid stuff of gold and silver, Quesnay insisted that wealth sprang from production and that it flowed through the nation, from hand to hand, replenishing the body social like the circulation of blood. The *tableau* made a vast impression—Mirabeau the elder characterized it as an invention deserving of equal rank with writing and money. But the trouble with Physiocracy was that it insisted that only the agricultural worker *produced* true wealth because Nature labored at his side, whereas the manufacturing worker merely altered its form in a "sterile" way. Hence Quesnay's system had but limited usefulness for practical policy. True, it advocated a policy of *laissez-faire*—a radical departure for the times. But in describing the industrial sector as performing only a sterile manipulation, it failed to see that labor could produce wealth wherever it performed, not just on the land.

To see that labor, not nature, was the source of "value," was one of Smith's greatest insights. Perhaps this was the consequence of having grown up in a country that bustled with trade, rather than in the overwhelmingly agricultural setting of France. Whatever the cause, Smith could not accept the agricultural bias of the Physiocratic cult (Quesnay's followers, like Mirabeau, were nothing if not adulatory). Smith had a profound personal admiration for the French doctor—had it not been for Quesnay's death, *The Wealth of Nations* would have been dedicated to him—but Physiocracy was fundamentally uncongenial to Smith's Scottish vision.

In 1766 the tour was brought to an abrupt halt. The

duke's younger brother, who had joined them, caught a fever, and despite the frantic attentions of Smith (who called in Quesnay), died in a delirium. His Grace returned to his estates at Dalkeith, and Smith went first to London, and then to Kirkcaldy. Despite Hume's entreaties, there he stayed, for the better part of the next ten years, while the great treatise took shape. Most of it he dictated, standing against his fireplace and nervously rubbing his head against the wall until his pomade had made a dark streak on the paneling. Occasionally he would visit his former charge on his estates at Dalkeith, and once in a while he would go to London to discuss his ideas with the literati of the day. One of them was Dr. Samuel Johnson, to whose select club Smith belonged, although he and the venerable lexicographer had hardly met under the most amiable of circumstances. Sir Walter Scott tells us that Johnson, on first seeing Smith, attacked him for some statement he had made. Smith vindicated the truth of his contention. "What did Johnson say?" was the universal inquiry. "Why, he said," said Smith, with the deepest impression of resentment, "he said, 'You lie!'" "And what did you reply?" "I said, 'You are a son of a—!'" On such terms, says Scott, did these two great moralists first meet and part, and such was the classical dialogue between two great teachers of philosophy.

Smith met as well a charming and intelligent American, one Benjamin Franklin, who provided him with a wealth of facts about the American colonies and a deep appreciation of the role that they might someday play. It is undoubtedly due to Franklin's influence that Smith subsequently wrote of the colonies that they constituted a nation "which, indeed, seems very likely to become one of the greatest and most formidable that ever was in the world."

In 1776, *The Wealth of Nations* was published. Two years later Smith was appointed Commissioner of Customs for Edinburgh, a sinecure worth six hundred pounds a year. With his mother, who lived until she was ninety, Smith lived out his bachelor's life in peace and quiet; serene, content, and in all likelihood absent-minded to the end.

little or no work
for income ooth

And the book?

It has been called "the outpouring not only of a great mind, but of a whole epoch." Yet it is not, in the strict sense of the word, an "original" book. There is a long line of observers before Smith who have approached his understanding of the world: Locke, Steuart, Mandeville, Petty, Cantillon, Turgot, not to mention Quesnay and Hume again. Smith took from all of them: there are over a hundred authors mentioned by name in his treatise. But where others had fished here and there, Smith spread his net wide; where others had clarified this and that issue, Smith illuminated the entire landscape. *The Wealth of Nations* is not a wholly original book, but it is unquestionably a masterpiece.

It is, first of all, a huge panorama. It opens with a famous passage describing the minute specialization of labor in the manufacture of pins, and covers, before it is done, such a variety of subjects as "the late disturbances in the American colonies" (evidently Smith thought the Revolutionary War would be over by the time his book reached the press), the wastefulness of the student's life at Oxford, and the statistics on the herring catch since 1771.

A glance at the index compiled for a later edition by Cannan shows the range of Smith's references and thoughts. Here are a dozen entries from the letter A:

Abassides, opulence of Saracen empire under
Abraham, weighed shekels
Abyssinia, salt money
Actors, public, paid for the contempt attending their profession
Africa, powerful king much worse off than European peasant
Alehouses, the number of, not the efficient cause of drunkenness
Ambassadors, the first motive of their appointment
America [a solid page of references follows]
Apprenticeship, the nature . . . of this bond servitude explained
Arabs, their manner of supporting war

Army, . . . no security to the sovereign against a disaffected clergy.

In fine print the index goes on for sixty-three pages; before it ends it has touched on everything: "Riches, the chief
enjoyment of, consists in the parade of; Poverty, sometimes
urges nation to inhuman customs; Stomach, desire for food
bounded by narrow capacity of the; Butcher, brutal and odi-
ous business." When we have finished the nine hundred
pages of the book we have a living picture of England in the
1770s, of apprentices and journeymen and rising capitalists,
of landlords and clergymen and kings, of workshops and
farms and foreign trade.

The book is heavy going. It moves with all the deliberation of an encyclopedic mind, but not with the precision of an
orderly one. This was an age when authors did not stop to
qualify their ideas with *ifs, ands,* and *buts,* and it was an era
when it was quite possible for a man of Smith's intellectual
stature virtually to embrace the great body of knowledge of
his times. Hence *Wealth* ducks nothing, minimizes nothing,
fears nothing. What an exasperating book! Again and again it
refuses to wrap up in a concise sentence a conclusion it has
laboriously arrived at over fifty pages. The argument is so full
of detail and observation that one constantly has to chip away
the ornamentation to find the steel structure that holds it
together underneath. Coming to silver, Smith detours for
seventy-five pages to write a "digression" on it; coming to religion, he wanders off in a chapter on the sociology of morality. But for all its weightiness, the text is shot through with
insights, observations, and well-turned phrases that imbue
this great lecture with life. It was Smith who first called England "a nation of shopkeepers"; it was Smith who wrote, "By
nature a philosopher is not in genius and disposition half so
different from a street porter, as a mastiff is from a greyhound." And of the East India Company, which was then ravaging the East, he wrote: "It is a very singular government in
which every member of the administration wishes to get out
of the country . . . as soon as he can, and to whose interest,
the day after he has left it and carried his whole fortune with

him, it is perfectly indifferent though the whole country as swallowed up by an earthquake."

The Wealth of Nations is in no sense a textbook. Adam smith is writing to his age, not to his classroom; he is expounding a doctrine that is meant to be of importance in running an empire, not an abstract treatise for academic distribution. The dragons that he slays (such as the Mercantilist philosophy, which takes over two hundred pages to die) were alive and panting, if a little tired, in his day.

And finally, the book is a revolutionary one. To be sure, Smith would hardly have countenanced an upheaval that disordered the gentlemanly classes and enthroned the common poor. But the import of *The Wealth of Nations* is revolutionary, nonetheless. Smith is not, as is commonly supposed, an apologist for the up-and-coming bourgeois; as we shall see, he is an admirer of their work but suspicious of their motives, and mindful of the needs of the great laboring mass. But it is not his aim to espouse the interests of any class. He is concerned with promoting the wealth of the entire nation. And wealth, to Adam Smith, consists of the goods that *all* the people of society consume, although not, of course, in equal amounts. There will be poverty as well as wealth in the Society of Natural Liberty.

Nonetheless, this is a democratic, and hence radical, philosophy of wealth. Gone is the notion of gold, treasures, kingly hoards; gone the prerogatives of merchants or farmers or working guilds. We are in the modern world, where the flow of goods and services consumed by everyone constitutes the ultimate aim and end of economic life.

And now, what of the vision? As we shall see, it cannot be so simply described as Hobbes's principle of sovereign power. Smith's vision is more like a blueprint for a whole new mode of social organization, a mode called Political Economy, or, in today's terminology, economics.

At the center of this blueprint are the solutions to two problems that absorb Smith's attention. First, he is interested in laying bare the mechanism by which society hangs together. How is it possible for a community in which everyone is busily following his self-interest not to fly apart from sheer centrifugal force? What is it that guides each individual's private business so that it conforms to the needs of the group? With no central planning authority and no steadying influence of age-old tradition, how does society manage to get those tasks done which are necessary for survival?

These questions lead Smith to a formulation of the laws of the market. What he sought was "the invisible hand," as he called it, whereby "the private interests and passions of men" are led in the direction "which is most agreeable to the interest of the whole society."

But the laws of the market will be only a part of Smith's inquiry. There is another question that interests him: whither society? The laws of the market are like the laws that explain how a spinning top stays upright; but there is also the question of whether the top, by virtue of its spinning, will be moved along the table.

To Smith and the great economists who followed him, society is not conceived as a static achievement of mankind which will go on reproducing itself, unchanged and unchanging, from one generation to the next. On the contrary, society is seen as an organism that has its own life history. Indeed, in its entirety *The Wealth of Nations* is a great treatise on history, explaining how "the system of perfect liberty" (also called "the system of natural liberty")—the way Smith referred to commercial capitalism—came into being, as well as how it worked.

But until we have followed Smith's unraveling of the laws of the market, we cannot turn to this larger and more fascinating problem. For the laws of the market themselves will be an integral part of the larger laws that cause society to prosper or decay. The mechanism by which the heedless individual is kept in line with everybody else will affect the mechanism by which society itself changes over the years.

Hence we begin with a look at the market mechanism. It is not the stuff that excites the imagination or stirs the pulse. Yet, for all its dryness, it has an immediacy that should lead us to consider it with a respectful eye. Not only are the laws of the market essential to an understanding of the world of

Adam Smith, but these same laws will underlie the very different world of Karl Marx, and the still different world in which we live today. Since we are all, knowingly or otherwise, under their sovereignty, it behooves us to scrutinize them rather carefully.

Adam Smith's laws of the market are basically simple. They tell us that the outcome of a certain kind of behavior in a certain social framework will bring about perfectly definite and foreseeable results. Specifically they show us how the drive of individual self-interest in an environment of similarly motivated individuals will result in competition; and they further demonstrate how competition will result in the provision of those goods that society wants, in the quantities that society desires, and at the prices society is prepared to pay. Let us see how this comes about.

It comes about in the first place because self-interest acts as a driving power to guide men to whatever work society is willing to pay for. "It is not from the benevolence of the butcher, the brewer, or the baker that we expect our dinner," says Smith, "but from their regard to their self-interest. We address ourselves, not to their humanity, but to their self-love, and never talk to them of our necessities, but of their advantages."

But self-interest is only half the picture. It drives men to action. Something else must prevent the pushing of profit-hungry individuals from holding society up to exorbitant ransom: a community activated only by self-interest would be a community of ruthless profiteers. This regulator is competition, the conflict of the self-interested actors on the market-place. For each man, out to do his best for himself with no thought of social consequences, is faced with a flock of similarly motivated individuals who are engaged in exactly the same pursuit. Hence, each is only too eager to take advantage of his neighbor's greed. A man who permits his self-interest to run away with him will find that competitors have slipped in to take his trade away; if he charges too much for his wares or if he refuses to pay as much as everybody else for his workers, he will find himself without buyers in the one case and without employees in the other. Thus very much as in *The*

Theory of Moral Sentiments, the selfish motives of men are transmuted by interaction to yield the most unexpected of results: social harmony.

Consider, for example, the problem of high prices. Suppose we have one hundred manufacturers of gloves. The self-interest of each one will cause him to wish to raise his price above his cost of production and thereby to realize an extra profit. But he cannot. If he raises his price, his competitors will step in and take his market away from him by underselling him. Only if all glove manufacturers combine and agree to maintain a solid front will an unduly high price be charged. And in this case, the collusive coalition could be broken by an enterprising manufacturer from another field—say, shoemaking—who decided to move his capital into glove manufacture, where he could steal away the market by shading his price.

But the laws of the market do more than impose a competitive price on products. They also see to it that the producers of society heed society's demands for the *quantities* of goods it wants. Let us suppose that consumers decide they want more gloves than are being turned out, and fewer shoes. Accordingly the public will scramble for the stock of gloves on the market, while the shoe business will be dull. As a result glove prices will tend to rise as consumers try to buy more of them than there are ready at hand, and shoe prices will tend to fall as the public passes the shoe stores by. But as glove prices rise, profits in the glove industry will rise, too; and as shoe prices fall, profits in shoe manufacture will slump. Again self-interest will step in to right the balance. Workers will be released from the shoe business as shoe factories contract their output; they will move to the glove business, where business is booming. The result is quite obvious: glove production will rise and shoe production fall.

And this is exactly what society wanted in the first place. As more gloves come on the market to meet demand, glove prices will fall back into line. As fewer shoes are produced, the surplus of shoes will soon disappear and shoe prices will again rise up to normal. Through the mechanism of the market, society will have changed the allocation of its elements of production to fit its new desires. Yet no one has issued a dictum, and no planning authority has established schedules of output. Self-interest and competition, acting one against the other, have accomplished the transition.

And one final accomplishment. Just as the market regulates both prices and quantities of *goods* according to the final arbiter of public demand, so it also regulates the *incomes* of those who cooperate to produce those goods. If profits in one line of business are unduly large, there will be a rush of other businessmen into that field until competition has lowered surpluses. If wages are out of line in one kind of work, there will be a rush of men into the favored occupation until it pays no more than comparable jobs of that degree of skill and training. Conversely, if profits or wages are too low in one trade area, there will be an exodus of capital and labor until the supply is better adjusted to the demand.

All this may seem somewhat elementary. But consider what Adam Smith has done, with his impetus of self-interest and his regulator of competition. First he has explained how prices are kept from ranging arbitrarily away from the actual cost of producing a good. Second, he has explained how society can induce its producers of commodities to provide it with what it wants. Third he has pointed out why high prices are a self-curing disease, for they cause production in those lines to increase. And finally, he has accounted for a basic similarity of incomes at each level of the great producing strata of the nation. In a word, he has found in the mechanism of the market a self-regulating system for society's orderly provisioning.

Note "self-regulating." The beautiful consequence of the market is that it is its own guardian. If output or prices or certain kinds of remuneration stray away from their socially ordained levels, forces are set into motion to bring them back to the fold. It is a curious paradox that thus ensues the market, which is the acme of individual economic freedom, is the strictest taskmaster of all. One may appeal the ruling of a planning board or win the dispensation of a minister; but there is no appeal, no dispensation, from the anonymous pressures of the market mechanism. Economic freedom is thus more illusory than at first appears. One can do as one pleases in the market. But if one pleases to do what the market disapproves, the price of individual freedom is economic ruination.

Does the world really work this way? To a very real degree it did in the days of Adam Smith. Even in his time, of course, there were already factors that acted as restraints against the free operation of the market system. There were combinations of manufacturers who rigged prices artificially high and associations of journeymen who resisted the pressures of competition when it acted to lower their wages. And already there were more disquieting signs to be read. The Lombe brothers' factory was more than a mere marvel of engineering and a source of wonderment to the visitor: it betokened the coming of large-scale industry and the emergence of employers who were immensely powerful individual actors in the market. The children in the cotton mills could surely not be considered market factors of equal power with the employers who bedded, boarded, and exploited them. But for all its deviations from the blueprint, eighteenth-century England approached, even if it did not wholly conform to, the model that Adam Smith had in mind. Business *was* competitive, the average factory *was* small, prices *did* rise and fall as demand ebbed and rose, and changes in prices *did* invoke changes in output and occupation. The world of Adam Smith has been called a world of atomistic competition, a world in which no agent of the productive mechanism, on the side of labor or capital, was powerful enough to interfere with or to resist the pressures of competition. It was a world in which each agent was forced to scurry after its self-interest in a vast social free-for-all.

And today? Does the competitive market mechanism still operate?

This is not a question to which it is possible to give a simple answer. The nature of the market has changed vastly since the eighteenth century. We no longer live in a world of atomistic competition in which no man can afford to swim against the current. Today's market mechanism is characterized by the huge size of its participants: giant corporations and strong labor unions obviously do not behave as if they

were individual proprietors and workers. Their very bulk enables them to stand out against the pressures of competition,
to disregard price signals, and to consider what their self-
interest shall be in the long run rather than in the immediate
press of each day's buying and selling.

That these factors have weakened the guiding function
of the market mechanism is apparent. But for all the attributes of modern-day economic society, the great forces of self-
interest and competition, however watered down or hedged
about, still provide basic rules of behavior that no participant
in a market system can afford to disregard entirely. Although
the world in which we live is not that of Adam Smith, the
laws of the market can still be discerned if we study its operations.

But the laws of the market are only a description of the
behavior that gives society its cohesiveness. Something else
must make it go. Ninety years after *The Wealth of Nations,*
Karl Marx was to discover "laws of motion" that described
how capitalism proceeded slowly, unwillingly, but ineluctably
to its doom. But *The Wealth of Nations* already had its own
laws of motion. However, altogether unlike the Marxist prognosis, Adam Smith's world went slowly, quite willingly, toward—although, as we shall see, never quite all the way
to Valhalla. *? what?*
Valhalla would have been the last destination that most
observers would have predicted. Sir John Byng, touring the
North Country in 1792, looked from his coach window and
wrote: "Why, here now, is a great flaring mill . . . all the Vale
is disturb'd. . . . Sir Richard Arkwright may have introduced
Much Wealth into his Family and into his Country, but, as a
Tourist, I execrate his Schemes, which having crept into
every Pastoral Vale, have destroyed the course, and the
Beauty of Nature." "Oh! What a dog's hole is Manchester,"
said Sir John on arriving there.

In truth, much of England was a dog's hole. The three
centuries of turmoil which had prodded land, labor, and capital into existence seemed to have been only a preparation for
still further upheaval, for the recently freed agents of produc-

tion began to be combined in a new and ugly form: the factory. And with the factory came new problems. Twenty years before Sir John's tour, Richard Arkwright, who had gotten together a little capital peddling women's hair to make wigs, invented (or stole) the spinning throstle. But, having constructed his machine, he found it was not so easy to staff it. Local labor could not keep up with the "regular celerity" of the process—wage-work was still generally despised, and some capitalists found their new-built factories burned to the ground out of sheer blind hatred. Arkwright was forced to turn to children—"their small fingers being active." Furthermore, since they were unused to the independent life of farming or crafts, children adapted themselves more readily to the discipline of factory life. The move was hailed as a philanthropic gesture—would not the employment of children help to alleviate the condition of the "unprofitable poor"?

For if any problem absorbed the public mind, besides its mixed admiration of and horror at the factory, it was this omnipresent problem of the unprofitable poor. In 1720, England was crowded with a million and a half of them—a staggering figure when we realize that her total population was only twelve or thirteen million. Hence the air was full of schemes for their disposition. Despairing schemes, mostly. For the common complaint was the ineradicable sloth of the pauper, and this was mixed with consternation at the way in which the lower orders aped their betters. Workpeople were actually drinking tea! The common folk seemed to prefer wheaten bread to their traditional loaf of rye or barley! Where would all this lead to, asked the thinkers of the day; were not the wants of the poor ("which it would be prudence to relieve, but folly to cure," as the scandalous Mandeville put it in 1723) essential for the welfare of the state? What would happen to Society if the indispensable gradations of society were allowed to disappear?

Consternation still described the prevailing attitude of his day toward the great, fearful problem of the "lower orders," but it certainly did not describe Adam Smith's philosophy. "No society can surely be flourishing and happy, of which by far the greater part of the numbers are poor and

miserable," he wrote. And not only did he have the temerity
to make so radical a statement, but he proceeded to demonstrate that society was in fact constantly improving; that it was
being propelled, willy-nilly, toward a positive goal. It was not
moving because anyone willed it to, or because Parliament
might pass laws, or England win a battle. It moved because
there was a concealed dynamic beneath the surface of things
which powered the social whole like an enormous engine.

For one salient fact struck Adam Smith as he looked at
the English scene. This was the tremendous gain in productivity which sprang from the minute division and specialization of labor. Early in *The Wealth of Nations*, Smith
comments on a pin factory: "One man draws out the wire, another straights it, a third cuts it, a fourth points it, a fifth
grinds it at the top for receiving the head; to make the head
requires two or three distinct operations; to put it on is a peculiar business; to whiten it is another; it is even a trade by
itself to put them into paper. . . . I have seen a small
manufactory of this kind where ten men only were employed
and where some of them consequently performed two or
three distinct operations. But though they were very poor,
and therefore but indifferently accommodated with the necessary machinery, they could, when they exerted themselves,
make among them about twelve pounds of pins in a day.
There are in a pound upwards of four thousand pins of a mid-
dling size. Those ten persons, therefore, could make among
them upwards of forty-eight thousand pins in a day. . . . But if
they had all wrought separately and independently . . . they
certainly could not each of them make twenty, perhaps not
one pin a day. . . ."

There is hardly any need to point out how infinitely
more complex present-day production methods are than
those of the eighteenth century. Smith, for all his disclaimers,
was sufficiently impressed with a small factory of ten people
to write about it; what would he have thought of one employing ten thousand! But the great gift of the division of labor is
not its complexity—indeed it simplifies most toil. Its advantage lies in its capacity to increase what Smith calls "that universal opulence which extends itself to the lowest ranks of

the people." That universal opulence of the eighteenth century looks like a grim existence from our modern vantage point. But if we view the matter in its historical perspective, if we compare the lot of the workingman in eighteenth-century England with that of his predecessor a century or two before, it is clear that, mean as his existence was, it constituted a considerable advance. Smith makes the point vividly:

> Observe the accommodation of the most common artificer or day labourer in a civilized and thriving country, and you will perceive that the number of people of whose industry a part, though but a small part, has been employed in procuring him this accommodation, exceeds all computation. The woollen coat, for example, which covers the day-labourer, as coarse and rough as it may seem, is the produce of the joint labour of a great multitude of workmen. The shepherd, the sorter of the wool, the wool-comber or carder, the dyer, the scribbler, the spinner, the weaver, the fuller, the dresser, with many others, must all join their different arts in order to complete even this homely production. How many merchants and carriers, besides, must have been employed ... how much commerce and navigation ... how many ship-builders, sailors, sail-makers, rope makers. . . .
>
> Were we to examine, in the same manner, all the different parts of his dress and household furniture, the coarse linen shirt which he wears next to his skin, the shoes which cover his feet, the bed which he lies on ... the kitchen-grate at which he prepares his victuals, the coals which he makes use of for that purpose, dug from the bowels of the earth, and brought to him perhaps by a long sea and a long land carriage, all the other utensils of his kitchen, all the furniture of his table, the knives and forks, the earthen or pewter plates upon which he serves up and divides his victuals, the different hands employed in preparing his bread and his beer, the glass window which lets in the heat and the light, and keeps out the wind and the rain, with all the knowledge and art

requisite for preparing that beautiful and happy invention . . . ; if we examine, I say, all those things . . . we
shall be sensible that without the assistance and cooperation of many thousands, the very meanest person in a
civilized country could not be provided, even according
to what we very falsely imagine, the easy and simple
manner in which he is commonly accommodated. Compared indeed with the more extravagant luxury of the
great, his accommodation must no doubt appear extremely simple and easy; and yet it may be true, perhaps,
that the accommodation of a European prince does not
always so much exceed that of an industrious and frugal
peasant, as the accommodation of the latter exceeds that
of many an African king, the absolute master of the lives
and liberties of ten thousand naked savages.

What is it that drives society to this wonderful multipli-
cation of wealth and riches? Partly it is the market mechanism itself, for the market harnesses man's creative powers in
a milieu that encourages him, even forces him, to invent, innovate, expand, take risks. But there are more fundamental
pressures behind the restless activity of the market. In fact,
Smith sees two deep-seated laws of behavior which propel
the market system in an ascending spiral of productivity.

The first of these is the Law of Accumulation. *Laws of Accum.*

Let us remember that Adam Smith lived at a time when
the rising industrial capitalist could and did realize a fortune
from his investments. Richard Arkwright, apprenticed to a
barber as a young man, died in 1792 leaving an estate of
£500,000. Samuel Walker, who started a forge going in an old
nailshop in Rotherham, left a steel foundry on that site worth
£200,000. Josiah Wedgwood, who stumped about his pottery
factory on a wooden leg scrawling "This won't do for Jos.
Wedgwood" wherever he saw evidence of careless work, left
an estate of £240,000 and much landed property. The Industrial Revolution in its earliest stages already provided a veritable grab bag of riches for whoever was quick enough,
shrewd enough, industrious enough to ride with its current.

And the object of the great majority of the rising capital-

ists was first, last, and always, to *accumulate* their savings. At
the beginning of the nineteenth century, £2,500 was collected in Manchester for the foundation of Sunday schools.
The sum total contributed to this worthy cause by the single
largest employers in the district, the cotton spinners, was
£90. The young industrial aristocracy had better things to do
with its money than contribute to unproductive charities—it
had to accumulate, and Adam Smith approved wholeheartedly. Woe to him who did not accumulate. And as for one
who encroached on his capital—"like him who perverts the
revenues of some pious foundation to profane purposes, he
pays the wages of idleness with those funds which the frugal-
ity of his forefathers had, as it were, consecrated to the main-
tenance of industry."

But Adam Smith did not approve of accumulation for accumulation's sake. He was, after all, a philosopher, with a
philosopher's disdain for the vanity of riches. Rather, in the
accumulation of capital Smith saw a vast benefit to society.
For capital—if put to use in machinery—provided just that
wonderful division of labor which multiplies man's productive energy. Hence accumulation becomes another of Smith's
two-edged swords: the avarice of private greed again re-
dounding to the welfare of the community. Smith is not worried over the problem that will face twentieth-century
economists: will private accumulations actually find their way
back into more employment? For him the world is capable of
indefinite improvement and the size of the market is limited
only by its geographical extent. Accumulate and the world
will benefit, says Smith. And certainly in the lusty atmosphere of his time there was no evidence of any unwillingness
to accumulate on the part of those who were in a position to
do so.

But—and here is a difficulty—accumulation would soon
lead to a situation where further accumulation would be impossible. For accumulation meant more machinery, and
more machinery meant more demand for workmen. And this
in turn would sooner or later lead to higher and higher
wages, until profits—the source of accumulation—were
eaten away. How is this hurdle surmounted?

• •

It is surmounted by the second great law of the system: the Law of Population.

To Adam Smith, laborers, like any other commodity, could be produced according to the demand. If wages were high, the number of workpeople would multiply; if wages fell, the numbers of the working class would decrease. Smith put it bluntly: ". . . the demand for men, like that for any other commodity, necessarily regulates the production of men."

Nor is this quite so naïve a conception as it appears at first blush. In Smith's day infant mortality among the lower classes was shockingly high. "It is not uncommon," says Smith, ". . . in the Highlands of Scotland for a mother who has borne twenty children not to have two alive." In many places in England, half the children died before they were four, and almost everywhere half the children lived only to the age of nine or ten. Malnutrition, evil living conditions, cold, and disease took a horrendous toll among the poorer element. Hence, although higher wages might have affected the birth rate only slightly, they could be expected to have a considerable influence on the number of children who would grow to working age.

Hence, if the first effect of accumulation would be to raise the wages of the working class, this in turn would bring about an increase in the number of workers. And now the market mechanism takes over. Just as higher prices on the market will bring about a larger production of gloves and the larger number of gloves in turn press down the higher prices of gloves, so higher wages will bring about a larger number of workers, and the increase in their numbers will set up a reverse pressure on the level of their wages. Population, like glove production, is a self-curing disease—as far as wages are concerned.

And this meant that accumulation might go safely on. The rise in wages which it caused and which threatened to make further accumulation unprofitable is tempered by the rise in population. Accumulation leads to its own undoing, and then is rescued in the nick of time. The obstacle of higher wages is undone by the growth in population which those very higher wages made feasible. There is something fascinating in this automatic process of aggravation and cure, stimulus and response, in which the very factor that seems to be leading the system to its doom is also slyly bringing about the conditions necessary for its further health.

And now observe that Smith has constructed for society a giant endless chain. As regularly and as inevitably as a series of interlocked mathematical propositions, society is started on an upward march. From any starting point the probing mechanism of the market first equalizes the returns to labor and capital in all their different uses, sees to it that those commodities demanded are produced in the right quantities, and further ensures that prices for commodities are constantly competed down to their costs of production. But further than this, society is dynamic. From its starting point accumulation of wealth will take place, and this accumulation will result in increased facilities for production and in a greater division of labor. So far, all to the good. But accumulation will also raise wages as capitalists bid for workers to man the new factories. As wages rise, further accumulation begins to look unprofitable. The system threatens to level off. But meanwhile, workmen will have used their higher wages to rear their children with fewer mortalities. Hence the supply of workmen will increase. As population swells, the competition among workmen will press down on wages again. And so accumulation will continue, and another spiral in the ascent of society will begin.

This is no business cycle that Smith describes. It is a long-term process, a secular evolution. And it is wonderfully certain. Provided only that the market mechanism is not tampered with, everything is inexorably determined by the preceding link. A vast reciprocating machinery is set up with all of society inside it: only the tastes of the public—to guide producers—and the actual physical resources of the nation are outside the chain of cause and effect.

But observe that what is foreseen is not an unbounded improvement of affairs. There will assuredly be a long period of what we call economic growth—Smith does not use the term—but the improvement has its limits. These do not im-

mediately affect the working man. True, the rise in population will eventually force wages back toward subsistence, but
for many years, in Smith's opinion, the working class would
improve its lot.

But Smith was above all a realist. In the *very* long run,
well beyond the horizon, he saw that a growing population
would push wages back to their "natural" level. When would
that time come? Clearly, it would arrive when society had
run out of unused resources and introduced as fine a division
of labor as possible. In a word, growth would come to an end
when the economy had extended its boundaries to their limits, and then fully utilized its increased economic "space."

But why could not that boundary be further expanded?
The answer is that Smith saw the all-important division of
labor as a once-for-all, not a continuing, process. As has been
recently pointed out, he did not see the organizational and
technological core of the division of labor as a self-generating
process of change, but as a discrete advance that would im-
part its stimulus and then disappear. Thus, in the very long
run the growth momentum of society would come to a halt—
Smith once mentions two hundred years as the longest period over which a society could hope to flourish. Thereafter
the laborer would return to his subsistence wages, the capitalist to the modest profits of a stable market, and the landlord alone might enjoy a somewhat higher income as food
production remained at the levels required by a larger, although no longer growing, population. For all its optimistic
boldness, Smith's vision is bounded, careful, sober—for the
long run, even sobering.

No wonder, then, that the book took hold slowly. It was
eight years before it was quoted in Parliament, the first to do
so being Charles James Fox, the most powerful member of
Commons (who admitted later that he had never actually
read the book). It was not until 1800 that the book achieved
full recognition. By that time it had gone through nine English editions and had found its way to Europe and America.
Its protagonists came from an unexpected quarter. They
were the rising capitalist class—the very class that Smith had

excoriated for its "mean rapacity," and of whose members he had said that they "neither are, nor ought to be, the rulers of mankind." All this was ignored in favor of the great point that Smith made in his inquiry: *let the market alone*.

What Smith had meant by this was one thing; what his proponents made him out to mean was another. Smith, as we have said, was not the proponent of any one class. He was a slave to his system. His whole economic philosophy stemmed from his unquestioning faith in the ability of the market to guide the system to its point of highest return. The market—that wonderful social machine—would take care of society's needs *if it was left alone*, so that the laws of evolution might take over to lift society toward its promised reward. Smith was neither antilabor nor anticapital; if he had any bias it was in favor of the consumer. "Consumption is the sole end and purpose of all production," he wrote, and then proceeded to castigate those systems that placed the interest of the producer over that of the consuming public.

But in Smith's panegyric of a free and unfettered market the rising industrialists found the theoretical justification they needed to block the first government attempts to remedy the scandalous conditions of the times. For Smith's theory does unquestionably lead to a doctrine of *laissez-faire*. To Adam Smith the least government is certainly the best: governments are spendthrift, irresponsible, and unproductive. And yet Adam Smith is not necessarily opposed—as his posthumous admirers made him out to be—to government action that has as its end the promotion of the general welfare. He warns, for example, of the stultifying effect of mass production—"the understandings of the greater part of men are necessarily formed in their employments. The man whose whole life is spent in performing a few simple operations . . . generally becomes as stupid and ignorant as it is possible for a human creature to become"—and prophesies a decline in the manly virtues of the laborer, "unless the government takes some pains to prevent it."

Indeed, far from being opposed to all government undertakings, Smith specifically stresses three things that government should do in a society of natural liberty. First, not

surprisingly, it should protect that society against "the violence and invasion" of other societies. Second, it should provide an "exact administration of justice" for all citizens. And
third, government has the duty of "erecting and maintaining
those public institutions and those public works which may
be in the highest degree advantageous to a great society," but
which "are of such a nature that the profit could never repay
the expense to any individual or small number of individuals."

Put into today's language, Smith explicitly recognizes the
usefulness of public investment for projects that cannot be
undertaken by the private sector—he mentions roads and education as two examples. Needless to say, this is an idea that
has grown considerably in scope since Smith's day—one
thinks of flood control, ecological repair, scientific research—but the idea itself, like so much else, is implicit, not
explicit, in Smith's underlying vision.

What Smith *is* against is the meddling of the government
with the market mechanism. He is against restraints on im-
ports and bounties on exports, against government laws that
shelter industry from competition, and against government
spending for unproductive ends. Notice that these activities
of the government all bear against the proper working of the
market system. Smith never faced the problem that was to
cause such intellectual agony for later generations of whether
the government is weakening or strengthening that system
when it steps in with welfare legislation. Aside from poor relief, there was virtually no welfare legislation in Smith's
day—the government was the unabashed ally of the govern-
ing classes, and the great tussle within the government was
whether it should be the landowning or the industrial classes
who should most benefit. The question of whether the working class should have a voice in the direction of economic affairs simply did not enter any respectable person's mind.

The great enemy to Adam Smith's system is not so much
government *per se* as monopoly in any form. "People of the
same trade seldom meet together," says Adam Smith, "but
the conversation ends in a conspiracy against the public, or in
some diversion to raise prices." And the trouble with such
goings-on is not so much that they are morally reprehensible

in themselves—they are, after all, only the inevitable consequence of man's self-interest—as that they impede the fluid
working of the market. And of course Smith is right. If the
working of the market is trusted to produce the greatest
number of goods at the lowest possible prices, anything that
interferes with the market necessarily lowers social welfare.
If, as in Smith's time, no master hatter anywhere in England
can employ more than two apprentices or no master cutler in
Sheffield more than one, the market system cannot possibly
yield its full benefits. If, as in Smith's time, paupers are tied
to their local parishes and prevented from seeking work
where work might be found, the market cannot attract labor
where labor is wanted. If, as in Smith's time, great companies
are given monopolies of foreign trade, the public cannot realize the full benefits of cheaper foreign produce.

Hence, says Smith, all these impediments must go. The
market must be left free to find its own natural levels of
prices and wages and profits and production; whatever interferes with the market does so only at the expense of the true
wealth of the nation. But because any act of the government—even such laws as those requiring the whitewashing
of factories or preventing the shackling of children to machines—could be interpreted as hampering the free operation of the market. *The Wealth of Nations* was liberally
quoted to oppose the first humanitarian legislation. Thus, by
a strange injustice, the man who warned that the grasping
eighteenth-century industrialists "generally have an interest
to deceive and even to oppress the public" came to be regarded as their economic patron saint. Even today, in blithe
disregard of his actual philosophy, Smith is generally regarded as a *conservative* economist, whereas in fact he was
more avowedly hostile to the *motives* of businessmen than
are most contemporary liberal economists.

In a sense the vision of Adam Smith is a testimony to the
eighteenth-century belief in the inevitable triumph of rationality and order over arbitrariness and chaos. Don't try to do
good, says Smith. Let good emerge as the by-product of selfishness. How like the philosopher to place such faith in a vast
social machinery and to rationalize selfish instincts into social

virtues! There is nothing halfhearted about Smith's abiding trust in the consequence of his philosophical beliefs. He urges that judges should be paid by the litigants rather than by the state, since in that way their self-interest will lead them to expedite the cases brought before them. He sees little future for the newly emerging business organizations called joint-stock companies (corporations), since it seems highly improbable that such impersonal bodies could muster the necessary self-interest to pursue complex and arduous undertakings. Even the greatest humanitarian movements, such as the abolition of slavery, are defended in his own terms; best abolish slavery, says Adam Smith, since to do so will probably be cheaper in the end.

The complex irrational world is thus reduced to a kind of rational scheme where human particles are magnetized in a simple polarity toward profit and away from loss. The great system works, not because man directs it, but because self-interest and competition line up the filings in the proper way; the most that man can do is to help this natural social magnetism along, to remove whatever barriers stand before the free working-out of this social physics, and to cease his misguided efforts to escape from its thralldom.

And yet, for all its eighteenth-century flavor, its belief in rationality, natural law, and the mechanized chain of human action and reaction, the world of Adam Smith is not without its warmer values. Do not forget that the great intended beneficiary of the system is the consumer—not the producer. For the first time in the philosophy of everyday life, the consumer is king.

Of the whole, what has survived?

Not the great scheme of evolution. We shall see that profoundly altered by the great economists to follow. But let us not regard the world of Adam Smith as merely a primitive attempt to arrive at formulations that were beyond his grasp. Smith was the economist of preindustrial capitalism; he did not live to see the market system threatened by enormous enterprises, or his laws of accumulation and population upset by sociological developments fifty years off. When Smith

lived and wrote, there had not yet been a recognizable phenomenon that might be called a "business cycle." The world
he wrote about actually existed, and his systematization of it
provides a brilliant analysis of its expansive propensities.

Yet something must have been missing from Smith's
conception. For although he saw an evolution for society, he
did not see a revolution—the Industrial Revolution. Smith
did not see in the ugly factory system, in the newly tried cor-
porate form of business organization, or in the weak attempts
of journeymen to form protective organizations, the first appearance of new and disruptively powerful social forces. In a
sense his system presupposes that eighteenth-century England will remain unchanged forever. Only in quantity will it
grow: more people, more goods, more wealth; its quality will
remain unchanged. His are the dynamics of a static community; it grows but it never matures.

But, although the system of evolution has been vastly
amended, the great panorama of the market remains as a
major achievement. To be sure, Smith did not "discover" the
market; others had preceded him in pointing out how the interaction of self-interest and competition brought about the
provision of society. But Smith was the first to understand
the full philosophy of action that such a conception demanded, the first to formulate the entire scheme in a wide
and systematic fashion. He was the man who made England,
and then the whole Western world, understand just how the
market kept society together, and the first to build an edifice
of social order on the understanding he achieved. Later
economists will embroider Smith's description of the market
and will inquire into the serious defects that subsequently appeared in it. None will improve on the richness and life with
which Smith imbued this aspect of the world.

For Smith's encyclopedic scope and knowledge there
can be only admiration. It was only in the eighteenth century
that so huge, all-embracing, secure, caustic, and profound a
book could have been written. Indeed, *The Wealth of Nations* and *The Theory of Moral Sentiments*, together with his
few other essays, reveal that Smith was much more than just
an economist. He was a philosopher-psychologist-historian-

sociologist who conceived a vision that included human motives and historic "stages" and economic mechanisms, all of which expressed the plan of the Great Architect of Nature (as Smith called him). From this viewpoint, *The Wealth of Nations* is more than a masterwork of political economy. It is part of a huge conception of the human adventure itself.

Moreover, *Wealth* constantly startles us with its piercing observations. Smith anticipated Veblen by a hundred and fifty years when he wrote, "With the greater part of rich people, the chief enjoyment of riches consists in the parade of riches, which in their eye is never so complete as when they appear to possess those decisive marks of opulence which nobody can possess but themselves." He was a statesman ahead of his time when he wrote, "If any of the provinces of the British Empire cannot be made to contribute towards the support of the whole empire, it is surely time that Great Britain should free herself from the expense of defending those provinces in time of war, and of supporting any part of their civil or military establishments in time of peace, and endeavour to accommodate her future views and designs to the real mediocrity of her circumstances." *resistance to authority*

Perhaps no economist will ever again so utterly encompass his age as Adam Smith. Certainly none was ever so serene, so devoid of contumacy, so penetratingly critical without rancor, and so optimistic without being utopian. To be sure, he shared the beliefs of his day; in fact, he helped to forge them. It was an age of humanism and reason; but while both could be perverted for the cruelest and most violent purposes, Smith was never chauvinist, apologist, or compromiser. "For to what purpose," he wrote in *The Theory of Moral Sentiments*, "is all the toil and bustle of this world? What is the end of avarice and ambition, of the pursuit of wealth, of power, and pre-eminence?" *The Wealth of Nations* provides his answer: all the grubby scrabbling for wealth and glory has its ultimate justification in the welfare of the common man.

At the end of his life, Smith was ripe with honors and respect. Burke traveled to Edinburgh to see him; he was elected Lord Rector at his old University of Glasgow; he saw

Wealth translated into Danish, French, German, Italian, Spanish. Only Oxford ignored him; it never deigned to give him an honorary degree. At one time Pitt the younger, then Prime Minister, was meeting with Addington, Wilberforce, and Grenville, and Adam Smith had been invited to attend. As the old philosopher walked into the room, everyone rose. "Be seated, gentlemen," he said. "No," replied Pitt, "we will stand until you are first seated, for we are all your scholars."

In 1790 Smith died; he was sixty-seven. Curiously, his passing attracted relatively little notice; perhaps people were too busy worrying about the French Revolution and the repercussions it might have on the English countryside. He was buried in the Canongate churchyard with an unpretentious tombstone; it states that Adam Smith, author of *The Wealth of Nations,* lies here. It would be hard to conceive of a more durable monument.

iv

The Gloomy Presentiments
of Parson Malthus
and David Ricardo

In addition to the omnipresent problem of poverty, a bother-some question worried England throughout most of the eighteenth century: the question of how many Englishmen there were. The worrisome aspect of the problem lay in the fact that England's natural enemies on the Continent bulged with what, to British eyes, must have appeared as a veritable flood of humanity, while England, with her slender resources, was convinced that her own population was on the decline.

Not that England was any too sure exactly how many Britishers there were; in hypochondriacal fashion, she preferred to worry in a factual vacuum. It would not be until 1801 that the first real census would be held, and when it came it would be heralded as "totally subversive of the last remnants of English liberty." Hence, Britain's earlier knowledge about the state of her human resources depended on the efforts of amateur statisticians: Dr. Price, a Nonconformist minister; Houghton, an apothecary and dealer in coffee and tea; and Gregory King, by trade a maker of maps.

Drawing on records of hearth taxes and baptismal registers, King, in 1696, reckoned up the number of souls in England and Wales as something near five and a half million—what seems to have been an extraordinarily accurate estimate. But King was concerned not only with the contemporary state of affairs. Looking into the future he wrote:

"In all probability, the next doubling of the people of England will be in about six hundred years to come, or by the year of our Lord 2300. . . . The next doubling after that will be, in all probability, in less than twelve or thirteen hundred years, or by the year of our Lord 3500 or 3600. At which time the kingdom will have 22 million souls . . . in case," the mapmaker added circumspectly, "the world should last so long."

But by the time of Adam Smith, King's projection of a gently rising population had given way to another view. Comparing eighteenth-century records of hearth-money taxes with those of an earlier day, Dr. Price proved conclusively that the population of England had *declined* by over 30 percent since the Restoration. The validity of his computation was obviously suspect, and other investigators hotly disputed his findings; nevertheless, what Dr. Price believed to be so was largely taken as fact, although, with the political exigencies of the times, a highly unpalatable fact. "The decay of population," moaned William Paley, the theologian-reformer, "is the greatest evil the state can suffer, and the improvement of it the object which ought . . . to be aimed at, in preference to every other political purpose whatsoever." Paley was not alone in his belief; the younger Pitt, the Prime Minister, even introduced a new poor-relief bill for the specific purpose of boosting the population. The bill was to pay liberal allowances for children, since it was quite apparent to Pitt that by having children a man "enriched" his country, even if his offspring should turn out to be paupers.

What is striking about the population question to our modern eyes is not whether England actually was or was not in danger of petering out as a nation. In retrospect, what is interesting is how harmonious either view of the population problem was with a vision that puts its faith in natural law, reason, and progress. Was the population declining? Then it should be encouraged to grow, as it "naturally" would under the benign auspices of the laws that Adam Smith had shown to be the guiding principles of a free market economy. Was the population growing? All to the good, since everyone agreed that a growing population was a source of national wealth. No matter which way one cut the cake, the result was favorable to an optimistic prognosis for society; or, to put it differently, there was nothing in the population question, as it was understood, to shake men's faith in their future.

Perhaps no one summed up this optimistic outlook so naïvely and completely as William Godwin. Godwin, a minister and pamphleteer, looked at the heartless world about him and shrank back in dismay. But he looked into the future and what he saw was good. In 1793 he published *Political Justice,* a book that excoriated the present but gave promise of a distant future in which "there will be no war, no crime, no administration of justice, as it is called, and no government. Besides this there will be no disease, anguish, melancholy, or resentment." What a wonderful vision! It was, of course, highly subversive, for Godwin's utopia called for complete equality and for the most thoroughgoing anarchic communism: even the property contract of marriage would be abolished. But in view of the high price of the book (it sold for three guineas) the Privy Council decided not to prosecute the author, and it became the fashion of the day in the aristocratic salons to discuss Mr. Godwin's daring ideas.

One home in which this debate took place was Albury House, not far from Guildford, where there resided a curious old gentleman who was described by *Gentleman's Magazine* on his death in 1800 as "an eccentric character in the strictest sense of the term." This eccentric was Daniel Malthus, a friend of David Hume and a passionate admirer of Rousseau, with whom he had gone on local botanizing walks and from whom he had received a herbarium and a set of books in one of the French philosopher's recurrent urges for self-dispossession. Like so many leisurely but inquiring gentlemen of his day, Daniel Malthus enjoyed nothing better than a stimulating intellectual dialogue, and for an opponent he usually turned to his gifted son, the Reverend Thomas Robert Malthus.

Quite naturally, Godwin's paradise came up for consideration, and as might perhaps be expected of a well-disposed oddball, Malthus the elder felt sympathetically inclined toward the supremely rational utopia. But young Malthus was not so hopeful as his father. In fact, as the argument progressed, he began to see an insurmountable barrier between human society as it existed and this lovely imaginary land of everlasting peace and plenty. To convince his father he wrote his objections down at length, and so impressed was Daniel Malthus with his son's ideas that he suggested the thesis be published and presented to the public.

Consequently, in 1798 an anonymous treatise of fifty thousand words appeared on the scene. It was entitled *An Essay on the Principle of Population as It Affects the Future Improvement of Society*, and with it perished at one blow all the fond hopes of a harmonious universe. In a few pages young Malthus pulled the carpet from under the feet of the complacent thinkers of the times, and what he offered them in place of progress was a prospect meager, dreary, and chilling.

For what the essay on population said was that there was a tendency in nature for population to outstrip all possible means of subsistence. Far from ascending to an ever higher level, society was caught in a hopeless trap in which the human reproductive urge would inevitably shove humanity to the very brink of the precipice of existence. Instead of being headed for Utopia, the human lot was forever condemned to a losing struggle between ravenous and multiplying mouths and the eternally insufficient stock of Nature's cupboard, however diligently that cupboard might be searched.

No wonder that after he read Malthus, Carlyle called economics "the dismal science," and that poor Godwin complained that Malthus had converted friends of progress into reactionaries by the hundreds.

In one staggering intellectual blow Malthus undid all the hopes of an age oriented toward self-satisfaction and a comfortable vista of progress. But, as if this were not enough, at the same time a quite different kind of thinker was also preparing the *coup de grâce* for yet another of the lulling assumptions of the late eighteenth and early nineteenth centuries. David Ricardo, an astonishingly successful trader in stocks, was soon to outline a theory of economics which, while less spectacular than Malthus's inundation of humanity, would be in its own quiet way just as devastating to the prospects of improvement held out by Adam Smith.

For what Ricardo foresaw was the end of a theory of society in which everyone moved together up the escalator of progress. Unlike Smith, Ricardo saw that the escalator worked with different effects on different classes, that some rode triumphantly to the top, while others were carried up a few steps and then were kicked back down to the bottom. Worse yet, those who kept the escalator moving were not those who rose with its motion, and those who got the full benefit of the ride did nothing to earn their reward. And to carry the metaphor one step further, if you looked carefully at those who were ascending to the top, you could see that all was not well here either; there was a furious struggle going on for a secure place on the stairs.

Society to Adam Smith was a great family; to Ricardo it was an internally divided camp, and small wonder that he should have seen it as such. In the forty years since *The Wealth of Nations* England had divided into two hostile factions: the rising industrialists, busy with their factories and fighting for parliamentary representation and social prestige, and the great landowners, a rich, powerful, and entrenched aristocracy, who looked resentfully at the encroachments of the brassy *nouveaux riches*.

It was not that the capitalists were making money which enraged the landowners. It was the damnable fact that they kept insisting that food prices were too high. What had happened in the short space of time since Adam Smith was that England, long a grain-exporting nation, was being forced to buy foodstuffs from abroad. Despite the mutterings of Dr. Price, who saw England's population rapidly dwindling away, the actual growth of population had caused the demand for grain to exceed the supply and had *quadrupled* the price of a bushel of wheat. And as prices rose, so did agricultural profits; on a farm in East Lothian, Scotland, profits and rent together averaged 56 percent of invested capital; on another farm of three hundred acres—a very typical medium-sized establishment—profits were £88 in 1790, £121 in 1803, and

£160 ten years later. In the country at large all witnesses agreed rents had at least doubled over the preceding twenty to twenty-five years.

As grain soared, enterprising merchants began to buy wheat and corn abroad and bring them into the country. Quite naturally, the landlord looked on this practice with dismay. Farming was not merely a way of life for the aristocracy, it was a business—a big business. On the Reevesby estate in Lincolnshire in 1799, for instance, Sir Joseph Banks needed two rooms for his offices, separated them with a fireproof wall and an iron door, and was proud of the fact that it took a hundred and fifty-six drawers to classify all the papers pertaining to the farm. Although such a landlord lived on his land and loved the land, although he saw his tenants daily and joined societies for the purpose of discussing crop rotation and the virtues of competing fertilizers, he did not lose sight of the fact that his income depended on the price at which he sold his crop.

Hence the flow of inexpensive grain from overseas was hardly viewed in a tolerant light. But fortunately for the landlord, the means were readily at hand to combat this distressing development. Dominating Parliament, the landlord simply legislated himself an ironclad system of protection. He passed the Corn Laws, which imposed sliding duties on the importation of grain; the lower the foreign price fell, the higher went the duty. In effect, a floor was established to keep low-priced wheat permanently out of the English market.

But by 1813 the situation had gotten out of hand. Bad crops and the war with Napoleon conspired to bring about virtual famine prices. Wheat sold at a price of 117 shillings a quarter—approximately 14 shillings per bushel. Thus a bushel of wheat sold for a price equal to nearly *twice* a workman's *whole weekly wage* (to put this into perspective, compare the highest price ever reached by American wheat before the 1970s: $3.50 per bushel in 1920 when weekly wages averaged $26.00).

Patently, the price of grain was fantastic, and what to do about it became a question of enormous moment to the country. Parliament studied the situation carefully—and came up with the solution that the duty on foreign grain should be raised still higher! The rationale was that higher prices in the short run would act to stimulate a larger production of English wheat in the long run.

This was too much for the industrialists to take. Contrary to the landed proprietors, the capitalists wanted cheap grain, for the price of food largely determined the amount they would have to pay for labor. It was not out of humanitarian motives that the industrialist fought for cheaper food. A great London banker, Alexander Baring, declared in Parliament that "the labourer has no interest in this question; whether the price be 84 shillings or 105 shillings a quarter, he will get dry bread in the one case and dry bread in the other." By this Baring meant that regardless of the price of bread, the laborer would get wages enough to buy his crust and no more. But from the point of view of those who met payrolls and sought after profits, it made a vast deal of difference whether grain—and wages—were cheap or dear.

The business interests organized; Parliament found itself flooded with more petitions than it had ever received before. In view of the temper of the country, it became obviously inexpedient to push through new higher Corn Laws without some deliberation. New committees were appointed in Commons and in Lords, and the issue was temporarily shelved. Fortunately, the next year saw the defeat of Napoleon, and grain prices subsided again toward more normal levels. But it is an index to the political power of the landholding class that thirty years would have to pass until the Corn Laws were finally wiped from the books and cheap grain was permitted to come freely into Britain.

It is not difficult to understand why David Ricardo, writing in the midst of such a period of crisis, saw economics in a different and far more pessimistic light than Adam Smith. Smith had looked at the world and had seen in it a great concert; Ricardo saw a bitter conflict. To the author of *The Wealth of Nations* there was good reason to believe that everyone could share in the benefits of a benign providence; to the inquiring stockbroker writing about a half-century later, not only was society rent into warring groups, but it

seemed inescapable that the rightful winner of the conflict—
the hardworking industrialist—was bound to lose. For Ricardo believed that the only class that could possibly benefit
from the progress of society was the landlord—unless his
hold on the price of grain was broken.

"The interest of the landlords is always opposed to the
interest of every other class in the community," he wrote in
1815, and with that unequivocal sentence an undeclared war
became recognized as the crucial political struggle of a growing market system. And with the open declaration of hostili-
ties there perished the last forlorn hope that this might after
all turn out to be the best of all possible worlds. Now it
seemed that if society did not drown in the Malthusian
swamp, it would tear itself to pieces on David Ricardo's
treacherous moving stairs.

We must look more closely at the profoundly disturbing
ideas of the gloomy parson and the skeptical trader. But first
let us look at the men themselves.

It would be hard to imagine two persons more widely
separated in background and career than Thomas Robert
Malthus and David Ricardo. Malthus, as we know, was the
son of an eccentric member of the English upper middle
class; Ricardo was the son of a Jewish merchant-banker who
had immigrated from Holland. Malthus was tenderly tutored
for a university under the guidance of a philosophically
minded father (one of his tutors went to jail for expressing
the wish that the French revolutionaries would invade and
conquer England); Ricardo went to work for his father at the
age of fourteen. Malthus spent his life in academic research;
he was the first professional economist, teaching at the
college founded in Haileybury by the East India Company
to train its young administrators; Ricardo set up in business
for himself at the age of twenty-two. Malthus was never well-
to-do; by the time he was twenty-six, Ricardo—who had
started with a capital of £800—was financially independent,
and in 1814, at the age of forty-two, he retired with a fortune
variously estimated to be worth between £500,000 and
£1,600,000.

Yet oddly enough it was Malthus, the academician, who was interested in the facts of the real world, and Ricardo, the man of affairs, who was the theoretician; the businessman cared only for invisible "laws" and the professor worried whether these laws fitted the world before his eyes. And as a final contradiction, it was Malthus with his modest income who defended the wealthy landowner, and Ricardo, a man of wealth and later a landlord himself, who fought against their interests.

Different as they were in background, training, and career, so they were accorded utterly different receptions. As for poor Malthus, in the words of a biographer, James Bonar, "He was the best abused man of his age. Bonaparte himself was not a greater enemy of his species. Here was a man who defended small-pox, slavery, and child-murder—a man who denounced soup-kitchens, early marriages, and parish allowances—a man who 'had the impudence to marry after preaching against the evils of a family.' " "From the first," says Bonar, "Malthus was not ignored. For thirty years it rained refutations."

Such abuse was bound to befall a man who urged "moral restraint" on the world. And yet Malthus was neither a prude (by the standards of his times) nor, certainly, an ogre. It is true that he urged the abolition of poor relief and even opposed housing projects for the working classes. But all this was done with the sincerest interest of the poorer classes at heart—and indeed may be contrasted with the view of some contemporary social theorists who suggested blandly that the poor be allowed to die peacefully in the streets.

Hence Malthus's position was not so much a hardhearted as a supremely logical one. Since according to his theory the basic trouble with the world was that there were too many people in it, anything that tended to promote "early attachments" only aggravated the sum of mankind's misery. A man for whom "at Nature's mighty feast there is no vacant cover" might be kept alive by charity; but since he would then propagate, such charity was only cruelty in disguise.

But logic does not always win popularity, and someone who points out the gloomy end of society can hardly expect to

gain popular esteem. No doctrine was ever so reviled: Godwin declared that "the express object of Mr. Malthus's writing was to prove how pernicious was their error, who aimed
at my considerable and essential improvement in human society." It is not surprising that Malthus was regarded as beyond the pale of decent-thinking people.

Ricardo, on the other hand, was a man on whom Fortune
smiled from the start. A Jew by birth, he had broken with his
family and became a Unitarian to marry a handsome Quaker
girl with whom he had fallen in love; but in a day when tolerance was hardly the rule—his father had traded in a part of
the Exchange known as the Jews' Walk—Ricardo achieved
both social status and widespread private respect. Later in
life, when he was in Commons, he was called on to speak
from both sides of the House. "I have no hope," he said, "of
conquering the alarm with which I am assailed the moment I
hear the sound of my own voice." That voice was described
by one witness as "harsh and screamy," by another as "sweet
and pleasant" although "pitched extremely high"; but when it
spoke, the House listened. With his earnest and brilliant expositions, which ignored the toss of events and concentrated
on the basic structure of society "as if he had dropped from
another planet," Ricardo became known as the man who educated Commons. Even his radicalism—he was a strong supporter of freedom of speech and assembly, and an opponent
of Parliamentary corruption and Catholic persecution—did
not detract from the veneration in which he was held.

It is doubtful whether his admirers grasped much of
what they read, for there is no more difficult economist to
understand than Ricardo. But although the text might have
been complex and involved, its import was plain: the interests
of the capitalists and the landlords were irrevocably opposed
and the interests of the landlords were inimical to the community. Hence, whether they understood him or not, the industrialists made him their champion: political economy even
became so popular with them that ladies who hired gov-
ernesses inquired whether they could teach its principles to
their children.

But while Ricardo, the economist, walked like a god (although he was a most modest and retiring person), Malthus was relegated to a lower status. His essay on population was read, admired, and then disproved again and again—the very vehemence of the disproofs a disquieting testimony to the strength of his thesis. And while Ricardo's ideas were avidly discussed, Malthus's contributions to economics—aside from his essay on population—were largely looked on with a kind of benevolent tolerance, or ignored. For Malthus had a sense that all was not well with the world, but he was utterly incapable of presenting his arguments in a clear-cut logical fashion: he was even heretical enough to suggest that depressions—"general gluts," he called them—might upset society, an idea that Ricardo had no trouble proving absurd. How exasperating for a modern reader! Intuitive and fact-minded, Malthus had a nose for trouble, but his wooly-headed expositions had no chance against the incisive brilliance of the financial trader who saw the world only as a great abstract mechanism.

Hence they argued about everything. When Malthus published his *Principles of Political Economy* in 1820, Ricardo went to the trouble of taking some 220-odd pages of notes to point out the flaws in the Reverend's arguments, and Malthus positively went out of his way in his book to expose the fallacies he was sure were inherent in Ricardo's point of view.

Strangest of all, the two were the closest of friends. They met in 1809 after Ricardo had published a series of masterful letters to the *Morning Chronicle* on the question of the price of bullion, and then had demolished a Mr. Bosanquet, who was rash enough to venture an opposing view. First James Mill and then Malthus sought out the author of the letters, and a friendship formed among all three which endured to the ends of their lives. A stream of correspondence passed between them, and they visited each other endlessly. "They hunted together in search of the Truth," wrote Maria Edgeworth, a contemporary writer, in a charming diary, "and huzzaed when they found her, without caring who found her first."

Mention of Maria Edgeworth warrants an additional

word. The daughter of an economist, she was perhaps the first woman to express opinions about the workings of the economy. These initially took the form of moral tales for children, but in 1800 she produced a novel, *Castle Rackrent,* about a landed family that squandered its fortune, largely by indifference to the needs of its tenants. "Rackrent" became a widely used term for such practices. Perhaps of greater interest for this account, Maria corresponded regularly with Ricardo and urged him to come to Ireland to see for himself the realities of the rent problem about which he wrote from Olympian heights. He did not take up her invitation. Incidentally, it would be a century until women became important economists in considerable numbers.

It was not all serious discussion; these were very human beings. Malthus, whether out of deference to his theories or other reasons, had married late, but he was fond of social gatherings. After his death, someone who had known him mused on his life at East India College: "The subdued jests and external homage and occasional insurrections of the young men; the archery of the young ladies; the curious politeness of the Persian professor . . . and the somewhat old-fashioned courtesies of the summer evening parties are all over now."

The pamphleteers compared him with Satan, but Malthus was a tall and handsome man and a gentle soul; his students called him "Pop" behind his back. He had one odd defect: from his great-great-grandfather he had inherited a cleft palate and his speech was difficult to understand; *l* was his worst letter, and there is an amusing account of his saying into the ear trumpet of a deaf and famous lady: "Would not you like to have a look at the lakes of Killarney?" This defect and the indissoluble association of his name with overpopulation led one acquaintance to write:

Philosopher Malthus was here last week. I got an agreeable party for him of unmarried people . . . he is a good natured man and, if there are no signs of approaching fertility, is civil to every lady. . . . Malthus is a real moral philosopher, and I would almost consent to speak as inarticulately, if I could think and act as wisely.

Ricardo at home also loved to entertain; his breakfasts were famous, and he seems to have indulged in a fondness for charades. In her *Life and Letters*, Miss Edgeworth tells of one round:

> *coxcomb*—Mr. Smith, Mr. Ricardo, Fanny, Harriet,— and Maria, *crowing*. Ditto, ditto, *combing* hair. Mr. Ricardo, solus strutting, a *coxcomb*, very droll.

He was extraordinarily gifted as a businessman. "The talent for obtaining wealth," wrote his brother, "is not held in much estimation, but perhaps in nothing did Mr. R. more evince his extraordinary powers than he did in business. His complete knowledge of all its intricacies—his surprising quickness at figures and calculation—his capability of getting through, without any apparent exertion, the immense transactions in which he was concerned—his coolness and judgment—enabled him to leave all his contemporaries at the Stock Exchange far behind." Sir John Bowring later declared that Ricardo's success was based upon his observation that people in general exaggerated the importance of events. "If therefore, dealing as he dealt in stocks, there was reason for a small advance, he bought, because he was certain the unreasonable advance would enable him to realize; so when stocks were falling, he sold in the conviction that alarm and panic would produce a decline not warranted by circumstances."

It was a curiously upside-down arrangement: the theoretical dealer in securities versus the practical divine—particularly curious since the theoretician was at home in the world of money whereas the man of facts and figures was utterly at sea.

During the Napoleonic Wars, Ricardo was an underwriter in a syndicate that bought government securities from the Treasury and then offered them to the subscribing public. Ricardo often did Malthus a favor and carried him for a small block of securities on which the parson made a modest profit. On the eve of Waterloo, Malthus thus found himself a small "bull" on the Exchange, and the strain was too much for his nerves. He wrote to Ricardo urging him "unless it is

wrong or inconvenient . . . to take an early opportunity of re-
alizing a small profit on the share you have been good
enough to promise me." Ricardo did, but with the stronger
staying power of the professional speculator bought himself
into a maximum bull position. Wellington won; Ricardo
made an immense killing, and poor Malthus could not help
being discomfited. Ricardo, on the other hand, wrote casually
to the Reverend, "This is as great an advantage as ever I expect or wish to make by a rise. I have been a considerable
gainer by the loan. . . . Now for a little of our old subject,"
and he plunged back into a discussion of the theoretical
meaning of a rise in the price of commodities.

Their endless debate went on, by letter and visit, until
1823. In his last letter to Malthus, Ricardo wrote: "And now,
my dear Malthus, I have done. Like other disputants, after
much discussion, we each retain our own opinions. These
discussions, however, never influence our friendship; I
should not like you more than I do if you agreed in opinion
with me." He died that year suddenly, at the age of fifty-one;
Malthus was to go on until 1834. As for his opinion of David
Ricardo: "I never loved anybody out of my own family so
much."

Although Malthus and Ricardo disagreed on almost
everything, they did not disagree about what Malthus had to
say about population. For in his celebrated *Essay* in 1798,
Malthus seemed not only to elucidate the question once for
all but also to shed a great deal of light on the terrible and
persistent poverty that haunted the English social scene.
Others had vaguely felt that somehow population and
poverty were related and a popular if apocryphal story of the
day concerned an island off the coast of Chile where one
Juan Fernandez landed two goats in case he should later wish
to find meat there. On revisiting the island he found that the
goats had multiplied beyond reason, so he then landed a pair
of dogs who also multiplied and cut down the goats. "Thus,"
wrote the author, a Reverend Joseph Townshend, "a new
kind of balance was restored. The weakest of both species
were the first to pay the debt of nature; the most active and

vigorous preserved their lives." To which he added: "It is the quantity of food which regulates the number of the human species."

But while this paradigm recognized the balance that must be struck in nature, it still failed to draw the final devastating conclusions implicit in the problem. This was left for Malthus to do.

He began with a fascination in the sheer numerical possibilities contained in the idea of *doubling*. His appreciation of the staggering multiplicative powers of reproduction has been amply supported by other, later scholars. One biologist has calculated that a pair of animals, each pair producing ten pairs annually, would at the end of twenty years be responsible for 700,000,000,000,000,000,000,000 offspring; and Havelock Ellis mentions a minute organism that, if unimpeded in its division, would produce from one single tiny being a mass a million times larger than the sun—in thirty days.

But such examples of the prolific power of nature are meaningless for our purposes. The vital question is: how great is the normal reproductive power of a human being? Malthus made the assumption that the human animal would tend to double its numbers in twenty-five years. In the light of his times this was a relatively modest assumption. It necessitated an average family of six, two of whom were presumed to die before reaching the age of marriage. Turning to America, Malthus pointed out that the population there had in fact doubled itself every twenty-five years for the preceding century and a half, and that in some backwoods areas where life was freer and healthier, it was doubling every fifteen years!

But against the multiplying tendencies of the human race—and it is inconsequential to the argument whether it tended to double in twenty-five years or in fifty—Malthus opposed the obdurate fact that land, unlike people, cannot be multiplied. Land can be added to laboriously, but the rate of progress is slow and hesitant; unlike population, land does not *breed*. Hence, while the number of mouths grows geometrically, the amount of cultivable land grows only arithmetically.

And the result, of course, is as inevitable as a proposition in logic: the number of people is bound, sooner or later, to outstrip the amount of food. "Taking the population of the world at any number, a thousand millions, for instance," wrote Malthus in his *Essay*, ". . . the human species would increase in the ratio of 1, 2, 4, 8, 16, 32, 64, 128, 256, 516, etc. and subsistence as 1, 2, 3, 4, 5, 6, 7, 8, 9, 10, etc. In two centuries and a quarter the population would be to the means of subsistence as 512 to 10; in three centuries as 4096 to 13, and in two thousand years the difference would be incalculable."

Such a dreadful view of the future would be enough to discourage any man: "The view," Malthus wrote, "has a melancholy hue." The troubled Reverend was driven to the conclusion that the incorrigible and irreconcilable divergence between mouths and food could have only one result: the larger portion of mankind would forever be subjected to some kind of misery or other. For somehow the huge and ever potentially widening gap must be sealed: population, after all, cannot exist without food. Hence among the primitives such customs as infanticide; hence war, disease, and, above all, poverty.

And if these are not enough: "Famine seems to be the last, the most dreadful resource of nature. The power of population is so superior to the power of the earth to provide subsistence . . . that premature death must in some shape or other visit the human race. The vices of mankind are active and able ministers of depopulation. . . . But should they fail in this war of extermination, sickly seasons, epidemics, pestilence, and plague advance in terrific array and sweep off their thousands and tens of thousands. Should success still be incomplete, gigantic inevitable famine stalks in the rear, and with one mighty blow, levels the population with the food of the world."

No wonder poor Godwin complained that Malthus had converted friends of progress into reactionaries. For this is truly the doctrine of despair. Nothing, *nothing* can rescue mankind from the constant threat of drowning under its own weight but the frail reed of "moral restraint." And how dependable is moral restraint against the great passion of sex?

•   •

Was Malthus right?

As recently as the early 1970s the general outlook for world population growth seemed to confirm the prescience of his expectations, at least in the less developed portions of the world. In those years demographers spoke of a possible world population of 20 billion—*five times* the population in 1970—if the momentum of population growth went unchecked for another fifty years.

Today the pendulum has swung somewhat to the other side. In fact, thinking on the population problem has always swung between poles of opinion: it is striking that Malthus himself was much more sanguine in a second edition of his famous essay published only five years after the first, pinning his hopes on the belief that the laboring classes would learn to exercise voluntary "restraint" by postponing their age of marriage.

Today's cautious optimism is based to a large extent on technological breakthroughs, especially the so-called Green Revolution which has raised crop yields dramatically in countries like India. India today produces enough foodstuffs to be a modest exporter. Hence, although agronomists still hold their breath each year until the crops are in, the terrible prospect of global famine, brought about by Malthus's arithmetic of supply and demand, is no longer regarded as a realistic prognosis. Horrified TV watchers in the 1980s who saw pictures of skeletonlike human beings in Ethiopia and the sub-Saharan belt were not witnessing Malthus's predictions come true, but the consequences of localized conditions, such as droughts and inadequate transportation networks.

Nonetheless, more is needed to set aside the Malthusian specter than an increase in food production. Even if global famine no longer seems imminent, experts warn that population pressures are still immense. In a Nobel symposium on population problems in 1981, demographers spoke of the threatened emergence of some fifteen mega-cities of over 20 million each in the underdeveloped world. "Spreading like scabrous growths, these human warrens surely pose the supreme political challenge to that world," commented one observer. "How are these urban masses to be kept from the rot of apathy, or restrained from the temptations of anarchy and disorder?"

Perhaps more important, we must not forget that Malthus was right in claiming that population growth, proceeding exponentially, inherently has the *capability* of swamping increases in agricultural productivity. Thus there remains the necessity to master the demand side of the equation as well as the supply side. What is required is control over the production of children as well as food.

Is worldwide population control possible? The answer seems to be a surprising yes. It is surprising because demographers have long doubted that the nations worst afflicted with the population "disease" could surmount the barriers of peasant ignorance, organized religious opposition, and political apathy. Now a more sanguine outlook prevails. During the last years, countries as different as Mexico and China have switched from indifference or outright hostility to an enthusiastic endorsement of birth control. Even India, long the despair of the demographers, has made a determined—indeed, at times a ruthless—effort to introduce planned parenthood.

And the effort has begun to pay off. In the years 1970—1975, despite the prevailing gloom, the rate of growth of population slowed down *for the first time in history*. The growth of population has not yet stopped by any means—U.N. experts predict that today's world population of some 5 billion may grow to between 9 to 10 billion before it levels off. But at least and at last, the growth rate *is* slowing down, and the leveling may come sooner than was imaginable only a decade ago. The trouble is that the victory will not be equally shared. In Europe, for example, we already have something close to ZPG—zero population growth, except for immigration. Fifty years hence, the United States own population, today roughly 275 million, may well number over 390 million, including some 800,000 immigrants. This is a total that will surely add to urban crowding, although it is not likely to overstrain total resources.

But in the poorest parts of the world, where food is scarcest, the forecast is not so reassuring. Birthrates are slowly dropping there, too, but more slowly than in the West, and from a higher starting point. The Malthusian specter will not disappear for a long time.

Curiously, Malthus himself did not aim his shafts at those parts of the world where the problem is so severe today. He was concerned about England and the Western world, not about the continents of the East and South. And here, happily, Malthus was quite mistaken. In 1860 in Great Britain, about 60 percent of all married couples had families of four or more. By 1925 only one couple in five had a family that size. Conversely, the number of families with only one or two children increased over the same time span, from 10 percent of the total to more than half.

What saved the West from Malthus's projected doublings and redoublings? Birth control undoubtedly played a central role. Originally it was called Neo-Malthusianism, a name that would have made Malthus wince, for he disapproved of the practice. Actually, birth control seems to have been practiced by the upper classes all through history, which is one reason why the rich got richer and the poor got children. As England and the West enjoyed a gradually widening affluence, the poor not only ate and clothed themselves better, but they also learned how to limit their offspring like the wealthier classes.

Equally important in confuting Malthus's prediction in the West was its enormous urbanization. On the farm, children can be assets; in the city they are liabilities. Thus economic considerations joined with increasing knowledge of birth control practices to prevent the feared population explosion from taking place.

So the worst of the predictions did not come true for England, and the terrible logic of Malthus's calculations was confined to those parts of the world where wealth and progress lagged. None of this, of course, was even dimly visible in Malthus's own day. In 1801, despite severe misgivings and rumors to the effect that it was the prelude to a military dictatorship, the first census was undertaken in Britain. John Rickman, a civil servant and statistician, calculated that England's population had increased by 25 percent in three decades. Although this was far from doubling, no one doubted that were it not for the disease and poverty of the masses, the population would have grown like an avalanche. No one saw the future slowing-down of the birthrate; rather it seemed as if Britain were forever to face the mean poverty that sprang from a relentlessly spawning humanity scrabbling for an insufficient supply of food. Poverty no longer seemed accidental, or an act of God, or the result even of human indifference. It was as though some malign providence had condemned the human race to eternal dolor, as if all of mankind's efforts toward self-improvement were made a farce through the stinginess of nature.

It was all very discouraging. Paley, who had urged a larger population "in preference to every other political purpose whatsoever," now became a convert to Malthus's banner; Pitt, who had wanted his country enriched with more children, now withdrew his bill for higher poor relief in deference to the parson's opinions. Coleridge summed up the doleful outlook. "Finally, behold this mighty-nation," he wrote, "its rulers and wise men listening to—Paley and—to Malthus! It is mournful, mournful."

Anyone who was not sufficiently depressed by Malthus had only to turn to David Ricardo.

At first glimpse his was not a particularly terrifying world—at least not after the Malthusian. The universe of David Ricardo, set forth in his *Principles of Political Economy* in 1817, is dry, spare, and condensed; there is none of the life, the lively detail of Adam Smith. Here is nothing but principle, abstract principle, expounded by an intellect that is focused on something more permanent than the changing flux of daily life. This is as basic, bare, unadorned, and architectural as Euclid, but, unlike a set of pure geometrical propositions, this system has human overtones: it is a *tragic* system.

To understand that tragedy, we must take a moment to introduce the main characters in the drama. They are not, as we have said, *people:* they are prototypes. Nor do these prototypes, in the everyday sense of the word, *live:* they follow "laws of behavior." There is none of the bustle of Adam Smith's world here; instead we watch a puppet show in which the real world has been stripped of everything but its economic motivations.

Whom do we meet? First, there are the workers, undifferentiated units of economic energy, whose only human aspect is a hopeless addiction to what is euphemistically called "the delights of domestic society." Their incurable penchant for these delights causes every rise in wages to be promptly met with an increase in population. The workers get their dry crust, as Alexander Baring put it, for without it they could not perpetuate themselves. But over the long run they are condemned by their own weakness to a life at the margin of subsistence. Like Malthus, Ricardo saw only "self-restraint" as a solution for the working masses, and although he wished the workers well, he did not put too much faith in their powers of self-control.

Next we meet the capitalists. They are not Adam Smith's conniving merchants. They are a gray and uniform lot, whose entire purpose on earth is to accumulate—that is, to save their profits and to reinvest them by hiring more men to work for them; and this they do with unvarying dependability. But the capitalists' lot is not an easy one. For one thing, by competing among themselves they quickly erase any undue profits that might accrue to a lucky soul who invented a new process or found an unusually profitable channel of trade. For another thing, their profits depend largely on the wages they have to pay, and as we shall see, this leads them into considerable difficulties.

But so far, save for the lack of realistic detail, it is not a world too far removed from that of Adam Smith. It was when Ricardo came to the landlord that things were different.

For Ricardo saw the landlord as a unique beneficiary in the organization of society. The worker worked, and for this he was paid a wage; the capitalist ran the show, and for this he gained a profit. But the landlord benefited from the powers of the soil, and his income—rent—was not held in line either by competition or by the power of population. In fact, he gained at everyone else's expense.

We must pause for a moment to understand how Ricardo came to this conclusion, for his bleak outlook for society hangs on his definition of the landlord's rent. Rent, to Ricardo, was not just the price one paid for the use of the soil, much as interest was the price of capital, and wages the price of labor. Rent was a very special kind of return which had its origin in the demonstrable fact that not all land was equally productive.

Suppose, says Ricardo, there are two neighboring landlords. On one landlord's fields the soil is fertile, and with the labor of a hundred men and a given amount of equipment he can raise fifteen hundred bushels of grain. On the second landlord's fields, the soil is less fecund; the same men and their equipment will raise only one thousand bushels. This is merely a fact of nature, but it has an economic consequence: grain will be cheaper, per bushel, on the fortunate landlord's estate. Obviously since both landlords must pay out the same wages and capital expenses, there will be an advantage in cost to the man who secures five hundred more bushels than his competitor.

It is from this *difference* in costs that rent springs, according to Ricardo. For if the demand is high enough to warrant tilling the soil on the less productive farm, it will certainly be a very profitable operation to raise grain on the more productive farm. Indeed, the greater the difference between the two farms, the greater will be the differential rent. If, for example, it is just barely profitable to raise grain at a cost of $2.00 a bushel on very bad land, then certainly a fortunate landowner whose rich soil produces grain at a cost of only 50 cents a bushel will gain a large rent indeed. For both farms will sell their grain in the market at the same price— say $2.10—and the owner of the better ground will therefore be able to pocket the difference of $1.50 in their respective costs of production.

All this seems innocuous enough. But now let us fit it into the world that Ricardo envisaged, and its portentous consequences will become quite clear.

To Ricardo, the economic world was constantly tending to expand. As capitalists accumulated, they built new shops and factories. Therefore, the demand for laborers increased. This boosted wages, but only temporarily, for better pay would soon tempt the incorrigible working orders to avail themselves of those treacherous delights of domestic society and so to undo their advantage by flooding the market with still more workers. But here is where the world of Ricardo turns sharply away from the hopeful prospects of Adam Smith. As population expanded, said Ricardo, *it would become necessary to push the margin of cultivation out further.* More mouths would demand more grain, and more grain would demand more fields. And quite naturally, the new fields put into seed would not be so productive as those already in use, for it would be a foolish farmer who had not already used the best soil available to him.

Thus, as the growing population caused more and more land to be put into use, the cost of producing grain would rise. So, of course, would the selling price of grain, and so too would the rents of well-situated landlords. And not only rents, but wages would rise as well. For, as grain became more expensive to produce, the laborer would have to be paid more, just to enable him to buy his dry crust and stay alive.

And now see the tragedy. The capitalist—the man responsible for the progress of society in the first place—has been put in a double squeeze. First, the wages he has to pay are higher, since bread is dearer. Secondly, the landlords are much better off, since rents have been rising on good land, as worse and worse land has got pushed into use. And as the landlord's share in society's fruit increases, there is only one class that can get elbowed aside to make room for him—the capitalist.

What a different conclusion from Adam Smith's great pageant of progress! In Smith's world everybody gradually became better off as the division of labor increased and made the community more wealthy. We can now see that this conclusion hinged on Smith's failure to perceive land as a bottleneck to progress. In Smith's vision there is no shortage of fertile soil, hence no margin behind which rents would rise along with population.

By way of contrast, in Ricardo's world *only* the landlord stood to gain. The worker was forever condemned to subsistence, for he chased after every wage rise with a flock of children and thereby competed most of his gains away. The capitalist, who worked and saved and invested, found that all his trouble was for nothing; his wage costs were higher and his profits smaller. As for the landlord, who did nothing but collect his rents—he sat back and watched them increase.

No wonder that Ricardo fought against the Corn Laws and showed the advantages of free trade in bringing cheap grain into Britain. No wonder the landlords fought tooth and nail for thirty years to keep cheap grain out of the country. And how natural that in Ricardo's exposition the young industrialist class saw the theory that just fitted their needs. Were they responsible for low wages? No, since it was only the worker's own blindness that drove him to multiply his numbers. Were they responsible for the progress of society? Yes, and what did it avail them to expend their energies and save their profits for still further adventures in production? All they got for their pains was the dubious satisfaction of watching rents and money wages rise, and their own profits shrink. It was they who drove the economic machine, and the landlord lolling in the back seat who gained all the pleasure and reward. Indeed a sensible capitalist would really have to ask himself if the game was worth the candle.

Now who was to pop up and say that Ricardo was unfair to the landlords but Parson Malthus!

Let us remember that Malthus was not just an expert on the population question. He was first and foremost an economist, and he had, as a matter of fact, propounded the "Ricardian" theory of rent before it was taken up and refined by Ricardo himself. But Malthus did not draw the same conclusions from his theory as his friend. "Rents," said Malthus, in his *Principles of Political Economy*, which appeared three years after Ricardo's, "are the reward of present valour and wisdom, as well as of past strength and cunning. Every day lands are purchased with the fruits of industry and talent." "In fact," Malthus adds in a footnote, "Mr. Ricardo himself is a landlord and a good example of what I mean."

It was not a very convincing rebuttal. Ricardo did not paint the landlord as a machinating figure of evil. He was very well aware that landlords often improved the productivity of their farms, although he pointed out that in so doing they were actually performing the functions of a capitalist. But with irrefutable logic he showed that as land *owners,* even if they neglected their land, they stood to gain from the higher price of grain. Without anyone's having willed it, the forces of economic growth simply operated to channel gain into the pockets of the class that owned the land.

We cannot stop here to trace all the permutations of this debate. What is important is that the dire *implications* of rent envisioned by Ricardo never came to pass. For the industrialists finally did break the power of the landlords and they did finally secure the importation of cheap food. The hillsides up which the wheatfields were ominously climbing in Ricardo's day were, within a few decades, returned to pasture. Equally important, the population never grew so fast as to swamp the resources of the country. For the Ricardian theory says that rent arises from the inequalities between the best land and the worst; obviously, if the population problem is under control, this difference will not develop to such a degree that rental returns assume socially alarming proportions. But consider for a moment the situation if Britain today were forced to feed a population of, say, a hundred million entirely from the produce of home-grown crops. And suppose the old Corn Laws had never been repealed. Is there any doubt that Ricardo's picture of a landlord-dominated society would be a frightening reality? The problem of rent has become almost an academic side issue in the modern Western world. But this is not because Ricardo's analysis was faulty; we have been spared the Ricardian dilemma only because the tempo of industrial life has rescued us from the Malthusian plight: industrialism has not only given us a brake on births, but it has enormously increased our ability to raise food from the land at our disposal.

Meanwhile, Malthus found yet another cause for concern. He was worried over the possibility of what he called a "general glut"—a flood of commodities without buyers.

Such an idea is by no means foreign to us, but it appeared foolish beyond belief to Ricardo. England had had upsets in trade, but all of these appeared to be traceable to some specific cause—a bank failure, or a burst of unwarranted speculation, or a war. More important, for Ricardo's mathematical mind, the concept of a general "glut" could be shown to be *logically impossible*. Therefore, it could never happen.

Ricardo's proof had been discovered by a young Frenchman named Jean-Baptiste Say. Say had two very simple propositions. First, he believed that the *desire* for commodities was infinite. The desire for food might be limited by the capacity of a man's stomach, as Adam Smith had said, but his desire for clothes, furniture, luxuries, and ornaments seemed incalculably large. But not only was demand infinitely large, said Say, but the *ability* to purchase was guaranteed as well. For every good that was produced cost something—and every cost was some man's income. Whether that cost was wages, rent, or profits, its sale price accrued as *someone's* income. And so how could a general glut ever occur? The *demand* for goods existed, and the *incomes* to buy them existed as well. Only passing misjudgments could prevent the market from finding the buyers it needed to clear its wares.

But although Ricardo accepted this as valid on the face of it, Malthus did not. It was not an easy argument to puncture, for it *did* seem logically watertight. But Malthus looked behind the process of swapping commodities for incomes, and came up with a strange idea. Was it not possible, he said, for the act of *saving* to make the demand for goods too small for the supply?

Again, to the modern world, this seems like a disturbingly fruitful line of inquiry. But Ricardo said it was plain and simple nonsense. "Mr. Malthus never appears to remember that to save is to spend, as surely, as what he exclusively calls spending," writes Ricardo in a reproving note. What he meant was that it was inconceivable to him that a man would bother to save his profits for any reason except to spend them for more labor and equipment, in order to earn still more profits.

This put Malthus in a quandary. Like Ricardo, he believed that saving meant spending—for industrial purposes, of course. But still, there seemed to be *something* in his argument—if only he could put his finger on it. He never could. He wrote, for example, to prove that accumulation was not *quite* so essential as Ricardo thought:

> Many a merchant has made a large fortune although, during the acquisition of this fortune, there was perhaps hardly a single year in which he did not rather increase than diminish his expenditure on objects of luxury, enjoyment, and liberality.

To which Ricardo penciled this annihilatory comment:

> True, but a brother merchant who avoided an increased expenditure on objects of luxury, enjoyment, and liberality with the same profits, would get rich faster than him.

Poor Malthus! He never came off best in the exchange. His arguments *were* confused, as perhaps he knew himself. He once wrote, "I have so very high an opinion of Mr. Ricardo's talents as a political economist, and so entire a conviction of his perfect sincerity and love of truth, that I frankly own I have sometimes felt almost staggered by his authority, while I have remained unconvinced by his reasonings." Alas for future generations, Malthus was never able to make his own reasonings cogent or entirely comprehensible. For he was stumbling on a phenomenon that would one day absorb the main attention of economists—the problem of boom and depression—whereas Ricardo was entirely taken up with the quite different problem of distribution. For Malthus, the issue was the immensely important one of How Much Is There? For Ricardo it was the explosive issue of Who Gets What? No wonder they disagreed so endlessly; they were talking about different things.

One last question remains to be examined. How can we explain the change in vision and analysis that separates both Malthus and Ricardo from Adam Smith? The answer tells us something more about the process by which the raw material of perception is reduced to the architecture of thought. For curiously enough, despite the striking differences in their analyses—their expectations and recommendations—at a basic level the vision of both Malthus and Ricardo is *not* fundamentally at odds with that of Smith!

What was that basic vision? It was a view of "society" as a great social mechanism driven by the imperative of a search for profit, disciplined by the omnipresent pressures of competition, and careful both to give government its sphere— and to hold it within that sphere. Why, then, did they come to such differing conclusions? No doubt personality played a role—it always does. But there is another explanation based on something more substantial. It has to do with differences in the workings of the society observed by Smith, compared with that observed by Malthus and Ricardo. The differences lie not in their respective profit motives, role of markets, or place of government—these are the same for all three. They stem from changes in the effects of technology.

For Smith, those effects are represented by the division of labor. We remember Smith's enthusiastic appraisal— mixed with some social misgivings—as to what that change could do for the production of a given product, such as pins. But we also recall that there is nothing in Smith's appraisal to suggest that once the division of labor had worked its wonders in the making of a given product, it would spread to *new* products—textiles, iron-making, who knows what next? Here is a technological reason why a country that had acquired its "full complement of riches," would thereafter stagnate or even decline.

No such limited prospects accompany the emerging industrial technology known to Malthus and Ricardo half a century later. The spinning jenny, the steam engine, the puddling of iron were immediately perceived as opening new avenues for economic growth. With this came an end to the Smithian view of finite expansion possibilities—and with it came as well a premonition of new problems arising from that very prospect. For one thing, population growth now took on a far more threatening aspect as economic expansion no longer enjoyed the brake of constrained capabilities. In

the same way, more expansive prospects for industrial economic growth also implied the further enrichment of the
landlord. Thus it is plausible that the problem-ridden character of Malthusian and Ricardian economics can be traced to
the analytic consequences of a change in vision imposed by a
widening of technological horizons.

How shall we sum up the contributions of the two central figures of this chapter, at once so alike at some levels and
so different at others?

Ricardo's gift to the world was plain. Here was a world
stripped to its essentials and laid open for everyone to examine: the watchworks were exposed. In its very unreality lay its
strength, for not only did the bare structure of a greatly simplified world reveal the laws of rent, but it elucidated as well
vital questions of foreign trade, money, taxation, and economic policy. By building a model world, Ricardo gave the
powerful tool of abstraction to economics—a tool that is essential if the distraction of everyday life is to be pierced and
its underlying mechanism understood. To be sure, as some
observers said in his own day, the tool of abstraction could
also be used to ignore awkward facts and not always "rational" behavior—a problem that has become known as the
Ricardian Vice. Nonetheless, it is to Ricardo's gift for abstraction that we owe the claim of economics to be considered as a
science. Perhaps it is to this very penchant for oversimplifica-
tion that we also owe its rather spotty record *as* a science.

Malthus was never so successful in building an abstract
world, and so his long-lasting academic contribution is
smaller. But he pointed out the appalling problem of population, and for that reason alone, his name is still alive. And he
sensed, even if he could not explain, the problem of general
depression which would occupy economists a century after
his book appeared.

Yet, in retrospect, perhaps the main contribution of the
two lay outside their technical accomplishments. For quite
without intending it, Malthus and Ricardo did one astonishing thing. They changed the viewpoint of their age from optimism to pessimism. No longer was it possible to view the

universe of mankind as an arena in which the natural forces of society would inevitably bring about a better life for everyone. On the contrary, those natural forces that once seemed teleologically designed to bring harmony and peace into the world now seemed malevolent and menacing. If humanity did not groan under a flood of hungry mouths, it seemed that it might suffer under a flood of commodities without takers. And in either event, the outcome of a long struggle for progress would be a gloomy state where the worker just barely subsisted, where the capitalist was cheated of his efforts, and where the landlord gloated.

Indeed, here is another common element to be recognized in the visions of Smith as well as Malthus and Ricardo, besides the structure of what we would call a capitalist economy. This was the vision of the working class as essentially passive. There is no hint in any of the three that the laboring poor might ever take it into their heads to introduce changes in the system—indeed, to build a new system of their own. But that leads us into the next chapter, where we will watch a new vision guide the course of the worldly philosophy.

V

The Dreams of
the Utopian Socialists

It is not difficult to understand why Malthus and Ricardo should have conceived of the world in gloomy terms. England in the 1820s was a gloomy place to live; it had emerged triumphant from a long struggle on the Continent, but now it seemed locked in an even worse struggle at home. For it was obvious to anyone who cared to look that the burgeoning factory system was piling up a social bill of dreadful proportions and that the day of reckoning on that bill could not be deferred forever.

Indeed, a recital of the conditions that prevailed in those early days of factory labor is so horrendous that it makes a modern reader's hair stand on end. In 1828, *The Lion,* a radical magazine of the times, published the incredible history of Robert Blincoe, one of eighty pauper-children sent off to a factory at Lowdham. The boys and girls—they were all about ten years old—were whipped day and night, not only for the slightest fault, but to stimulate their flagging industry. And compared with a factory at Litton where Blincoe was subsequently transferred, conditions at Lowdham were rather humane. At Litton the children scrambled with the pigs for the slops in a trough; they were kicked and punched and sexually abused; and their employer, one Ellice Needham, had the chilling habit of pinching the children's ears until his nails met through the flesh. The foreman of the plant was even worse. He hung Blincoe up by his wrists over a machine so that his knees were bent and then he piled heavy weights on his shoulders. The child and his co-workers were almost naked in the cold of winter and (seemingly as a purely gratuitous sadistic flourish) their teeth were filed down!

Without a doubt such frightful brutality was the exception rather than the rule; indeed we suspect a little of the reformer's zeal has embellished the account. But with full discount for exaggeration, the story was nonetheless all too illustrative of a social climate in which practices of the most callous inhumanity were accepted as the natural order of events and, even more important, as nobody's business. A sixteen-hour working day was not uncommon, with the working force tramping to the mills at six in the morning and trudging home at ten at night. And as a crowning indignity, many factory operators did not permit their work-people to carry their own watches, and the single monitory factory clock showed a strange tendency to accelerate during the scant few minutes allowed for meals. The richest and most farsighted of the industrialists might have deplored such excesses, but their factory managers or hard-pressed competitors seem to have regarded them with an indifferent eye.

And the horrors of working conditions were not the only cause for unrest. Machinery was now the rage, and machinery meant the displacement of laboring hands by uncomplaining steel. As early as 1779 a mob of eight thousand workers had attacked a mill and burned it to the ground in unreasoning defiance of its cold implacable mechanical efficiency, and by 1811 such protests against technology were sweeping England. Wrecked mills dotted the countryside, and in their wake the word went about that "Ned Ludd had passed." The rumor was that a King Ludd or a General Ludd was directing the activities of the mob. It was not true, of course. The Luddites, as they were called, were fired by a purely spontaneous hatred of the factories that they saw as prisons and the wagework that they still despised.

But the disturbances raised a real apprehension in the country. Ricardo almost alone among the respectable people admitted that perhaps machinery did not always operate to the immediate benefit of the workman, and for this opinion he was regarded as having slipped, for once, from his usual acumen. To most observers, the sentiment was less reflective: the lower orders were getting out of hand and should be severely dealt with. And to the gentler classes, the situation seemed to indicate the coming of a violent and terrifying Armageddon. Southey, the poet, wrote, "At this moment nothing but the Army preserves us from that most dreadful of all calamities, an insurrection of the poor against the rich, and how long the Army may be depended upon is a question which I scarcely dare ask myself"; and Walter Scott lamented, ". . . the country is mined beneath our feet."

But all through this dark and troubled period, one spot in Britain shone like a beacon through the storm. In the dour mountains of Scotland, a good day's post from Glasgow, in country so primitive that the tollgate keepers at first refused gold coins (never having seen them before), stood the gaunt seven-story brick mills of a little community called New Lanark. Over the hilly roads from Glasgow rode a constant stream of visitors—twenty thousand signed the guestbook at New Lanark between 1815 and 1825—and the visiting crowds included such dignitaries as the Grand Duke Nicholas, later to be Tsar Nicholas I of Russia, Princes John and Maximilian of Austria, and a whole covey of parish deputations, writers, reformers, sentimental ladies, and skeptical businessmen.

What they came to see was the living proof that the squalor and depravity of industrial life were not the only and inevitable social arrangement. Here at New Lanark were neat rows of workers' homes with *two* rooms in every house; here were streets with the garbage neatly piled up awaiting disposal instead of being strewn in filthy disarray. And in the factories a still more unusual sight greeted the visitors' eyes. Over each employee hung a little cube of wood with a different color painted on each side: black, blue, yellow, and white. From lightest to darkest, the colors stood for different grades of deportment: white was excellent; yellow, good; blue, indifferent; black, bad. At a glance the factory manager could judge the deportment of his work force. It was mainly yellow and white.

For another surprise there were no children in the factories—at least none under the age of ten or eleven—and those that did work toiled only a short ten-and-three-quarter-hour day. Furthermore, they were never punished; no one in fact was punished, and save for a few adult incorrigibles who had to be expelled for chronic drunkenness or some such vice, discipline seemed to be wielded by benignity rather than fear. The door of the factory manager stood open, and anyone could (and did) present his objections to any rule or regulation. Everyone could inspect the book that contained the detailed report of his deportment and thus served as referent for the assignment of his colored cube, and he could appeal if he felt that he had been unjustly rated.

Most remarkable of all were the little children. Instead of running wild and fierce through the streets, they were found by the visitors to be fast at work and play in a large schoolhouse. The littlest were learning the names of the rocks and trees they found about them; the slightly older were learning grammar from a frieze where General Noun contested with Colonel Adjective and Corporal Adverb. Nor was it all work, delightful as the work seemed to be. Regularly the children gathered to sing and dance under the tutelage of young ladies who had been instructed that no child's question was ever to go unanswered, that no child was ever bad without reason, that punishment was never to be inflicted, and that children would learn faster from the power of example than from admonition.

It must have been a wonderful and, indeed, an inspiring sight. And for the business-minded gentlemen who were less likely to be carried away by the sight of happy children than the tenderhearted ladies, there was the irrefutable fact that New Lanark was profitable, marvelously profitable. This was an establishment run not only by a saint but by an eminently practical one, at that.

It was not only a practical saint who was responsible for New Lanark but a most improbable one. Like so many of the early nineteenth-century reformers on whom we look back as the Utopian Socialists, Robert Owen, the "benevolent Mr. Owen of New Lanark," was a strange mixture of practicality and naïveté, achievement and fiasco, common sense and lunacy. Here was a man who advocated the abandonment of the plow in favor of the spade; a man who from scratch became a great capitalist and from a great capitalist a violent opponent of private property; a man who advocated benevolence because it would pay dividends, and who then urged the abolition of money.

It is hard to believe that one man's life could take so many twists. It began as a chapter straight from Horatio Alger. Born of poor parents in Wales in 1771, Robert Owen left school at the age of nine to become apprenticed to a linen draper with the unlikely name of McGuffog. He might have stayed a linen draper always and watched the store name change to McGuffog and Owen, but in true business-hero style, he chose to go to Manchester; and there, at the age of eighteen and on the strength of £100 borrowed from his brother, he set himself up as a tiny capitalist manufacturing textile machinery. But the best was yet to come. A Mr. Drinkwater, the owner of a large spinning establishment, found himself one morning without a factory manager and advertised in the local paper for applicants. Owen had no knowledge of spinning mills, but he got the post in a fashion that might have provided a test for countless writers on the virtues of Pluck and Luck. "I put on my hat," wrote Owen over a half-century later, "and proceeded straight to Mr. Drinkwater's counting house. 'How old are you?' 'Twenty this May,' was my reply. 'How often do you get drunk in the week?' . . . 'I was never,' I said, 'drunk in my life,' blushing scarlet at this unexpected question. 'What salary do you ask?' 'Three hundred a year,' was my reply. 'What?' Mr. Drinkwater said, with some surprise, repeating the words, 'Three hundred a year! I have had this morning I know not how many seeking the situation and I do not think all their askings together would amount to what you require.' 'I cannot be governed by what others seek,' said I, 'and I cannot take less.' "

It was a characteristic Owen gesture and it succeeded. At twenty he became the boy wonder of the textile world— an engaging young man with a rather straight nose in a very long face, and with large, frank eyes that advertised his candor. Within six months Mr. Drinkwater offered him a quarter interest in the business. But this was still only the prelude to a fabulous career. Within a few years Owen had heard of a set of mills for sale in the squalid village of New Lanark—coincidentally they were owned by a man with whose daughter he had fallen in love. To acquire either the mills or the hand of the daughter looked like an impossible feat: Mr. Dale, the mill-owner, was a fervid Presbyterian who would never approve of Owen's radical free-thinking ideas, and then there was the question of how to find the capital to buy the mills. Nothing daunted, Owen marched up to Mr. Dale as he had once marched up to Mr. Drinkwater and the impossible became done. He borrowed the money, bought the mills, and won the hand of the daughter in the bargain.

Matters might well have rested there. Within a year Owen had made New Lanark a changed community; within five years it was unrecognizable; in ten years more it was world famous. It would have been accomplishment enough for most men, for in addition to winning a European reputation for farsightedness and benevolence, Robert Owen had made a fortune of at least £60,000 for himself.

But matters did not rest there. Despite his meteoric rise, Owen conceived of himself as a man of ideas rather than as a mere man of action; New Lanark had never been for him an idle exercise of philanthropy. Rather, it was an opportunity to test out theories that he had evolved for the advancement of humanity as a whole. For Owen was convinced that mankind was no better than its environment and that if that environment was changed, a real paradise on earth might be achieved. In New Lanark he could, as it were, test his ideas in a laboratory, and since they succeeded beyond all measure, there seemed no reason why they should not be given to the world.

He soon had his chance. The Napoleonic Wars subsided and in their wake came trouble. A succession of what

Malthus would have called "general gluts" wracked the country; from 1816 to 1820 with the exception of a single year, business was very bad. The misery threatened to explode: "bread and blood" riots broke out, and a kind of hysteria gripped the country. The Dukes of York and Kent and a body of notables formed a committee to look into the causes of the distress, and purely as a matter of course they called upon Mr. Owen, the philanthropist, to present his views.

The committee was hardly prepared for what it got. It had no doubt expected a plea for factory reform, for Mr. Owen was widely known for his championship of a shorter working day and the abolition of child labor. Instead the notables found themselves reading a blueprint for social reorganization on a sweeping scale.

What Owen suggested was that the solution to the problem of poverty lay in making the poor productive. To this end he advocated the formation of Villages of Cooperation in which eight hundred to twelve hundred souls would work together on farm and in factory to form a self-sustaining unit. The families were to live in houses grouped in parallelograms—the word immediately caught the public eye—with each family in a private apartment but sharing common sitting rooms and reading rooms and kitchens. Children over the age of three were to be boarded separately so that they could be exposed to the kind of education that would best mold their characters for later life. Around the school were gardens to be tended by the slightly older children, and around them in turn would stretch out the fields where crops would be grown—needless to say with the aid of spades and without the use of plows. In the distance, away from the living areas, would be a factory unit; in effect this would be a planned garden city, a kibbutz, a commune.

The committee of notables was considerably taken aback. It was hardly prepared to urge the adoption of planned social communities in a day of untrammeled *laissez-faire*. Mr. Owen was thanked and Mr. Owen's ideas were carefully ignored. But Owen was nothing if not single-purposed. He insisted upon a review of the applicability of his plans and flooded Parliament with tracts expounding his views. Again his determination won the day. In 1819 a special committee (including David Ricardo) was put together for the purpose of trying to raise the necessary £96,000 to establish one full-fledged experimental Village of Cooperation.

Ricardo was skeptical, although willing to give the plan a trial, but the country was not skeptical at all; it found the idea an abomination. One editorialist wrote: "Robert Owen, Esq., a benevolent cotton-spinner . . . conceives that all human beings are so many plants which have been out of the earth for a few thousand years, and require to be reset. He accordingly determines to dibble them in squares after a new fashion."

William Cobbett, then in exile in America for his own radical ideas, was even more scornful. "This gentleman," he wrote, "is for establishing *communities* of paupers! . . . Wonderful peace, happiness, and national benefit are to be the result. How the little matters of black eyes, bloody noses, and pulling of caps are to be *settled*, I do not exactly see. Mr. Owen's scheme has, at any rate, the recommendation of perfect novelty, for of such a thing as a *community of paupers*, I believe no human being has ever before heard. . . . Adieu, Mr. Owen of Lanark."

Owen did not, of course, envision a community of paupers. He believed, on the contrary, that paupers could become the producers of wealth if they were given a chance to work, and that their deplorable social habits could be easily transformed into virtuous ones under the influence of a decent environment. And it was not only paupers who were to be thus elevated. The Villages of Cooperation were to be so manifestly superior to the turmoil of industrial life that other communities would naturally follow suit.

But it was obvious that Owen held his views alone. Serious-minded people saw in Owen's scheme a disturbing threat to the established order of things, and radical-minded people saw in it only a farce. The necessary money for the trial Village was never raised, but now there was no stopping the indomitable philanthropist. He had been a humanist; now he became a professional humanitarian. He had made a fortune; now he dedicated it to the realization of his ideas. He sold his interest in New Lanark and in 1824 set about building his own community of the future. Not unnaturally he chose America for his milieu, for where better to build utopia than in the midst of a people who had known political liberty for fifty years?

For a site he bought from a religious sect of Germans known as Rappites a tract of thirty thousand acres on the banks of the Wabash in Posey County, Indiana. On the Fourth of July, 1826, he dedicated it with a Declaration of Mental Independence—independence from Private Property, Irrational Religion, and Marriage—and then left it to shift for itself with its lovely wishful name of New Harmony.

It could not and did not succeed. Owen had envisioned a utopia sprung full-blown into the world, and he was not prepared to wean one from the imperfect environment of the old society. There was no planning: eight hundred settlers poured in, helter-skelter, within a few weeks. There was not even elementary precaution against fraud. Owen was bilked by an associate who piled insult upon injury by setting up a whiskey distillery on land that he had unfairly taken. And since Owen was not there, rival communities sprang up: Macluria under one William McClure, and others under other dissidents. The pull of acquisitive habit was too strong for the bond of ideas; in retrospect it is only astonishing that the community managed to exist for as long as it did.

By 1828 it was apparent that the enterprise was a failure. Owen sold the land (he had lost four-fifths of his entire fortune in the venture) and went off to talk about his schemes to President Jackson and then to Santa Anna in Mexico. Neither of these gentlemen expressed more than polite interest.

Owen now returned to England. He was still the benevolent (if slightly cracked) Mr. Owen, and his career was about to take its final unexpected twist. For while most opinion had mocked at his Villages of Cooperation, his teachings had sunk deep into one section of the country: the working classes. This was the time of the first trade unions, and the leaders of the spinners and the potters and the builders had come to regard Owen as a man who could speak for their interests—

indeed, as their leader. Unlike his peers, they took his teachings seriously—while the Villages of Cooperation were being
debated by committees of notables, real working cooperative
societies based on his tracts were springing up throughout
the country on a more modest scale: producers' cooperatives
and consumers' cooperatives and even a few ill-fated attempts to follow Mr. Owen's ideas to the letter and do away
with money.

Without exception, the producers' cooperatives failed
and the moneyless exchanges ended in moneyless but equally
final bankruptcies. But one aspect of the cooperative movement took root. Twenty-eight devoted men who called
themselves the Rochdale Pioneers began the *consumer* cooperative movement. To Owen it was only of passing interest,
but with time it grew to be one of the great sources of
strength of the Labour party in Great Britain. Curiously, the
movement in which he took least interest was to survive all
the projects into which he poured his heart and strength.

Owen had no time for cooperatives, for a good reason;
on his return from America he had conceived a huge moral
crusade, and he plunged into it with a typical vigorous abandon. The onetime poor boy, onetime capitalist, one-time social architect, now drew around him the leaders of the
working-class movement. He bestowed a properly impressive
name on his project: the Grand National Moral Union of the
Productive and Useful Classes. The name was soon short-
ened to the Grand National Consolidated Trades Union, and
since that was still quite a mouthful, to the Grand National.
Under its banner the trade-union leaders rallied, and in 1833
the English working-class movement was officially launched.

It was a nationwide union—the precursor of the industrial trade unions of our day. Its membership was five hundred thousand—a mammoth figure for that time—and it
embraced virtually every important union in all of England.
But, unlike a modern union, its goals were not limited to
hours and wages or even to management prerogatives. The
Grand National was to be an instrument not only of social
betterment but of deep social change. Hence, while its program asked for better wages and working conditions, it went

on to expound a fuzzy amalgam of Villages of Cooperation, the abolition of money, and a number of other ideas from the potpourri of Owen's writing.

Owen stumped the country for his final cause. It was a fiasco. England was no more prepared for a national trade union than America for a local paradise. Local unions could not control their members, and local strikes weakened the national body. Owen and his lieutenants fell out; they accused him of atheism, and he charged them with fomenting class hatred. The government stepped in and with violence and vengeance did its best to disrupt the growing movement. The employing classes heard in the Grand National the knell of private property and called for prosecution under anti-union laws. No youthful movement could have withstood such an onslaught. Within two years the great union was dead, and Owen at the age of sixty-four had played his last historical role.

He continued for another twenty years, the grand old man of labor, urging his cooperative ideas, his preference for the spade, his naive distrust of money. In 1839 he had an audience with Queen Victoria despite the protests of a group of the best people known as the Society for Peaceably Repressing Infidelity. But he was finished. In his last years he found a refuge in spiritualism, in endless tracts endlessly the same, and in his wonderful *Autobiography*. In 1858, eighty-seven years old and still hopeful, he died.

What a romantic and fantastic story! And looking back, it is his story rather than his ideas which interests us. Owen was never a truly original and certainly never a flexible thinker. "Robert Owen is not a man to think differently of a book for having read it," was the devastating way in which one contemporary writer characterized him, and Macaulay, who fled at the sound of his voice, called him "always a gentle bore."

He was not, by any stretch of the imagination, an economist. But he was more than that; he was an economic innovator who reshaped the raw data with which economists have to deal. Like all the Utopian Socialists, Owen wanted the world changed; but while others wrote, powerfully or otherwise, he went ahead and tried to change it.

And on second thought, perhaps he did leave one great idea behind him. It is charmingly illustrated in this anecdote from the autobiography of his son, Robert Dale Owen.

"When the child screams from temper, my dear Caroline," said his father (Robert Owen), "set him in the middle of the nursery floor and be sure you don't take him up until he stops crying." "But my dear, he'll go on crying by the hour." "Then let him cry." "It may hurt his little lungs, and perhaps throw him into spasms." "I think not. At all events, it will hurt him more if he grows into an ungovernable boy. Man is the creature of circumstances."

"Man is the creature of circumstances." And who makes the circumstances but man himself? The world is not inevitably good or bad but to the extent that we make it so. In that thought Owen left behind him a philosophy of hope more powerful than all his fanciful notions about spades and plows or money or Villages of Cooperation.

Robert Owen is certainly the most romantic of that group of nineteenth-century protesters against raw capitalism, but he is by no means the most peculiar. For sheer perversity of character, honors must go to Count Henri de Rouvroy de Saint-Simon, and for indisputable eccentricity of ideas there is no peer of Charles Fourier.

Saint-Simon, as his rolling name suggests, was an aristocrat; his family claimed descent from Charlemagne. Born in 1760, he was brought up to be conscious of the nobility of his ancestry and of the importance of maintaining the luster of his name; every morning, as a youth, he was awakened by his valet, who would cry: "Arise, Monsieur le Comte, you have great things to do today."

The knowledge that one is a chosen vessel of history can do strange things to a man. In Saint-Simon's case, it provided the excuse for an extravagant self-indulgence. Even as a boy he confused a devotion to principle with sheer pigheadedness; it is said that when a passing wagon interfered with a childhood game, he threw himself down across the road and obstinately refused to budge—and who was to throw a young count into the ditch? Later this same obstinacy led him to refuse to go to communion at his father's behest—but the father, perhaps more used to his son's intransigence and certainly less awed by it, promptly threw him into jail.

His self-indulgence might have turned him toward that most self-indulgent of all political groups, the court of Louis XVI. But it was redeemed by a love for a most uncourtly idea: democracy. In 1778 the young count went to America and distinguished himself in the Revolutionary War. He fought in five campaigns, won the Order of Cincinnatus, and most important of all, became a passionate disciple of the new ideas of freedom and equality.

But this did not yet constitute Great Things. The Revolutionary War left him in Louisiana; thence he went to Mexico to urge the Viceroy to build a canal that would have preceded the Panama. That might have made his name, but the idea came to naught—it was, of course, nine tenths idea and one tenth plan—and the young revolutionary noble returned to France.

He was just in time for the Revolution there, and he threw himself into it with fervor. His townspeople of Falvy in Peronne asked him to be mayor and he refused, saying that the election of the old nobility would be a bad precedent; then when they chose him for the National Assembly anyway, he proposed the abolition of titles and renounced his own to become plain Citoyen Bonhomme. His democratic predilections were not a pose; Saint-Simon had a genuine feeling for his fellow man. Before the Revolution he had been posting to Versailles one day, in the height of style, when he came across a farmer's cart mired in the road. Saint-Simon got down from his carriage, put his elegantly clad shoulder to the wheel, and then found the farmer's conversation so interesting that he dismissed his own vehicle and rode to Orléans with his newfound peasant friend.

The Revolution dealt strangely with him. On the one hand he speculated adroitly in Church lands and made himself a modest fortune; on the other he busied himself with a gigantic educational scheme that, because it threw him into contact with foreigners, brought him into disfavor and resulted in his being put in protective custody. He escaped and then, in a gesture both romantic and truly noble, surrendered himself again when he found that his hotel proprietor had been unjustly accused of collaborating in his escape.

This time he went to jail. But there, in his cell, there came to him the revelation for which he had, in a sense, been waiting all his life. The revelation came, as such visitations do, in a dream; Saint-Simon described it thus:

"During the cruelest period of the Revolution, and during a night of my imprisonment at Luxembourg, Charlemagne appeared to me and said: 'Since the world began no family has enjoyed the honor to produce both a hero and philosopher of first rank. This honor was reserved for my house. My son, your successes as a philosopher will equal mine as a soldier and a statesman.'"

Saint-Simon asked for no more. He obtained a release from prison, and the money he had accumulated now poured forth in a fantastic search for knowledge. This man actually set out to know everything there was to know—scientists, economists, philosophers, politicians, all the savants of France were invited to his house, financed in their work, and endlessly queried that Saint-Simon might encompass the world's intellectual scope. It was a bizarre endeavor. At one time, having come to the conclusion that he still lacked a firsthand acquaintance with family life for the pursuance of his social studies, he married—on a three-year contract. One year was enough: his wife talked too much and his guests ate too much, and Saint-Simon decided that marriage as an educational institution had its limitations. Instead he sought the hand of the most brilliant woman in Europe, Mme. de Staël; she was the only woman, he declared, who would understand his plans. They met, but it was an anticlimax; she found him full of *esprit* but hardly the greatest philosopher in the world. In the circumstances, his enthusiasm also waned.

But the search for encyclopedic knowledge, while stimulating, was financially disastrous. His expenditures had been lavish to the point of recklessness; his marriage unexpectedly expensive. He found himself reduced first to modest circumstances and then to real poverty; he was forced to find a clerical job and then to depend on the kindness of an old servant for board and lodging. Meanwhile he was writing, furiously writing an endless stream of tracts, observations, exhortations, and examinations of society. He sent his works to the leading patrons of the day with a pathetic note:

MONSIEUR:
Be my saviour, I am dying of hunger. . . . For 15 days I have lived on bread and water . . . sold everything but my clothes, to pay for the expense of copies of my work. It is the passion for knowledge and the public welfare, the desire to find a peaceful means of ending the frightful crisis which engages all European society which has brought me to this state of distress. . . .

No one subscribed. In 1823, although his family now accorded him a small pension, he shot himself in despair. But he could never quite do anything as he wished. He succeeded only in losing an eye. He lived two more years, ill, impoverished, dedicated, and proud. When the end came, he gathered his few disciples around him and said, "Remember that in order to do great things one must be impassioned!"

But what had he done to justify such an operatic end? A strange thing: he had founded an industrial religion. He had not done it through his books, which were voluminous enough but unread, nor through lectures, nor through doing "great things." Somehow the man himself had inspired a sect, had gathered a small band of followers, and had given society a new image of what it might be.

It was a strange, semimystical, and disorganized religion, and little wonder, for it was built on an unfinished and lopsided edifice of ideas. It was not even meant to be a religion as such—although after his death there was actually a Saint-Simonian Church with six departmental churches in France and with branches in Germany and England. Perhaps it is better compared with an order of brotherhood; his disciples dressed in shades of blue and ranked each other as "fathers and sons." And as a nice symbol of what the founder himself

had stood for, they wore a special waistcoat that could be neither put on nor taken off unassisted and that thus emphasized the dependence of every man on his brothers. But the
church soon degenerated into little more than a cult, for the
latter-day Saint-Simonians devised their own code of morality, which in some instances was little more than a re-
spectably codified immorality.

The gospel that Saint-Simon had preached is hardly
shocking to modern eyes. It proclaimed that "man must
work" if he is to share in society's fruits. But compared with
the conclusions drawn from this premise, Robert Owen's society of parallelograms was clarity itself.

"We suppose," writes Saint-Simon, "that France suddenly loses her fifty leading physicists; her fifty leading
chemists, her fifty leading physiologists . . . mathematicians
. . . mechanics" and so on until three thousand savants,
artists, and artisans have been accounted for (Saint-Simon is
not noted for the economy of his style). What would be the
result? It would be a catastrophe that would rob France of
her very soul.

But now suppose, says Saint-Simon, that instead of losing these few individuals, France were to be deprived at
one blow of its social upper crust: suppose it should lose M.
the brother to the king, the Duke de Berry, some duchesses,
the officers of the Crown, the ministers of state, its judges,
and the ten thousand richest proprietors of the land—thirty
thousand people in all. The result? Most regrettable, says
Saint-Simon, because these are all good people, but the loss
would be purely a sentimental one; the state would hardly
suffer. Any number of people could discharge the functions
of these lovely ornaments.

So the moral is clear. It is the workers—*les industrials*
—of all ranks and hierarchies who merit the highest rewards
of society, and the idlers who deserve the least. But what do
we find? By a strange miscarriage of justice, it is just the opposite: those who do the least get the most.

Saint-Simon proposes that the pyramid be set aright. Society is actually organized as a gigantic factory, and it should
carry out the factory principle to its logical conclusion. Gov-

ernment should be economic, not political; it should arrange things and not direct men. Rewards should be apportioned to one's social contribution; they should accrue to the active members of the factory and not to the lazy onlookers. It is not a revolution that Saint-Simon preaches, nor even socialism as we understand the word. It is a kind of paean of the industrial process and a protest that in a society of toil, idlers should take such a disproportionate share of the wealth.

Not a word about how this is to be done; the later Saint-Simonians went a step beyond their founder and urged the end of private property, but even this left them with little more than a vague program of social reformation. This was a religion of work, but it lacked a proper catechism; it pointed to grave injustices in the distribution of society's wealth, but it gave disappointingly little guidance to those who wanted to set things to rights.

Perhaps it was just this lack of a program which helped to account for the success of a man who was quite the opposite of Saint-Simon. Whereas the ax-nobleman had been inspired by a passion for the grand idea, Charles Fourier was inspired by a passion for trivia. Like Saint-Simon, Fourier believed the world was hopelessly disorganized, but the cure he proposed was explicit down to the tiniest detail.

Saint-Simon had been an adventurer in life; Fourier was an adventurer in imagination. His biography is largely a blank: born in 1772, the son of a tradesman of Besançon, he spent his days as an unsuccessful commercial traveler. In a sense he did nothing, not even marry. His passions were two: flowers and cats. It is only at the end of his life that he is appealing, for he spent his last years punctually sitting at advertised hours in his small room awaiting the visit of some great capitalist who would offer to finance his schemes to do over the world. After all, this little salesman had written, "I alone have confounded twenty centuries of political imbecility; and it is to me alone that present and future generations will look for the origin of their immense happiness." With such a responsibility resting on his shoulders, he could hardly afford not to be at hand when the appointed savior capitalist would arrive with his moneybags in train. But no one ever came.

Fourier, to be polite, was an eccentric; to be accurate, he was probably off his rocker. His world was a fantasy: the earth, he believed, had been given a life of eighty thousand years; forty thousand of ascending vibrations and the same number of descending. In between (never mind the arithmetic) lay eight thousand years of the Apogée du Bonheur. We lived in the fifth of eight stages of advancement, having pushed through Confusion, Savagery, Patriarchism, and Barbarousness. Ahead lay Guaranteeism (not a bad bit of insight), and then the upward slope of Harmony. After we reached utter bliss, however, the seesaw would tip and we would work our way right back down through all the stages to the beginning.

But as we worked our way ever deeper into Harmony, things would really begin to pop: a Northern Crown would encircle the Pole, shedding a gentle dew; the sea would become lemonade; six new moons would replace the old solitary satellite; and new species would emerge, better suited to Harmony: an antilion, a docile and most serviceable beast; an antiwhale, which could be harnessed to ships; an antibear; antibugs; and antirats. We would live to be one hundred and forty-four years old, of which one hundred and twenty years would be spent in the unrestricted pursuit of sexual love.

All this plus a firsthand description of the inhabitants of other planets gives to Fourier's writings the air of a madman. Perhaps he was. But when he turned his starry vision to this earth he saw in it chaos and unhappiness, and he saw, as well, a way to reorganize society.

His prescription was very exact. Society should be organized into phalanxes—the French word is *phalanstères*—which would consist of a kind of Grand Hotel arrangement, not too dissimilar from Owen's Villages of Cooperation. The hotel was carefully described: there would be a large central building (its various rooms and their dimensions were all thought out), and around it would be fields and industrial establishments. You could live in the hotel at the scale best suited to your purse; first, second, or third class, with just as much privacy as you desired (including meals in your rooms) and with just enough mingling to spread a leaven of culture. Efficiency would be achieved through centralization; Fourier, the old bachelor, paints a mouth-watering picture of the triumphs of the central cuisine.

Everyone would have to work, of course, for a few hours each day. But no one would shirk work, for each would do what he best liked. Thus the problem of dirty work was solved by asking who liked to do dirty work. The children, of course. So there would be Little Hordes who would go off gaily to the slaughterhouses or to mend the roads and have the time of their lives. And for the minority of children who shrank from dirty work, there would be Little Bands who would tend the flowers and correct their parents' bad pro- nunciation. Among the workers there would be amicable competition to see who did best: contests of pear growers and cultivators of spinach and finally (once the phalanstery principle had encircled the globe and the 2,985,984 necessary *phalanstères* established) great battles of omelette chefs and champagne bottlers. he's crazy

And the whole affair would be profitable in the extreme; gains would run to 30 percent. But it would be communal profit: the surplus would be divided five twelfths to labor, four twelfths to capital, and three twelfths to "ability," and everybody would be urged to become a part owner as well as a fellow worker.

Weird and fantastic as it seems, the Fourierist idea took some hold, even in that fortress of practicality and common sense, the United States. At one time there were over forty phalansteries in this country, and if one groups together the Owenite communities and the religious movements of various sorts, there were at least one hundred and seventy-eight actual Utopian groups with from fifteen to nine hundred members each.

Their variety was immense: some were pious, some impious; some chaste, some licentious; some capitalistic, others anarchic. There was Trumbull Phalanx in Ohio and Modern Times on Long Island; there were Oneida and Brook Farm and New Icaria and one rather remarkable phalanx—the North American Phalanx in New Jersey—which endured from 1843 to 1855 and then lingered on, half hotel, half community, until the late 1930s. Of all unlikely people, the critic Alexander Woollcott was born there.

None of the dream communities took solid root. Dream worlds have a difficult time contending with the frictions of reality, and of all the projected Utopian rearrangements of society, none was so far removed from practicality as the *phalanstère*. And yet, none is so beguiling. If we could live in a *phalanstère*, who would not like to? Fourier pointed with devastating truth to the miserable unhappiness of the world in which he lived, but his prescription was too much compounded of heavenly ingredients for the mortal ills he wished to cure.

Do they appear ridiculous, these Utopians? It is true that they were all dreamers—but, as Anatole France said, without dreamers, mankind would still live in caves. There was not one without a touch of madness: even Saint-Simon speculated solemnly on the possibility of the beaver, as the most intelligent animal, someday replacing humankind. But they are not noteworthy because they were eccentrics or because of the richness and appealing quality of their fantasies. They are worth our attention because they were courageous, and to appreciate their courage we must appraise and understand the intellectual climate in which they lived.

They lived in a world that was not only harsh and cruel but that rationalized its cruelty under the guise of economic law. Necker, the French financier and statesman, said at the turn of the century, "Were it possible to discover a kind of food less agreeable than bread but having double its substance, people would be reduced to eating only once in two days." Harsh as such a sentiment might have sounded, it did ring with a kind of logic. It was the world that was cruel, not the people in it. For the world was run by economic laws, and economic laws were nothing with which one could or should trifle; they were simply *there*, and to rail about whatever injustices might be tossed up as an unfortunate consequence of their working was as foolish as to lament the ebb and flow of the tides.

The laws were few but final. We have seen how Adam

Smith, Malthus, and Ricardo elaborated the laws of economic distribution. These laws seemed to explain not only
how the produce of society tended to be distributed but how
it *should* be distributed. The laws showed that profits were
evened out and controlled by competition, that wages were
always under pressure from population, and that rent accrued to the landlord as society expanded. And that was
that. One might not necessarily *like* the result, but it was
apparent that this result was the natural outcome of society's
dynamics: there was no *personal* ill-will involved nor any
personal manipulation. Economic laws were like the laws
of gravitation, and it seemed as nonsensical to challenge one
as the other. Hence a primer of elementary economic principles said: "A hundred years ago only savants could fathom
them [economic laws]. Today they are commonplaces of
the nursery, and the only real difficulty is their too great simplicity."

No wonder the Utopians went to such extremes. The
laws did look inviolable—and yet the state of society for
which they were held responsible was intolerable. So the
Utopians took their courage in both hands and said, in effect,
the whole system must change. If this is capitalism—with a
nod at Robert Blincoe chained to a machine—let us have
anything else—Villages of Cooperation, moral codes, or the
delightful resort atmosphere of a *phalanstère*. The Utopians—and there were many besides those mentioned in this
chapter—were reformers of the heart rather than the head.

This is one reason why we designate them as *Utopian*
Socialists. The "utopia" was not merely a matter of idealistic
ends; it was also a key to the means. In contradistinction to
the Communists, these were reformers who hoped to per-
suade the members of the *upper* classes that social change
would be for their own ultimate benefit. The Communists
talked to the masses and urged violence, if necessary, to encompass their ends; the Socialists appealed to their own
kind—to the intelligentsia, the *petit bourgeois*, the freethink-
ing middle-class citizen, or the intellectually emancipated
aristocrat—for adherents to their schemes. Even Robert
Owen hoped to get his brother mill-owners to see the light.

But secondly, note that these were Utopian *Socialists*. This meant they were *economic* reformers. Utopia builders had existed since Plato, but it was not until the French Revolution that they had begun to react to economic as well as political injustice. And since it was early capitalism that provided the chamber of horrors against which they revolted, not unnaturally they turned their backs on private property and the struggle for private wealth. Few of them thought of reform *within* the system: remember that this was the age of the very first watered-down factory legislation and that such grudging reforms as were painfully won were largely honored in the breach. The Utopians wanted something better than reform—they wanted a new society in which Love Thy Neighbor could somehow be made to take priority over the mean gouging of each for himself. In the communality of property, in the warmth of common ownership, were to be found the touchstones of human progress.

They were men of very good will. And yet, for all their good intentions and their earnest theories, the Utopians lacked the stamp of respectability; they needed the imprimatur of someone with them in heart but whose head would be somewhat more firmly attached to his shoulders. And they found such a person in the most unlikely place—in the ultimate conversion to socialism of the person who was by common consent the greatest economist of the age: John Stuart Mill.

Everyone in this chapter is a somewhat unbelievable character, but perhaps J. S. Mill is the most remarkable of them all. His father was James Mill, historian, philosopher, pamphleteer, friend and intimate of Ricardo and Jeremy Bentham, one of the leading intellects of the early nineteenth century. James Mill had definite ideas about almost everything, and especially about education. His son, John Stuart Mill, was the extraordinary result.

John Stuart Mill was born in 1806. In 1809 (not 1819) he began to learn Greek. At age seven he had read most of the dialogues of Plato. The next year he began Latin, having meanwhile digested Herodotus, Xenophon, Diogenes Laër-

tius, and part of Lucian. Between eight and twelve he finished Virgil, Horace, Livy, Sallust, Ovid, Terence, Lucretius,
Aristotle, Sophocles, and Aristophanes; had mastered geome-
try, algebra, and the differential calculus; written a Roman
History, an Abridgment of the Ancient Universal History, a
History of Holland, and a few verses. "I never composed at
all in Greek, even in prose, and but little in Latin," he wrote
in his famous *Autobiography*. "Not that my father could be
indifferent to the value of this practice . . . but because there
really was not the time for it."

At the ripe age of twelve, Mill took up logic and the work
of Hobbes. At thirteen he made a complete survey of all
there was to be known in the field of political economy.

It was a strange, and by our standards a dreadful, upbringing. There were no holidays "lest the habit of work
should be broken, and a taste for idleness acquired," no boyhood friends, and not even a real awareness that his education and rearing were significantly different from the normal.
The miracle is not that Mill subsequently produced great
works, but that he managed to avoid a complete destruction
of his personality. He did have a kind of nervous breakdown:
in his twenties; the delicate dry intellectual world of work
and effort on which he had been nourished suddenly became
sterile and unsatisfying, and while other youths had to discover that there could be beauty in intellectual activity, poor
Mill had to find that there could be beauty in beauty. He un-
derwent a siege of melancholy; then he read Goethe, then
Wordsworth, then Saint-Simon—all people who spoke of the
heart as seriously as his father had spoken of the brain. And
then he met Harriet Taylor.

There was, worse luck, a Mr. Taylor. He was ignored;
Harriet Taylor and Mill fell in love and for twenty years
wrote each other, traveled together, and even lived together—all (if we are to believe their correspondence) in
perfect innocence. Then the barrier of Mr. Taylor was removed by his death and the two finally married.

It was a superlative match. Harriet Taylor (and later, her
daughter, Helen) completed for Mill the emotional awaken-
ing that had begun so late; together, the two women opened

his eyes to women's rights and, even more importantly, to mankind's rights. After Harriet's death, when he was reflecting on the story of his life, he reviewed their converging influences on himself, and he wrote: "Whoever, either now or hereafter, may think of me and of the work I have done, must never forget that it is the product not of one intellect and conscience, but of three."

Mill, as we have seen, learned all the political economy there was to know at the age of thirteen. It was not until thirty years later that he wrote his great text, the two long, masterful volumes of the *Principles of Political Economy*. It was as if he had accumulated thirty years of knowledge just for this purpose.

The book is a total survey of the field: it takes up rent and wages and prices and taxes, and retreads the paths that had been first mapped by Smith and Malthus and Ricardo. But it is far more than a mere updating of doctrines that had by now received the stamp of virtual dogma. It goes on to make a discovery of its own, a discovery that Mill believed to be of monumental importance. Like so many great insights, the discovery was very simple. It consisted in pointing out that the true province of economic law was production and not distribution.

What Mill meant was very clear: the economic laws of production concern nature. There is nothing arbitrary about whether labor is more productive in this use or that, nor is there anything capricious or optional about such a phenomenon as the diminishing powers of productivity of the soil. Scarcity and the obduracy of nature are real things, and the economic rules of behavior which tell us how to maximize the fruits of our labor are as impersonal and as absolute as the laws of the expansion of gases or the interaction of chemical substances.

But—and this is perhaps the biggest *but* in economics—the laws of economics have nothing to do with distribution. Once we have produced wealth as best we can, we can do with it as we like. "The things once there," says Mill, "mankind, individually or collectively, can do with them as they please. They can place them at the disposal of whomso-

ever they please, and on whatever terms. . . . Even what a
person has produced by his individual toil, unaided by anyone, he cannot keep, unless by the permission of society. Not
only can society take it from him, but individuals could and
would take it from him, if society . . . did not . . . employ and
pay people for the purpose of preventing him from being disturbed in [his] possession. The distribution of wealth, therefore, depends on the laws and customs of society. The rules
by which it is determined are what the opinions and feelings
of the ruling portion of the community make them, and are
very different in different ages and countries, and might be
still more different, if mankind so chose. . . ."

It was a body blow to the followers of Ricardo who had
rigidified his objective findings into a straitjacket for society.
For what Mill said was transparently obvious—once it had
been said. Never mind if the "natural" action of society was
to depress wages or to equalize profits or to raise rents or
whatever. If society did not like the "natural" results of its activities, it had only to change them. Society could tax and
subsidize, it could expropriate and redistribute. It could give
all its wealth to a king, or it could run a gigantic charity ward;
it could give due heed to incentives, or it could—at its own
risk—ignore them. But whatever it did, there was no "correct" distribution—at least none that economics had any
claim to fathom. There was no appeal to "laws" to justify how
society shared its fruits: there were only men sharing their
wealth as they saw fit.

Actually, Mill's discovery was not quite so monumental as he believed. For as conservative economists quickly
pointed out, when men intervene into the distribution
process, they cannot help intervening into the production
process as well: a 100 percent tax on profits, for example,
would certainly have a terrific impact on how much there
was, as well as on who got it. And as Marx was to point out
from another perspective, one cannot separate distribution
and production as cleanly as Mill thought, because different
societies arrange their modes of payment as integral parts of
their modes of production: feudal societies, for example, do

not have "wages," any more than capitalist societies have feudal dues.

Thus from both Right and Left came the criticism that
there were *limits* on the freedom with which societies could
restructure their distribution—much narrower limits than
Mill implied. And yet it would be wrong to undervalue Mill's
insight, just as it is wrong to exaggerate it. For the existence
of limits means that there is room for maneuver, that capitalism is not beyond reform. Indeed, the New Deal and the
welfare capitalisms of Scandinavia are the direct expressions
of Mill's vision of a society that would try to remedy its "natural" workings by imposing its moral values. Who is to say
that this has not led to important social change, even if the
change is limited?

Certainly in Mill's own time, his findings came as a
breath of fresh air. In an age when smugness and cant were
the order of the day, Mill spoke out with a voice of extraordinary moral clarity. In his *Principles,* for example, after making his great division between Production and Distribution,
he went on to examine the contemporary schemes of "communism" proposed by various Utopian reformers—not, let us
hasten to add, the communism of Marx, of whose existence
Mill was quite unaware.

Mill considered the various objections that could be
lodged against these "communistic" schemes, and saw some
merit in many of them. But then he summed up his opinion
in this thunderous paragraph:

> If . . . the choice were to be made between Communism
> with all its chances, and the present state of society with
> all its sufferings and injustices; if the institution of
> private property necessarily carried with it as a conse-
> quence, that the produce of labour should be appor-
> tioned as we now see it, almost in an inverse ratio to the
> labour—the largest portions to those who have never
> worked at all, the next largest to those whose work is al-
> most nominal, and so in a descending scale, the remu-
> neration dwindling as the work grows harder and more
> disagreeable, until the most fatiguing and exhausting

bodily labour cannot count with certainty on being able to earn even the necessaries of life; if this or Communism were the alternatives, all the difficulties, great or small, of Communism would be as dust in the balance.

But, Mill went on to add, this was not quite the choice. For the principle of private property, he believed, had not yet had a fair trial. The laws and institutions of Europe still reflected the violent feudal past, not the spirit of reform that Mill believed attainable through the application of the very principles he was writing about.

Thus in the end, he stopped short of advocating really revolutionary change for two reasons. First, he saw in the rough and harsh contest of daily life a necessary vent for the energies of mankind.

"I confess," he wrote, "I am not charmed with an ideal of life held out by those who think that the normal state of human beings is that of struggling to get on; that the trampling, crushing, elbowing, and treading on each other's heels, which form the existing type of social life, are the most desirable lot of human kind, or anything but the disagreeable symptoms of one of the phases of industrial progress."

But a distaste for acquisitiveness did not blind him to its usefulness: "That the energies of mankind should be kept in employment by the struggle for riches as they were formerly by the struggle for war, until the better minds succeed in educating the others into better things, is undoubtedly better than that they should rust and stagnate. While minds are coarse they require coarse stimuli and let them have them."

And then there was a second, perhaps more cogent, reservation. Weighing up the pros and cons of the imagined society of communism, Mill saw a difficulty that he expressed in these words:

The question is whether there would be any asylum left for individuality of character; whether public opinion would not be a tyrannical yoke; whether the absolute dependence of each on all, and the surveillance of each by all, would not grind all down into a tame uniformity of thoughts, feelings, and actions. . . . No society in which eccentricity is a matter of reproach can be in a wholesome state.

This is the "political" Mill speaking, later to be the author of the tract *On Liberty*, which is, perhaps, his greatest work. But we are interested here in the economist Mill. For his *Principles* was much more than an exploration of the possibilities for social reform. It was also a large-scale social model that projected a trajectory for the capitalist system, much as had the models of Smith and Ricardo before him. But Mill's model had a destination different from any theretofore. As we have seen, Mill was above all else a believer in the possibility of *changing* social behavior. Therefore he no longer swallowed the main mechanism of gloom for Ricardo—the population reflex that vitiated all chances for substantial working-class improvement. Instead, Mill thought that the working classes could be educated to understand their Malthusian peril, and that they would thereupon voluntarily regulate their numbers.

With the pressure of population on wages removed, Mill's model took a different turn from those of Ricardo and Smith. As before, the tendencies of the accumulation process would bid up wages, but this time there would be no flood of children to lessen the pressure of wages on profits. As a result, wages would rise and the accumulation of capital would come to an end. Thus Mill's system approached a high *stationary* plateau, just as Smith's or Ricardo's would have done had it not been for their relentless population pressures.

But now comes another departure. Rather than seeing a stationary state as the finale for capitalism and economic progress, Mill sees it as the first stage of a benign socialism, where mankind would turn its energies to serious matters of justice and liberty, not just to economic growth. Within this impending stationary society, great changes could be made. The state would prevent landlords from reaping unearned benefits, just as it would tax away inheritances. Associations of workmen would displace the organization of enterprises in which men were subordinate to masters. By their sheer competitive advantages, the workers' cooperatives would win the day. Capitalism would gradually disappear as former masters sold out to their workingmen and retired on annuities.

Is it all just a Utopian fantasy? Looking back on a century of enormous economic expansion that followed the last edition of the *Principles,* we can only smile when we realize that Mill believed England (and by extension, world capitalism) to be within a "hand's breadth" of a stationary state. And yet, looking ahead at the problems that will face capitalist expansion over the next generation or two, and reflecting again on the degree to which some capitalist nations, such as Holland or the Scandinavian trio, have managed to introduce a high level of social responsibility into their economic framework, we cannot dismiss his vision as mere Victorian wishful thinking. Perhaps because he *is* a Victorian, Mill is too easily dismissed, for his calm reasoned prose, restrained even in his heights of eloquence, does not speak in the tones that attract the modern ear. Yet, Mill has a way of returning—of finding his way to the back door after he has been ushered out the front.

So let us bid him a respectful adieu. He lived until 1873, a venerated, almost worshiped man, his mildly Socialistic leanings forgiven in exchange for his vista of hope and his removal of the pall of Malthusian and Ricardian despair. After all, what he advocated was not so shocking but that it could be embraced by many who were not Socialists: taxation of rents, and inheritance taxes, and the formation of workmen's cooperatives. He was not very sanguine about the possibilities of trade unions, and that was all to the good, as far as respectable opinion went. It was a doctrine English to the core: gradualist, optimistic, realistic, and devoid of radical overtones.

Principles of Political Economy was an enormous success. It went into seven editions in the expensive two-volume edition during his own lifetime, and, characteristic of Mill, he had it printed at his own expense in one cheap volume that would be within the reach of the working class. Five cheap editions also sold out before he died. Mill became the Great

Economist of his day; he was talked of as Ricardo's rightful successor and heir, and compared not unfavorably with Adam Smith himself.

And economics aside, the man himself was so respected. In addition to *On Liberty*, Mill was the author of *Logic*, of *Considerations on Representative Government*, and of *Utilitarianism*, all classics in their fields. And more than merely brilliant, he verged on being saintly. When Herbert Spencer, his great rival in the area of philosophy, found himself so straitened in circumstances that he was unable to complete his projected series on social evolution, it was Mill who offered to finance the project. "I beg that you will not consider this proposal in the light of a personal favor," he wrote his rival, "though even if it were I should still hope to be permitted to offer it. But it is nothing of the kind—it is a simple proposal of cooperation for an important public purpose, for which you give your labor and have given your health."

There was never a more typical gesture. Mill cared only for two things: his wife, for whom he conceived a devotion that his friends thought verged on blindness, and the pursuit of knowledge, from which nothing could deflect him. When he was elected to Parliament his defense of human rights exceeded the temper of the day; he was thereupon defeated, but he cared not a whit either way. As he saw the world, so he wrote and spoke, and the only person who mattered, as far as approval went, was his beloved Harriet.

After she died, there was her daughter, Helen, now equally indispensable. In gratitude, Mill wrote in his *Autobiography*: "Surely no one before was so fortunate as, after such a loss as mine, to draw another such prize in the lottery of life." He retired to spend his last days with Helen in Avignon, near Harriet's grave, a wonderfully wise and thoroughly great man.

One last coincidence. His masterwork on economics, with its message of progress and the opportunity for peaceful change and betterment, was published in 1848. Perhaps it was not an epoch-making book, but it was certainly an epoch-marking one. For by a curious quirk of fate another, far smaller book—a pamphlet—was published in the same year. It was entitled *The Communist Manifesto,* and in its few pages it undid, in bitter words, all the calm and buoyant reasonableness with which J. S. Mill had endowed the world.

vi

The Inexorable System
of Karl Marx

The *Manifesto* opened with ominous words: "A spectre is haunting Europe—the spectre of Communism. All the powers of old Europe have entered into a holy alliance to exorcise this spectre: Pope and Tsar, Metternich and Guizot, French Radicals and German police spies."

The specter certainly existed: 1848 was a year of terror for the old order on the Continent. There was a revolutionary fervor in the air and a rumble underfoot. For a moment—for a brief moment—it looked as if the old order might break down. In France the plodding regime of Louis Philippe, the portly middle-class king, wrestled with a crisis and then collapsed; the king abdicated and fled to the security of a Surrey villa, and the workingmen of Paris rose in a wild uncoordinated surge and ran up the Red Flag over the Hôtel de Ville. In Belgium a frightened monarch offered to submit his resignation. In Berlin the barricades went up and bullets whistled; in Italy mobs rioted; and in Prague and Vienna popular uprisings imitated Paris by seizing control of the cities.

"The Communists disdain to conceal their views and aims," cried the *Manifesto*. "They openly declare that their ends can be attained only by the forcible overthrow of all existing social relations. Let the ruling classes tremble at a Communist revolution. The proletarians have nothing to lose but their chains. They have a world to win."

136

The ruling classes did tremble, and they saw the threat of communism everywhere. Nor were their fears groundless. In the French foundries the workmen sang radical songs to the accompaniment of blows from their sledgehammers, and the German romantic poet Heinrich Heine, who was touring the factories, reported that "really people in our gentle walk of life can have no idea of the demonic note which runs through these songs."

But despite the clarion words of the *Manifesto,* the demonic note was not a call for a revolution of communism; it was a cry born only of frustration and despair. For all of Europe was in the grip of reaction compared with which conditions in England were positively idyllic. The French government had been characterized by John Stuart Mill as "wholly without the spirit of improvement and . . . wrought almost exclusively through the meaner and more selfish impulses of mankind," and the French had no monopoly on such a dubious claim to fame. As for Germany, well, here it was, the fourth decade of the nineteenth century, and Prussia still had no parliament, no freedom of speech or right of assembly, no liberty of the press or trial by jury, and no tolerance for any idea that deviated by a hair's breadth from the antiquated notion of the divine right of kings. Italy was a hodgepodge of anachronistic principalities. Russia under Nicholas I (despite the Tsar's one-time visit to Robert Owen's New Lanark) was characterized by the historian de Tocqueville as "the cornerstone of despotism in Europe."

Had the despair been channeled and directed, the demonic note might have changed into a truly revolutionary one. But, as it was, the uprisings were spontaneous, undisciplined, and aimless; they won initial victories, and then, while they were wondering what next to do, the old order rocked invincibly back into place. The revolutionary fervor abated, and where it did not, it was mercilessly crushed. At the price of ten thousand casualties, the Paris mobs were subdued by the National Guard, and Louis Napoleon took over the nation and soon exchanged the Second Republic for the Second Empire. In Belgium the country decided that it had better ask the king to stay after all; he acknowledged the tribute by abolishing the right of assembly. The Viennese and Hungarian crowds were cannonaded from their strongholds, and in Germany a constitutional assembly that had been bravely debating the question of republicanism broke down into factional bickering and then ignominiously offered the country to Frederick William IV of Prussia. Still more ignominiously, that monarch declared that he would accept no crown proffered by the ignoble hands of commoners.

The revolution was over. It had been fierce, bloody, but inconclusive. There were a few new faces in Europe, but the policies were much the same.

But to a little group of working-class leaders who had just formed the Communist League, there was no cause for deep despair. True, the revolution for which they had entertained high hopes had petered out and the radical movements pocketed throughout Europe were being more ruthlessly hounded than ever before. Yet all that could be regarded with a certain equanimity. For according to their understanding of history, the uprisings of 1848 were only the small-scale dress rehearsals of a gigantic production that was scheduled for the future, and of the eventual success of that awesome spectacle there could be not the shadow of a doubt.

The League had just published its statement of objectives and called it *The Communist Manifesto*. With all its slogans and its trenchant phrases, the *Manifesto* had not been written merely to whip up revolutionary sentiment or to add another voice of protest to the clamor of voices that filled the air. The *Manifesto* had something else in mind: a philosophy of history in which a Communist revolution was not only desirable but demonstrably *inevitable*. Unlike the Utopians, who also wanted to reorganize society closer to their desires, the Communists did not appeal to men's sympathies or to their addiction to building castles in the air. Rather, they offered men a chance to hitch their destinies to a star and to watch that star move inexorably across the historical zodiac. There was no longer a contest in which one side or the other ought to win for moral or sentimental reasons or because it thought the existing order was outrageous. Instead there was a cold analysis of which side *had* to win, and since that side was the proletariat, their leaders had only to wait. In the end, they could not lose.

The *Manifesto* was a program written for the future. But one thing would have surprised its authors. They were prepared to wait—but not for *seventy* years. They were already scanning Europe for the likeliest incubator of revolt. And they never even cast a glance in the direction of Russia.

The *Manifesto,* as everybody knows, was the brainchild of that angry genius, Karl Marx. More accurately, it was the result of collaboration between him and his remarkable companion, compatriot, supporter, and colleague, Friedrich Engels.

They are interesting, and, of course, enormously important men. The trouble is, they rapidly became not just men, but figures. At least until the Soviet debacle, Marx was widely considered a religious leader to rank with Christ or Mohammed, and Engels thus became a sort of Saint Paul or John. In the Marx-Engels Institute in Moscow, scholars pored over their works with the idolatry they ridiculed in the antireligious museums down the street. But while Marx and Engels were canonized in Stalinist Russia and, to a lesser extent, in Maoist China, they were regarded as creatures of the devil in much of the rest of the world.

They merit neither treatment, for they were neither saints nor devils. Nor is their work either Scripture or anathema. It belongs in the great line of economic viewpoints that have successively clarified, illuminated, and interpreted the world for us, and like the other great works on the shelf, it is not without flaw. The world has been preoccupied with Marx the Revolutionary. But had Marx not lived, there would have been other Socialists and other prophets of a new society. The real and lasting impact of Marx and Engels is not their revolutionary activity, none of which bore too much fruit during their own lifetimes. It is with the vision of Marx the Political Economist that capitalism must finally come to grips. For the final imprint he made on history was his prediction that capitalism must inevitably collapse. On that prediction, communism built its edifice, heedless of its own weaknesses.

But let us see the men.

They were very much opposites in appearance. Marx *looked* like a revolutionary. His children called him "The Moor," for his skin was dark and his eyes deep-set and flashing. He was stocky and powerfully built and rather glowering in expression with a formidable beard. He was not an orderly man; his home was a dusty mass of papers piled in careless disarray in the midst of which Marx himself, slovenly dressed, padded about in an eye-stinging haze of tobacco smoke. Engels, on the other hand, would pass for a member of his despised *bourgeoisie;* tall and fair and rather elegant, he had the figure of a man who liked to fence and to ride to hounds and who had once swum the Weser River four times without a break.

It was not only in their looks that they differed; their personalities were at opposite poles. Engels was gay and observant and gifted with a quick and facile mind; it was said that he could stutter in twenty languages. He had a taste for the bourgeois pleasures in life, including a good palate for wine, and it is amusing to note that although he turned to the proletariat for his amours, he spent much of his time romantically (and unsuccessfully) trying to prove that his working-class mistress, Mary Burns (and later, after her death, her sister Lizzie), were actually descended from the Scottish poet.

Marx was much more ponderous. He is the German scholar par excellence, slow, meticulous, and painstakingly, even morbidly, perfectionist. Engels could dash off a treatise in no time at all; Marx was always worrying one to death. Engels was fazed only by Arabic with its four thousand verb roots; Marx, after twenty years of practice, still spoke hideously Teutonic English. When he writes of the great "chock" which events have caused him, we can almost hear him speak. But for all his heaviness, Marx is the greater mind of the two; where Engels supplied breadth and dash, Marx provided the depth.

They met, for the second time, in 1844 in Paris, and their collaboration begins at this date. Engels had come merely to call on Marx, but they had so much to say to each other that their conversation lasted for ten days. Thereafter there is hardly a product of the one that was not edited or rewritten or at least debated with the other, and their correspondence fills volumes.

Their paths to that common meeting ground in Paris were widely divergent. Engels was the son of a pietist, Calvinist, narrow-minded father, a manufacturer in the Rhineland. When Friedrich as a young man had shown an incomprehensible taste for poetry, his father had packed him off to Bremen to learn the export business and to live with a cleric: religion and moneymaking, according to Caspar Engels, were good cures for a romantic soul. Engels had dutifully applied himself to business, but everything he saw was colored by a personality in revolt, a happy-go-lucky personality that was incompatible with his father's rigid standards. He went down to the docks in the course of business, but his observant eye took in not only the first-class accommodations "in mahogany ornamented with gold" but the steerage as well, where the people were "packed in like the paving-stones in the streets." He began to read the radical literature of his time, and by the age of twenty-two he was converted to the ideals of "communism"—a word that then had no very clear definition except insofar as it rejected the idea of private property as a means for organizing society's economic effort.

Then he went to Manchester to enter his father's textile business there. Manchester, like the ships in Bremen, seemed to Engels a façade. There were pleasant streets lined with shops and suburbs ringing the city with pleasant villas. But there was a second Manchester as well. It was hidden behind the first and laid out so that the mill owners never had to see it on their trips to their offices. It harbored a stunted population living in a state of filth and despair, turning to gin and evangelism and doping itself and its children with laudanum against a life that was hopeless and brutal. Engels had seen similar conditions in the factory towns of his Rhineland home, but now he explored Manchester until he knew every last hovel and each ratlike abode. He was to publish his findings in the most terrible verdict ever passed on the world of industrial slums: *The Condition of the Working Class in England in 1844.* One time he talked of the misery of the place to a gentleman friend and remarked that he had never seen so "ill-built a city." His companion listened to him quietly and then said, "And yet there is a great deal of money made here; good day, sir."

He was writing now—treatises to show that the great English economists were only apologists for the existing order—and one of his contributions made a special impression on a young man named Karl Marx, who was editing a radical philosophical magazine in Paris.

Unlike Engels, Marx came from a liberal, even mildly radical, family background. He was born in 1818 in Trier, Germany, the second son of a prosperous Jewish family that shortly thereafter adopted Christianity so that Heinrich Marx, an advocate, might be less restricted in his practice. Heinrich Marx was a respected man; he was, in fact, even appointed *Justizrat*, an honorary title for eminent lawyers, but in his day he had joined illegal banquet clubs that drank toasts to a republican Germany, and he had reared his young son on a diet of Voltaire, Locke, and Diderot.

Heinrich Marx hoped that his son would study law. But at the universities of Bonn and Berlin, young Marx found himself swept up in the great philosophical debate of the day. The philosopher Hegel had propounded a revolutionary scheme, and the conservative German universities found themselves split wide open over it. Change, according to Hegel, was the rule of life. Every idea, every force, irrepressibly bred its opposite, and the two merged into a "unity" that in turn produced its own contradiction. And history, said Hegel, was nothing but the expression of this flux of conflicting and resolving ideas and forces. Change—dialectical change—was immanent in human affairs. With one exception: when it came to the Prussian state, the rules no longer applied; the Prussian government, said Hegel, was like "a veritable earthly god."

This was a powerful stimulus for a young student. Marx joined a group of intellectuals known as the Young Hegelians who debated such daring questions as atheism and pure theoretical communism in terms of the Hegelian dialectic, and he decided to become a philosopher himself. He might have, had it not been for the action of that godlike state. Marx's favorite professor, Bruno Bauer, who was eager to procure an appointment for him at Bonn, was dismissed for proconstitutional and antireligious ideas (one evidently as bad as the other), and an academic career for young Dr. Marx became an impossibility.

He turned instead to journalism. The *Rheinische Zeitung,* a small middle-class liberal newspaper, to which he had been a frequent contributor, asked him to take on its editorship. He accepted; his career lasted exactly five months. Marx was then a radical, but his radicalism was philosophical rather than political. When Friedrich Engels came respectfully to call on him, Marx rather disapproved of that brash young man brimming with Communist ideas, and when Marx himself was accused of being a Communist, his reply was equivocal: "I do not know communism," he said, "but a social philosophy which has as its aim the defense of the oppressed cannot be condemned so lightly." But regardless of his disavowals, his editorials were too much for the authorities. He wrote a bitter denunciation of a law that would have prevented the peasants from exercising their immemorial rights to gather dead wood in the forests; for this he was censured. He wrote editorials deploring the housing situation; for this he was warned. And when he went so far as to say some uncomplimentary things about the Tsar of Russia, the *Rheinische Zeitung* was suppressed.

Marx went to Paris to take over another radical journal, which was to be almost as short-lived as the newspaper. But his interests were now turned in the direction of politics and economics. The undisguised self-interest of the Prussian government, the implacable resistance of the German *bourgeoisie* toward anything that might alleviate the condition of the German working classes, the almost caricaturesque attitudes of reaction which characterized the wealthy and ruling classes of Europe—all of this had coalesced in his mind to form part of a new philosophy of history. And when Engels came to visit him and the two struck up their strong rapport, that philosophy began to take formal shape.

The philosophy is often called dialectical materialism; *dialectical* because it incorporates Hegel's idea of inherent change, and *materialism* because it grounds itself not in the world of ideas, but on the terrain of social and physical environment.

"The materialist conception of history," wrote Engels many years later in a famous tract entitled "Anti-Dühring" (it was aimed against a German professor named Eugen Dühring) "starts from the principle that production, and with production the exchange of its products, is the basis of every social order; that in every society that has appeared in history the distribution of the products, and with it the division of society into classes or estates, is determined by what is produced and how it is produced, and how the product is exchanged. According to this conception, the ultimate causes of all social changes and political revolutions are to be sought, not in the minds of men, in their increasing insight into eternal truth and justice, but in changes in the mode of production and exchange; they are to be sought not in the *philosophy* but in the *economics* of the epoch concerned."

The reasoning is powerful. Every society, says Marx, is built on an economic base—the hard reality of human beings who must organize their activities to clothe and feed and house themselves. That organization can differ vastly from society to society and from era to era. It can be pastoral or built around hunting or grouped into handicraft units or structured into a complex industrial whole. But whatever the form in which men solve their basic economic problem, society will require a "superstructure" of noneconomic activity and thought—it will need to be bound together by laws, supervised by a government, inspired by religion and philosophy.

But the superstructure of thought cannot be selected at random. It must reflect the foundation on which it is raised. No hunting community would evolve or could use the legal framework of an industrial society, and similarly no industrial community could use the conception of law, order, and government of a primitive village. Note that the doctrine of materialism does not toss away the catalytic function and creativity of ideas. It only maintains that thoughts and ideas are the *product* of environment, even though they aim to change that environment.

Materialism by itself would reduce ideas to mere passive accompaniments of economic activity. That was never Marx's contention. For the new theory was *dialectical* as well as materialist: it envisaged change, constant and inherent change; and in that never-ending flux the ideas emanating from one period would help to shape another. "Men make their own history," wrote Marx, commenting on the *coup d'état* of Louis Napoleon in 1852, "but they do not make it just as they please; they do not make it under circumstances chosen by themselves, but under circumstances directly found, given, and transmitted from the past."

But the dialectical—the internal dynamism—aspect of this theory of history did not depend merely on the interplay of ideas and social structures. There was another and far more powerful agent at work. The economic world itself was changing; the bedrock on which the structure of ideas was built was itself in movement.

For example, the isolated markets of the Middle Ages began to lock fingers under the impetus of exploration and political unification, and a new commercial world was born. The old hand mill was replaced by the steam mill under the impetus of invention, and a new form of social organization called the factory came into being. In both cases the determining framework of economic life itself changed its form, and as it did, it forced a new social adaptation from the community in which it was embedded. "The hand-mill gives you society with the feudal lord," Marx wrote, "the steam-mill, society with the industrial capitalist."

And once such a change had taken place, it carried with it a whole train of consequences. The market and the factory were incompatible with the feudal way of life—even though they were born amidst it. They demanded a new cultural and

social context to go with them. And they helped in that difficult birthing process by creating their own new social classes:
the market nurtured a new merchant class, and the factory
gave birth to an industrial proletariat.

But the process of social change was not merely a matter
of new inventions pressing on old institutions: it was a matter
of new classes displacing old ones. For society, said Marx, is
organized into class structures, aggregates of individuals who
stand in some common relationship—favorable or otherwise—to the existing form of production. And economic
change threatens all of that. As the organizational and technical forces of production change—as factories destroy
handicraft industry, for example—the social relations of production change too; those on top may find the ground cut
from under them, while those who were on the bottom may
be carried higher. We have seen just such an upset of the rel-
ative position of social classes in Ricardo's day in England,
when the capitalists, riding the wave of the Industrial Revolution, were threatening to usurp the time-honored prerogatives of the landed gentry.

Hence conflict develops. The classes whose positions are
jeopardized fight the classes whose positions are enhanced:
the feudal lord fights the rising merchant, and the guild master opposes the young capitalist.

But the process of history pays no attention to likes and
dislikes. Gradually conditions change, and gradually, but
surely, the classes of society are rearranged. Amid turmoil
and anguish the division of wealth is altered. And thus history
is a pageant of ceaseless struggle between classes to partition
social wealth. For as long as the technics of society change,
no existing division of wealth is immune from attack.

What did this theory augur for the society of Marx and
Engels's day? It pointed to revolution—inevitable revolution.
For capitalism, according to this analysis, must also contain
"forces" and "relations" of production—a technological and
organizational foundation, and an architecture of law and political rights and ideology. And if its technical base was evolving, then necessarily its superstructure must be subject to
increasing strain.

That is exactly what Marx and Engels saw in 1848. The economic base of capitalism—its anchor in reality—was industrial production. Its superstructure was the system of private property, under which a portion of society's output went to those who owned its great technical apparatus. The conflict lay in the fact that the base and superstructure were incompatible.

Why? Because the base of industrial production—the actual making of goods—was an ever more organized, integrated, *interdependent* process, whereas the superstructure of private property was the most *individualistic* of social systems. Hence the superstructure and the base clashed: factories necessitated social planning, and private property abhorred it; *capitalism* had become so complex that it needed direction, but *capitalists* insisted on a ruinous freedom.

The result was twofold. First, capitalism would sooner or later destroy itself. The planless nature of production would lead to a constant disorganization of economic activity—to crises and slumps and the social chaos of depression. The system was simply too complex; it was constantly getting out of joint, losing step, and overproducing one good while underproducing another.

Secondly, capitalism must unknowingly breed its own successor. Within its great factories it would not only create the technical base for socialism—rationally planned production—but it would create as well a trained and disciplined *class* which would be the agent of socialism—the embittered proletariat. By its own inner dynamic, capitalism would produce its own downfall, and in the process, nourish its own enemy.

It was a profoundly important insight into history, not only for what it betokened for the future, but for the whole new perspective it opened upon the past. We have come to be familiar with the "economic interpretation" of history, and we can accept with equanimity a reevaluation of the past with respect to the struggle, say, of the nascent seventeenth-century commercial classes and the aristocratic world of land and lineage. But for Marx and Engels, this was no mere exercise in historical reinterpretation. The dialectic led to the future, and that future, as revealed by *The Communist Manifesto*, pointed to revolution as the destination toward which capitalism was moving. In somber words the *Manifesto* proclaimed: "The development of modern industry... cuts from under its feet the very foundation on which the bourgeoisie produces and appropriates products. What the bourgeoisie therefore produces, above all, are its own gravediggers. Its fall and the victory of the proletariat are equally inevitable."

The *Manifesto*, with its rumbling, inexorable interpretation of history, was not written in Paris. Marx's career had been brief in that city. He edited a caustic, radical magazine; he again rubbed the sensibilities of the Prussian government; and at its behest, he was expelled from the French capital.

He was married now—in 1843 he had married Jenny von Westphalen, who had lived next door to him as a child. Jenny was the daughter of a Prussian aristocrat and Privy Councillor, but Baron von Westphalen was nevertheless a humanist and liberal thinker. He had talked to young Marx about Homer and Shakespeare and even told him about the ideas of Saint-Simon despite their pronouncement as heresy by the local bishop. As for Jenny—she was the belle of the town. Beautiful and with suitors galore, she could easily have made a more "suitable" match than the dark young man next door. But she was in love with him, and both families smiled their approval. For the Marxes such a marriage would be a not inconsiderable social triumph, and for the Baron it was, perhaps, a happy vindication of his humanist ideas. One wonders if he would have given his consent could he have foreseen what was to happen to his daughter. For Jenny was to be forced to share the bed of a common prostitute in jail and would have to beg the money from a neighbor to buy a coffin to bury one of her children. In place of the pleasant comforts and the social prestige of Trier, she was to spend the years of her life in two dismal rooms in a London slum, sharing with her husband the calumny of a hostile world.

And yet it was a deeply devoted union. In his dealings with outsiders, Marx was unkind, jealous, suspicious, and wrathful; but he was a joyous father and a loving husband. At one period, when his wife was ill, Marx turned to Lenchen, the Westphalian family maid who stayed with them, unpaid, all their days, but even that infidelity—from which an unacknowledged child was born—could not undo a relationship of great passion. Later, much later, when Jenny was dying and Marx was ill, this lovely scene was witnessed by her daughter.

> Our dear mother lay in the big front room and the Moor lay in the little room next to it. . . . Never shall I forget the morning he felt himself strong enough to go into Mother's room. When they were together they were young again—she a young girl and he a loving youth, both on life's threshold, not an old disease-ridden man and an old dying woman parting from each other for life.

The Marxes had moved to London in 1849. Expulsion from Paris, four years before, had landed them in Brussels, where they stayed (and the *Manifesto* was composed) until the revolutionary outbursts in 1848. Then, when the Belgian king had secured a firm enough grip on his shaky throne, he rounded up the radical leaders in his capital, and Marx went briefly to Germany.

It was the same pattern all over again. Marx took over the editorship of a newspaper, and it was only a matter of time before the government closed it down. He printed the last edition in red—and sought a haven in London.

He was now in desperate financial shape. Engels was in Manchester, leading his strange double life (he was a respected figure on the Manchester Stock Exchange), and he supplied the Marxes with a never-ending stream of checks and loans. Had Marx been a financially orderly person, the family might have lived in decency. But Marx was never one to balance his books. Thus the children had music lessons—and the family went without heat. Life was a constant struggle against bankruptcy, and money worries were a suffocating presence always.

There were, in all, five of them including Lenchen. Marx

had no work—except his never-ending stint in the British Museum from ten o'clock every morning until seven o'clock at night. He tried to make a little money by writing articles on the political situation for the *New York Tribune*, whose editor, Charles A. Dana, was a Fourierist and not averse to a few slaps at European politics. It helped for a while, although it was Engels who bailed Marx out by composing many of his pieces for him—Marx meanwhile advising by letter as follows: "You must your war-articles colour a little more." When the articles stopped, he tried to get a clerical job with a railway, but was rejected for his atrocious handwriting. Thereafter he pawned what was left to his name, all the family silver and valuables having been sold long ago. At times his want was so intense that he was forced to sit home because his coat and even his shoes were in pawn; on other occasions he lacked the money to buy postage stamps to send his works to the publisher. And to compound his difficulties, he suffered from the most painful boils. When he arrived home one evening after writing in misery all day long in the Museum he remarked, "I hope the bourgeoisie as long as they live will have cause to remember my carbuncles." He had just composed the terrible chapter of *Das Kapital* which describes the Working Day.

There was only Engels to fall back on. Marx wrote him constantly, touching on economics, politics, mathematics, military tactics, on everything under the sun, but especially on his own situation. A typical excerpt reads:

> My wife is ill. Little Jenny is ill. Lenchen has a sort of nervous fever and I can't call in the doctor because I have no money to pay him. For about eight or ten days we have all been living on bread and potatoes and it is now doubtful whether we shall be able to get even that. . . . I have written nothing for Dana because I didn't have a penny to go and read the papers. . . . How am I to get out of this infernal mess? Finally, and this was most hateful of all, but essential if we were not to kick the bucket, I have, over the last 8–10 days, touched some German types for a few shillings and pence . . .

Only the last years were a little easier. An old friend left Marx a small bequest, and he was able to live in some comfort, and even to travel a bit for his health. Engels, too, finally came into an inheritance and left his business; in 1869 he went to his office for the last time and came over the fields to meet Marx's daughter, "swinging his stick in the air and singing, his face beaming."

In 1881 Jenny died; she had buried two of her five children, including her only son; she was old and tired. Marx was too ill to go to the funeral; when Engels looked at him he said, "The Moor is dead, too." Not quite; he lingered for two more years; disapproved of the husbands two of his daughters had chosen; grew weary of the bickering of the working-class movement and delivered himself of a statement that has never ceased to bedevil the faithful ("I am not a Marxist," he said one day); and then on a March afternoon, quietly slipped away.

What had he done, in these long years of privation?

He had produced, for one thing, an international working-class movement. As a young man, Marx had written: "The philosophers hitherto have only interpreted the world in various ways; the thing, however, is to change it." Marx and Engels had given the accolade to the proletariat in their interpretation of history; now they set about steering and guiding the proletariat so that it should exert its maximum leverage on history.

It was not an attempt crowned with much success. Coincident with the publication of the *Manifesto*, the Communist League had been formed, but it was never much more than a paper organization; the *Manifesto*, which was its platform, was not then even placed on public sale, and with the demise of the revolution of 1848, the League died too.

It was followed in 1864 with a far more ambitious organization, the International Workingmen's Association. The International boasted seven million members and was real enough to have a hand in a wave of strikes which swept the Continent and to earn for itself a rather fearsome reputation. But it, too, was doomed to have a brief history. The International did not consist of a tough and disciplined army of Communists, but a motley crew of Owenists, Proudhonists, Fourierists, lukewarm Socialists, rabid nationalists, and trade unionists who were leery of any kind of revolutionary theory whatsoever. With considerable skill Marx kept his crew together for five years, and then the International fell apart; some followed Bakunin, a giant of a man with a true revolutionist's background of Siberia and exile (it was said that his oratory was so moving that his listeners would have cut their throats if he had asked them to), while others turned their attention back to national affairs. The last meeting of the International was held in New York in 1874. It was a lugubrious failure.

But far more important than the creation of the First International was the peculiar tone which Marx injected into working-class affairs. This was the most quarrelsome and intolerant of men, and from the beginning he was unable to believe that anyone who did not follow his line of reasoning could possibly be right. As an economist his language was precise, as a philosopher-historian it was eloquent, as a revolutionary it was scurrilous. He stooped to anti-Semitism. He called his opponents "louts," "rascals," even "bedbugs." Early in his career, when he was still in Brussels, Marx had been visited by a German tailor named Weitling. Weitling was a tried son of the labor movement; he had scars on his legs from the irons of Prussian prisons and a long history of selfless and valiant efforts on behalf of the German workingman. He came to speak to Marx on such things as justice and brotherhood and solidarity; instead he found himself exposed to a merciless cross-examination on the "scientific principles" of socialism. Poor Weitling was confused, his answers were unsatisfactory. Marx, who had been sitting as the chief examiner, began to stride angrily about the room. "Ignorance has never helped anybody yet," he shouted. The audience was over.

Willich was another to be excommunicated. An ex-Prussian captain, he had fought in the German revolution and later was to become an outstanding general on the Union side of the American Civil War. But he clung to the "un-Marxist" idea that "pure will" could be the motive power of revolution instead of "actual conditions"; for this notion—

which Lenin was one day to prove was not so far-fetched after all—he, too, was dropped from the movement.

And the list could be extended endlessly. Perhaps no single incident was more provocative, more prophetic of a movement that was one day to degenerate into an internal witch-hunt for "deviationists" and "counterrevolutionaries" than the feud between Marx and Pierre Proudhon. Proudhon was the son of a French barrelmaker, a self-educated brilliant Socialist who had rocked the French intelligentsia with a book entitled *What Is Property?* Proudhon had answered, Property is Theft, and he had called for an end to huge private riches, although not to all private property. Marx and he had met and talked and corresponded, and then Marx asked him to join forces with himself and Engels. Proudhon's answer is so profoundly moving and so prescient that it is worth quoting at some length:

> Let us together seek, if you wish, the laws of society, the manner in which these laws are reached, the process by which we shall succeed in discovering them; but, for God's sake, after having demolished all the *a priori* dogmatisms, do not let us in our turn dream of indoctrinating the people. . . . I applaud with all my heart your thought of inviting all shades of opinion; let us carry on a good and loyal polemic, let us give the world the example of an informed and farsighted tolerance, but let us not—simply because we are at the head of a movement—make ourselves into the leaders of a new intolerance, let us not pose as the apostles of a new religion, even if it be the religion of logic, the religion of reason. Let us gather together and encourage all dissent, let us outlaw all exclusiveness, all mysticism, let us never regard a question as exhausted, and when we have used one last argument, let us if necessary begin again—with eloquence and irony. On these conditions, I will gladly enter into your association. Otherwise, no!

Marx's answer was this: Proudhon had written a book called *The Philosophy of Poverty;* Marx now annihilated it with a rejoinder entitled *The Poverty of Philosophy.*

The pattern of intolerance was never to disappear. The First International would be followed by the mild and well-meaning Second—which included Socialists of such caliber as Bernard Shaw, Ramsay MacDonald, and Pilsudski (as well as Lenin and Mussolini!), and then by the infamous Third, organized under the aegis of Moscow. And yet, the impact of these great movements is perhaps less than the persistence of that narrowness, that infuriating and absolute inability to entertain dissent, which communism has inherited from its single greatest founder.

Had Marx produced nothing more in his long years in exile than a revolutionary labor movement, he would not loom today so important a figure in the world. Marx was only one of a dozen revolutionaries and by no means the most successful; he was only one of at least that many prophets of socialism, and as a matter of fact he wrote next to nothing about what that new society might be like. His final contribution lies elsewhere: in his dialectical materialist theory of history, and even more important, in his pessimistic analysis of the outlook for a capitalist economy.

"The history of capitalism," we read in the Program of the Communist International adopted in 1929—a kind of latter-day restatement of *The Communist Manifesto*—"has completely confirmed the Marxist theory of the laws of development of capitalist society and of its contradictions, leading to the destruction of the entire capitalist system." What were those laws? What was Marx's prognosis for the system that he knew?

The answer lies in that enormous work *Das Kapital* (*Capital*). With Marx's agonizing meticulousness, it is remarkable that the work was ever finished—in a sense it never was. It was eighteen years in process; in 1851 it was to be done "in five weeks"; in 1859 "in six weeks"; in 1865 it was "done"—a huge bundle of virtually illegible manuscripts which took two years to edit into Volume I. When Marx died in 1883 three volumes remained: Engels put out Volume II in 1885 and the third in 1894. The final (fourth) volume did not emerge until 1910.

There are twenty-five hundred pages to read for anyone intrepid enough to make the effort. And what pages! Some deal with the tiniest of technical matters and labor them to a point of mathematical exhaustion; others swirl with passion and anger. This is an economist who has read *every* economist, a German pedant with a passion for dotting i's and crossing t's, and an emotional critic who can write that capital has a "vampire thirst for the living blood of labour," and who tells us that capital came into the world "dripping from head to foot, from every pore, with blood and dirt."

And yet one must not jump to the conclusion that this is merely an irascible text inveighing against the sins of the wicked money barons. It is shot through with remarks that betray the total involvement of the man with his theoretical adversary, but the great merit of the book, curiously enough, is its utter detachment from all considerations of morality. The book describes with fury, but it analyzes with cold logic. For what Marx has set for his goal is to discover the intrinsic tendencies of the capitalist system, its inner laws of motion, and in so doing, he has eschewed the easy but less convincing means of merely expatiating on its manifest shortcomings. Instead he erects the most rigorous, the purest capitalism imaginable, and within this rarefied abstract system, with an imaginary capitalism in which all the obvious defects of real life are removed, he seeks his quarry. For if he can prove that the best of all possible capitalisms is nonetheless headed for disaster, it is certainly easy to demonstrate that real capitalism will follow the same path, only quicker.

And so he sets the stage. We enter a world of perfect capitalism: no monopolies, no unions, no special advantages for anyone. It is a world in which every commodity sells at exactly its proper price. And that proper price is its *value*—a tricky word. For the value of a commodity, says Marx (essentially following Ricardo), is the amount of labor it has within itself. If it takes twice as much labor to make hats as shoes, then hats will sell for twice the price of shoes. The labor, of course, need not be direct manual labor; it may be overhead labor that is spread over many commodities, or it may be the labor that once went into making a machine and that the machine now slowly passes on to the products it shapes. But no matter what its form, everything is eventually reducible to labor, and all commodities, in this perfect system, will be priced according to the amount of labor, direct or indirect, that they contain.

In this world stand the two great protagonists of the capitalist drama: worker and capitalist—the landlord has by now been relegated to a minor position in society. They are not quite the same protagonists we have met earlier in similar economic tableaux. The worker is no longer the slave to his reproductive urge. He is a free bargaining agent who enters the market to dispose of the one commodity he commands—labor power—and if he gets a rise in wages he will not be so foolish as to squander it in a self-defeating proliferation of his numbers.

The capitalist faces him in the arena. His greed and lust for wealth are caustically described in those chapters that leave the abstract world for a look into 1860 England. But it is worth noting that he is not money hungry from mere motives of rapacity; he is an owner-entrepreneur engaged in an endless race against his fellow owner-entrepreneurs; he *must* strive for accumulation, for in the competitive environment in which he operates, one accumulates or one gets accumulated.

The stage is set and the characters take their places. But now the first difficulty appears. How, asks Marx, can profits exist in such a situation? If everything sells for its exact value, then who gets an unearned increment? No one dares to raise his price above the competitive one, and even if one seller managed to gouge a buyer, that buyer would only have less to spend elsewhere in the economy—one man's profit would thus be another man's loss. How can there be profit *in the whole system* if everything exchanges for its honest worth?

It seems like a paradox. Profits are easy to explain if we assume that there are monopolies that need not obey the leveling influences of competition or if we admit that capitalists may pay labor less than it is worth. But Marx will have none of that—it is to be ideal capitalism which will dig its own grave.

He finds the answer to the dilemma in one commodity that is different from all others. The commodity is labor power. For the laborer, like the capitalist, sells his product for exactly what it is worth—for its value. And its value, like the value of everything else that is sold, is the amount of labor that goes into it—in this case, the amount of labor that it takes to "make" labor-power. In other words, a laborer's salable energies are worth the amount of socially necessary labor it takes to keep that laborer going. Smith and Ricardo would have agreed entirely: the value of a workman is the money he needs in order to exist. It is his subsistence wage.

So far, so good. But here comes the key to profit. The laborer who contracts to work can ask only for a wage that is his due. What that wage will be depends, as we have seen, on the amount of labor-time it takes to keep a man alive. If it takes six hours of society's labor per day to maintain a workingman, then (if labor is priced at one dollar an hour), he is "worth" six dollars a day. No more.

But the laborer who gets a job does not contract to work only six hours a day. That would be just long enough to support himself. On the contrary, he agrees to work a full eight-hour, or in Marx's time, a ten- or eleven-hour day. Hence he will produce a full ten or eleven hours' worth of value and he will get paid for only six. His wage will cover his subsistence, which is his true "value," but in return he will make available to the capitalist the value he produces in a full working day. And this is how profit enters the system.

Marx called this layer of unpaid work "surplus value." The words do not imply moral indignation. The worker is entitled only to the *value* of his labor-power. He gets it in full. But meanwhile the capitalist gets the full value of his workers' whole working day, and this is longer than the hours for which he paid. Hence when the capitalist sells his products, he can afford to sell them at *their* true value and still realize a profit. For there is more labor time embodied in his products than the labor time for which he was forced to pay.

How can this state of affairs come about? It happens because the capitalists monopolize one thing—access to the means of production themselves. Under the legal arrangements of private property, capitalists "own" jobs, insofar as they own the machines and equipment without which men and women cannot work. If someone isn't willing to work the number of hours that a capitalist asks, he or she doesn't get a job. Like everyone else in the system, a worker has no right and no power to ask for more than his own worth as a commodity. The system is perfectly "equitable," and yet all workers are cheated, for they are forced to work a longer time than their own self-sustenance demands.

Does this sound strange? Remember that Marx is describing a time when the working day was long—sometimes unendurably long—and when wages were, by and large, little more than it took to keep body and soul together. The idea of surplus value may be hard to grasp in a country where sweatshops are, with some exceptions, a thing of the past, but it was not merely a theoretical construct at the time that Marx was writing. One example may suffice: at a Manchester factory in 1862 the average work week for a period of a month and a half was 84 hours! For the previous 18 months it had been 78½ hours.

But all this is still only the setting for the drama. We have the protagonists, we have their motives, we have the clue to the plot in the discovery of "surplus value." And now the play is set in motion.

All capitalists have profits. But they are all in competition. Hence they try to accumulate, to expand their scales of output, at the expense of their competitors. But expansion is not so easy. It requires more laborers, and to get them the capitalists must bid against one another for the working force. Wages tend to rise. Conversely, surplus value tends to fall. It looks as if the Marxian capitalists will soon be up against the dilemma faced by the capitalists of Adam Smith and David Ricardo—their profits will be eaten away by rising wages.

To Smith and Ricardo the solution to the dilemma lay in the propensity of the working force to increase its numbers with every boost in pay. But Marx, like Mill, rules out this possibility. Marx doesn't argue about it; he simply brands the Malthusian doctrine "a libel on the human race"—after all, the proletariat, which is to be the ruling class of the future, cannot be so shortsighted as to dissipate its gains through mere unbridled physical appetite. But he rescues his capitalists just the same. For he says that they will meet the threat of rising wages by introducing *laborsaving machinery* into their plants. This will throw part of the working force back onto the street, and there, as an Industrial Reserve Army, it will serve the same function as Smith's and Ricardo's population growth: it will compete wages back down to their former "value"—the subsistence level.

Now comes the crucial twist. It seems as though the capitalist has saved the day, for he has prevented wages from rising by creating unemployment through machinery. But not so fast. By the very process through which he hopes to free himself from one horn of the dilemma, he impales himself on the other.

For as he substitutes machines for men, he simultaneously substitutes nonprofitable means of production for profitable ones. Remember that in Marx's model of an ideal capitalist world, no one makes a profit by merely sharp bargaining. Whatever a machine will be worth to a capitalist, you can be sure that he paid full value for it. If a machine will create ten thousand dollars' worth of value over its whole life, our capitalist was presumably charged the full ten thousand dollars in the first place. It is only from his living labor that he can realize a profit, only from the unpaid-for hours of surplus working time. Hence, when he reduces the number or proportion of workers, he is killing the goose that lays the golden egg.

And yet, unhappy fellow, he has to. There is nothing Mephistophelean about his actions. He is only obeying his impulse to accumulate and trying to stay abreast of his competitors. As his wages rise, he *must* introduce laborsaving machinery to cut his costs and rescue his profits—if he does not, his neighbor will. But since he must substitute machinery for labor, he must also narrow the base out of which he gleans his profits. It is a kind of Greek drama where men go willy-nilly to their fate, and in which they all unwittingly cooperate to bring about their own destruction.

For now the die is cast. As his profits shrink, each capitalist will redouble his efforts to put new laborsaving, cost-cutting machinery in his factory. It is only by getting a step ahead of the parade that he can hope to make a profit. But since everyone is doing precisely the same thing, the ratio of living labor (and hence surplus value) to total output shrinks still further. The rate of profit falls and falls. And now doom lies ahead. Profits are cut to the point at which production is no longer profitable at all. Consumption dwindles as machines displace men and the number of employed fails to keep pace with output. Bankruptcies ensue. There is a scramble to dump goods on the market, and in the process smaller firms go under. A capitalist crisis is at hand.

A crisis does not mean the end of the game. Quite the contrary. As workers are thrown out of work, they are forced to accept subvalue wages. As machinery is dumped, the stronger capitalists can acquire machines for less than their true value. After a time, surplus value reappears. The forward march is taken up again. Thus each crisis serves to renew the capacity of the system to expand. Crisis—or a business slump or recession, in modern terminology—is therefore the way the system *works*, not the way it fails.

But the working is certainly very peculiar. Each renewal leads to the same ending: competition for workers; higher wages; labor-displacing machinery; a smaller base for surplus value; still more frenzied competition; another crisis—*worse than the preceding one.* For during each period of crisis, the bigger firms absorb the smaller ones, and when the industrial monsters eventually go down, the wreckage is far greater than when the little enterprises buckle.

Finally, the drama ends. Marx's picture of it has all the eloquence of a description of a Damnation:

> Along with the constantly diminishing number of the magnates of capital, who usurp and monopolize all advantages of this process of transformation, grows the mass of misery, oppression, slavery, degradation, exploitation; but with this too grows the revolt of the working-class, a class always increasing in numbers, and

disciplined, united, organized by the very mechanism of the process of capitalist production itself. . . . Centralization of the means of production and socialization of labour at last reach a point where they become incompatible with their capitalist integument. This integument bursts asunder. The knell of capitalist private property sounds. The expropriators are expropriated.

And so the drama ends in the sequence that Marx had envisioned in the dialectic. The system—the *pure* system—breaks down as it works upon itself to squeeze out its own source of energy, surplus value. The breakdown is hastened by the constant instability that arises from the essentially planless nature of the economy. Although there are forces at work that act to prolong its end, its final death struggle is inescapable.

How sharply all this contrasts with earlier views! For Adam Smith, the capitalist escalator climbed upward, at least as far as the eye could reasonably see. For Ricardo that upward motion was stalled by the pressure of mouths on insufficient crop land, which brought a stalemate to progress and a windfall to the fortunate landlord. For Mill the vista was made more reassuring by his discovery that society could distribute its product as it saw fit, regardless of what "economic laws" seemed to dictate. But for Marx even that saving possibility was untenable. For the materialist view of history told him that the state was only the political ruling organ of the economic rulers. The thought that it might act as a kind of referee, a third force balancing the claims of its conflicting members, would have seemed sheer wishful thinking. No, there was no escape from the inner logic, the dialectical development, of a system that would not only destroy itself but, in so doing, would give birth to its successor.

As to what that successor might look like, Marx had little to say. It would be "classless," of course—by which Marx meant that the basis for an economic division of society based on property would be removed once society owned all the means of production of goods. Just how society would "own" its factories; what was meant by "society"; whether there would or could be bitter antagonisms between the managers and the managed, between the political chieftains and the rank and file—none of this did Marx discuss. During a transitional period of "socialism" there would be a "dictatorship of the proletariat"; after that, "pure" communism itself.

Marx, it must be kept in mind, was not the architect of actual socialism. That formidable task would fall to Lenin. *Das Kapital* is the Doomsday Book of capitalism, and in all of Marx there is almost nothing that looks beyond the Day of Judgment to see what the future might be like.

What are we to make of his apocalyptic argument?

There is an easy way of disposing of the whole thing. Remember that the system is built on value—labor value—and that the key to its demise lies in that special phenomenon called surplus value. But the real world consists not of "values" but of real tangible prices. Marx must show that the world of dollars and cents mirrors, in some approximate fashion, the abstract world that he has created. But in making the transition from a value-world to a price-world, he lands in the most terrible tangle of mathematics. In fact he makes a mistake.

It is not an irreparable mistake, and by going through an even worse tangle of mathematics one can make the Marxist equations come out "right." But the critics who pointed out the error were hardly interested in setting the scheme aright, and their judgment that Marx was "wrong" was taken as final. When the equations were finally rectified, no one paid much attention. For regardless of its mathematical purity, there are problems galore in the Marxian model. Can we really use the concept of surplus value in a world of monopolies or in a setting of scientific technology? Has Marx really disposed of the difficulties of using "labor" as the measuring rod of value?

Questions such as these continue to agitate the world of Marxian scholars and have tempted most non-Marxist economists to toss the whole scheme to one side as awkward and inflexible. But to do so overlooks two extraordinary properties of Marx's analysis.

First, it was more than just another "model" of economics. Marx literally invented a new task for social inquiry—

the critique of economics itself. A great part of *Capital* is
devoted to showing that earlier economists had failed to understand the real challenge of the study they undertook.
Take, for example, the problem of value that had exercised
Smith and Ricardo. Both of them had sought, with varying
degrees of success, to show how prices reflected—or failed
to reflect—the amounts of labor-time embodied in different
commodities.

But this was not the really perplexing question, Marx
pointed out. The perplexing question was how one could
speak of "labor" as a common denominator of value when the
actual labors of men and women were so different. Ricardo
spoke of the hours of labor it took to catch a salmon and to
kill a deer as establishing their exchange ratios—that is, their
prices. But no deer was ever killed with a fishing rod and no
salmon caught by a hunter in the woods. How then could one
use "labor" as a common denominator to determine exchange ratios?

The answer, said Marx, is that capitalist society creates a
special kind of labor—abstract labor, labor that is detached
from the special personal attributes of a precapitalist world,
labor that can be bought and sold like so much wheat or coal.
Hence the real insight of a "labor theory of value" is not the
determination of prices, as Smith and Ricardo thought, *but
the identification of a kind of social system in which labor-
power becomes a commodity.* That society is capitalism,
where historical forces (such as the enclosure movement)
have created a propertyless class of workers who have no alternative but to sell their labor-power—their sheer ability to
work—as a commodity.

Thus Marx invented a kind of "socio-analysis" that puts
economics itself into a wholly new light. And beyond that signal contribution, Marx's model of capitalism, despite its
clumsiness, seemed to come alive, to unfold in an extraordinary manner. Given its basic assumptions—the *mise-en-
scène* of its characters, their motives and their milieu—the
situation it presented *changed,* and changed in a way that was
foreseeable. We have seen what these changes were: how
profits fell, how capitalists sought new machinery, how each

boom ended in a crash, how small businesses were absorbed in each debacle by the larger firms. Marx called these trends the "laws of motion" of a capitalist system—the path that capitalism would tread over future time. And the astonishing fact is that so many of these predictions have come true.

For profits *do* tend to fall in a capitalist economy. The insight was not original with Marx, nor do profits fall only for the reason he gave. But as Adam Smith or Ricardo or Mill pointed out—and as any businessman will vouchsafe—the pressures of competition and rising wages do indeed cut profits. Impregnable monopolies aside (and these are few), profits are both the hallmark of capitalism and its Achilles' heel, for no business can *permanently* maintain its prices much above its costs. There is only one way in which profits can be perpetuated: a business—or an entire economy—must grow.

But the need for growth implies the second prediction of the Marxist model: the ceaseless quest for new techniques. It was no accident that industrial capitalism dates from the Industrial Revolution, for as Marx made clear, technological progress is not merely an accompaniment of capitalism but a vital ingredient. Business *must* innovate, invent, and experiment if it is to survive; the business that rests content on its past achievements is not long for this enterprising world. Not untypically, one large chemical company recently announced that some three quarters of its income came from products that were unknown ten years ago; and although this is an exceptionally inventive industry, the relationship between industrial inventiveness and profitability generally holds.

The model showed three more tendencies for capitalism which have also come to pass. We hardly need document the existence of business crises over the past hundred years or the emergence of giant business enterprise. But we might remark on the daring of Marx's predictions. A propensity to crisis—what we would call *business cycles*—was not recognized as an inherent feature of capitalism by any other economist of Marx's time, although future events have certainly vindicated his prediction of successive boom and crash. And in the world of business, when *Capital* appeared, bigness was the exception rather than the rule, and small enterprise still ruled the roost. To claim that huge firms would come to dominate the business scene was as startling a prediction in 1867 as would be a statement today that fifty years hence America will be a land in which small-scale proprietorships will have displaced giant corporations.

Last, Marx believed that the small independent artisan or self-employed worker would be unable to resist the pressures of mass production, and that an ever larger fraction of the work force would have to sell its labor-power on the market—that is, to become a "proletarian." Has that come true? Well, in the first quarter of the nineteenth century about three-quarters of all Americans worked for themselves, on the farm or in small shops. Today only about 10 percent of the labor force is self-employed. We may not think of an office worker or a bus driver or a bank teller as a proletarian, but in Marx's terms these are all workers who must offer their labor-power to capitalists, unlike the farmer or the shoe cobbler, who own their own means of production.

All in all, the model displayed extraordinary predictive capacity. But note this: all these changes, vast and portentous as they were, could not have been unearthed purely by examining the world as it appeared to Marx's eyes. For there is no single representative figure for his vision—no farsighted labor leader, no hero of the revolution-to-come. Of course there are central players, above all the self-defeating capitalist and the ultimately triumphant worker, but both are pawns in the drama that brings one ultimately to defeat, the other to victory. The representative "figure" in Marx's scenario is not a person but a process. It is the dialectical force of things that is the centerpiece of his vision.

It was not, of course, exact. Marx thought that profits would not only fall *within* the business cycle, which they do, but that they would display a long downward secular trend; this does not appear to have taken place. But for all its shortcomings—and it is far from infallible, as we shall see—the Marxist model of how capitalism worked was extraordinarily prophetic.

But everything that Marx had predicted so far was, after

all, fairly innocuous. There remained the final prediction of the model; for, as the reader will remember, in the end Marx's "pure capitalism" *collapsed.*

Let it be said at the outset that this prediction as well cannot be lightly brushed aside. In Russia and Eastern Europe, capitalism was displaced by socialism; in Germany and Italy it drifted into fascism. And while wars, brute political power, exigencies of fate, and the determined efforts of revolutionaries have all contributed their share, the grim truth is that these changes occurred largely for the very reason Marx foresaw: capitalism broke down.

Why did it break down? Partly because it developed the instability Marx said it would. A succession of worsening business crises, compounded by a plague of wars, destroyed the faith of the lower and middle classes in the system. But that is not the entire answer. European capitalism failed not so much for economic as for *social* reasons—and Marx foresaw this too!

For Marx recognized that the economic difficulties of the system were not insuperable. Although antimonopoly legislation or anti-business-cycle policies were unknown in Marx's day, such activities were not inconceivable: there was nothing inevitable in the *physical* sense about Marx's vision. The Marxist prediction of decay was founded on a conception of capitalism in which it was *politically* impossible for a government to set the system's wrongs aright; ideologically, even emotionally, impossible. The cure for capitalism's failings would require that a government would have to rise above the interests of one class alone—and that was to assume that men could free themselves from the shackles of their immediate economic self-interest. Marx's analysis made that doubtful.

It is just this lack of social flexibility, this bondage to shortsighted interest, that weakened European capitalism—at least until after World War II. For one who has read the works of Marx it is frightening to look back at the grim determination with which so many nations steadfastly hewed to the very course that he insisted would lead to their undoing. It was as if their governments were unconsciously vindicating

Marx's prophecy by obstinately doing exactly what he said they would. When in Russia under the Tsars all democratic trade unionism was ruthlessly stamped out, when in England and Germany monopolies and cartels were officially encouraged, the Marxist dialectic looked balefully prescient indeed. All through the late nineteenth and early twentieth centuries, when one inspected the enormous gulf between rich and poor and saw evidence of the total indifference of the former for the latter, one had the uneasy feeling that the psychological stereotypes that Marx cast in his historical drama were all too truly drawn from life.

Things moved differently in America during those years. We too had our share of reactionaries and revolutionaries. The economic history of the United States contains more than enough exploitation and ugliness. But capitalism here evolved in a land untouched by the dead hand of aristocratic lineage and age-old class attitudes. To some degree this resulted in a harsher social climate in America than in Europe, for we clung to the credo of "rugged individualism" long after the individual had been hopelessly overwhelmed by the environment of massive industrialism, whereas in Europe a traditional noblesse oblige existed side by side with its unconcealed class divisions. Yet out of the American milieu came a certain pragmatism in dealing with power, private as well as public, and a general subscription to the ideals of democracy which steered the body politic safely past the rocks on which it foundered in so many nations abroad.

It is in these capabilities for change that the answer to Marxian analysis lies. Indeed, the more we examine the history of capitalism, especially in recent decades, the more we learn both to respect the penetration of Marx's thought and to recognize its limitations. The *problems* he diagnosed within capitalism are still very much with us, including above all a tendency to economic instability and to the concentration of wealth and power. Yet in different nations we find widely different responses to these problems. Thus, despite much higher unemployment rates than we find in the United States, many European countries provide free universal education (including college), health and pension benefits, and unemployment relief on scales that put ours to shame. As a result, the proportion of our population living in poverty is three and four times higher than theirs!

The point, in weighing Marx's powerful vision and the analytics that follow from it, is his failure to make allowances for the role of sociopolitical culture—an element he barely mentions. There is a spectrum of views and values on the prerogatives of capital, the centrality of the market, and the respective roles of the private and the public sectors in all nations whose institutions are capitalist—that is, that incorporate these defining beliefs. It is in this spectrum of institutions, behaviors, and attitudes that the successor vision to Marx must be sought.

Yet, shorn of its overtones of inevitable doom, the Marxist analysis cannot be disregarded. It remains the gravest, most penetrating examination the capitalist system has ever undergone. It is not an examination conducted along moral lines with head wagging and tongue clucking over the iniquities of the profit motive—this is the stuff of the Marxist revolutionary but not of the Marxist economist. For all its passion, it is a dispassionate appraisal, and it is for this reason that its somber findings remain pertinent.

Finally, we must remember that Marx was not just a great economist. In his graveside oration, Engels said that "just as Darwin discovered the law of evolution in organic nature, so Marx discovered the law of evolution in human history." This is certainly too much to claim, but Engels was not wrong in emphasizing the extraordinary importance of Marx's vision of the historic process as an arena in which social classes struggle for supremacy. Marx taught us not just to look at, but to look through, history, just as Freud taught us to look *through* the façade of personality to the psychic processes within us, or as Plato taught us to look through the screen of unexamined ideas to the veiled questions of philosophy.

That is why Marx's name, like those of Freud and Plato, remains contemporary. Marx is certainly not infallible, for all the idol worship to which he has been subjected. He is better thought of as *unavoidable*—a great explorer whose footprints have been indelibly imprinted on the continent of social thought that he discovered. All who wish to explore that continent further, whether or not they agree with Marx's findings, must pay their respects to the person who first claimed it for mankind.

vii

The Victorian World
and the Underworld
of Economics

Karl Marx pronounced his sentence of doom on capitalism in the *Manifesto* of 1848; the system was diagnosed as the victim of an incurable disease, and although no timetable was given, it was presumed to be close enough to its final death struggle for the next of kin—the Communists—to listen avidly for the last gasp that would signal their inheritance of power. Even before the appearance of *Capital* in 1867, the deathwatch had begun, and with each bout of speculative fever or each siege of industrial depression, the hopeful drew nearer to the deathbed and told each other that the moment of Final Revolution would now be soon at hand.

But the system did not die. True, many of the Marxist laws of motion were verified by the march of events: big business did grow bigger and recurrent depressions and unemployment did plague society. But along with these confirmations of the prognosis of doom, another highly important and portentously phrased Marxist symptom was remarkable by its absence: the "increasing misery" of the proletariat failed to increase.

Actually, there has been a long debate among Marxists as to what Marx meant by that phrase. If he meant only that more and more of the working class would experience the "misery" of becoming proletarians—wage workers—he was right, as we have seen. But if he meant that their physical misery would worsen, he was wrong.

Indeed, a Royal Commission convened to look into the slump of 1886 expressed particular satisfaction with the condition of the working classes. And this was not just the patronizing cant of class apologists. Conditions *were* better— perceptibly and significantly better. Looking back on the situation from the 1880s, Sir Robert Giffen wrote: "What we have to consider is that fifty years ago, the working man with wages on the average about half, or not much more than half what they are now, had at times to contend with a fluctuation in the price of bread which implied sheer starvation. Periodic starvation was, in fact, the condition of the masses of working men throughout the kingdom fifty years ago." But by the time Giffen wrote, although prices had risen, wages had risen faster. *For the first time,* the English workingman was making enough to keep body and soul together—a sorry commentary on the past, but a hopeful augury for the future.

And not only had wages gone up, but the very source of surplus value had diminished: hours were far shorter. At the Jarrow Shipyards and the New Castle Chemical Works, for example, the work week had fallen from sixty-one to fifty-four hours, while even in the sweated textile mills, the stint was reduced to only fifty-seven hours. Indeed the mill owners complained that their wage costs had risen by better than 20 percent. But while progress was expensive, it paid intangible dividends. For as conditions ameliorated, the mutterings of 1848 died down. "You cannot get them to talk of politics so long as they are well employed," testified a Staffordshire manufacturer on the attitude of his working force.

Even Marx and Engels had to recognize the trend. "The English proletariat is actually becoming more and more bourgeois," mourned Engels in a letter to Marx, "so that the ultimate aim of this most bourgeois of all nations would appear to be the possession, *alongside* the bourgeois, of a bourgeois aristocracy and a bourgeois proletariat."

Clearly, Marx was premature in his expectation of impending doom. For the faithful, of course, the disconcerting

turn of events could be swallowed in the comforting knowledge that "inevitable" still meant inevitable, and that a matter
of a generation or two came to little in the grand march
of history. But for the non-Marxist surveyors of the scene,
the great Victorian boom meant something else. The world
more and more appeared full of hope and promise, and the
forebodings of a dissenter like Karl Marx seemed merely the
ravings of a discontented radical. Hence the intellectual
bombshell that Marx had prepared went off in almost total silence; instead of a storm of abuse, Marx met the far more
crushing ignominy of indifference.

For economics had ceased to be the proliferation of
world views that, in the hands of now a philosopher, now a
financial trader, now a revolutionary, seemed to illuminate
the whole avenue down which society was marching. It
became instead the special province of professors, whose investigations threw out pinpoint beams rather than the wide-
searching beacons of the earlier economists.

There was a reason for this: as we have seen, Victorian
England had caught the steady trade winds of late-
nineteenth-century progress and optimism. Improvement
was in the air, and so quite naturally there seemed less
cause to ask disturbing questions about the nature of the
voyage. Hence the Victorian boom gave rise to a roster of
elucidators, men who would examine the workings of the
system in great detail, but not men who would express
doubt as to its basic merits or make troublesome prognosti-
cations as to its eventual fate. A new professordom took over
the main life of economic thought. Its contributions were
often important, yet not vital. For in the minds of men like
Alfred Marshall, Stanley Jevons, John Bates Clark, and the
proliferating faculties that surrounded them, there were no
wolves in the economic world anymore, and therefore no
life-and-death activities for economic theory to elucidate.
The world was peopled entirely with agreeable, if imaginary,
sheep.

The sheep were never more clearly delineated than in a
little volume entitled *Mathematical Psychics*, which appeared in 1881, just two years before Marx died. It was not

written by the greatest of academicians, but perhaps by the most revealing of them—a strange, shy professor named Francis Ysidro Edgeworth, a nephew of that Maria Edgeworth who had once played charades with Ricardo.

Edgeworth was undoubtedly a brilliant scholar. In his final examinations at Oxford, when he was asked a particularly abstruse question, he inquired of his examiners, "Shall I answer briefly, or at length?" and then proceeded to hold forth for half an hour, punctuating his reply with excursions into Greek while his examiners gaped.

But Edgeworth was not fascinated with economics because it justified or explained or condemned the world, or because it opened new vistas, bright or gloomy, into the future. This odd soul was fascinated because economics dealt with *quantities* and because anything that dealt with quantities could be translated into *mathematics!* The process of translation required the abandonment of that tension-fraught world of the earlier economists, but it yielded in return a world of such neat precision and lovely exactness that the loss seemed amply compensated.

To build up such a mathematical mirror of reality, the world obviously had to be simplified. Edgeworth's simplification was this assumption: *every man is a pleasure machine.* Jeremy Bentham had originated the conception in the early nineteenth century under the beguiling title of the Felicific Calculus, a philosophical view of humanity as so many living profit-and-loss calculators, each busily arranging his life to maximize the pleasure of his psychic adding machine. To this general philosophy Edgeworth now added the precision of mathematics to produce a kind of Panglossian Best of All Possible Worlds.

Of all men to have adopted such a view of society, Edgeworth seems a most unlikely choice. He himself was as ill-constructed a pleasure machine as can be imagined. Neurotically shy, he tended to flee from the pleasures of human company to the privacy of his club; unhappy about the burden of material things, he received few of the pleasures that for most people flow from possessions. His rooms were bare, his library was the public one, and his stock of material wealth did not include crockery, or stationery, or even stamps. Perhaps his greatest source of pleasure was in the construction of his lovely imaginary economic Xanadu.

But regardless of his motives, Edgeworth's pleasure-machine assumption bore wonderful intellectual fruit. For if economics was defined to be the study of human pleasure-mechanisms competing for shares of society's stock of pleasure, then it could be shown—with all the irrefutability of the differential calculus—that in a world of perfect competition each pleasure machine would achieve the highest amount of pleasure that could be meted out by society.

In other words, if this was not yet *quite* the best of all possible worlds, it could be. Unfortunately, the world was not organized as a game of perfect competition; men did have the lamentable habit of sticking together in foolish disregard of the beneficent consequences of stubbornly following their self-interest; trade unions, for example, were in direct controversion to the principle of each for himself, and the undeniable fact of inequalities of wealth and position did make the starting position of the game something less than absolutely neutral.

But never mind, said Edgeworth. Nature has taken care of that too. While trade unions might gain in the short run through combination, it could be shown that in the long run they must lose—they were only a transient imperfection in the ideal scheme of things. And if high birth and great wealth seemed at first to prejudice the outcome of the economic game, that could be reconciled with mathematical psychics, too. For while all individuals were pleasure machines, some were *better* pleasure machines than others. Men, for example, were better equipped to run up their psychic bank accounts than women, and the delicate sensibilities of the "aristocracy of skill and talent" were more responsive to the pleasures of good living than the clodlike pleasure machines of the laboring classes. Hence, the calculus of human mathematics could still function advantageously; indeed it positively justified those divisions of sex and status which one saw about him in the living world.

But mathematical psychics did more than rationalize the

tenets of conservatism. Edgeworth actually believed that his algebraic insight into human activity might yield helpful results in the world of flesh and blood. His analysis involved such terms as these:

$$\frac{d_2y}{dx^2} = \left(\frac{d\pi}{dx}\right)^2\left(\frac{d_2\pi}{dy_2}\right) - 2\,\frac{d\pi}{dx}\cdot\frac{d\pi}{dy}\left(\frac{d_2\pi}{dxdy}\right) + \ldots$$

"Considerations so abstract," wrote Edgeworth, "it would of course be ridiculous to fling upon the floodtide of practical politics. But they are not perhaps out of place when we remount to the little rills of sentiment and secret springs of motive where every course of action must be originated."

"The little rills of sentiment," indeed! What would Adam Smith have thought of this conversion of his pushy merchants, his greedy journeymen, and his multiplying laboring classes into so many categories of delicate pleasure-seekers? In fact, Henry Sidgwick, a contemporary of Edgeworth's and a disciple of J. S. Mill, angrily announced that he ate his dinner not because he had toted up the satisfactions to be gained therefrom, but because he was hungry. But there was no use protesting: the scheme of mathematical psychics was so neat, so beguiling, so bereft of troublesome human intransigences, and so happily unbesmirched with considerations of human striving and social conflict, that its success was immediate.

Edgeworth's was not the only such attempt to dehumanize political economy. Even during Marx's lifetime a whole mathematical school of economics had grown up. In Germany an economist named von Thünen came up with a formula that yielded, he claimed, the precise just wage of labor:

$$\sqrt{a \cdot p}$$

Von Thünen liked it well enough to have it engraved on his tombstone; we do not know what the workingmen thought of it. In France a distinguished economist named Léon Walras proved that one could deduce by mathematics the exact prices that would just exactly clear the market; of course, in order to do this, one had to have the equation for every single economic good on the market and then the ability to solve a problem in which the number of equations would run into the hundreds of thousands—indeed, into the millions. But never mind the difficulties; theoretically the problem could be done. At the University of Manchester, a professor named W. Stanley Jevons wrote a treatise on political economy in which the struggle for existence was reduced to "a Calculus of Pleasure and Pain." "My theory of Economics . . . is purely mathematical in character," wrote Jevons, and he turned out of his focus every aspect of economic life which was not reducible to the jigsaw precision of his scheme. Perhaps even more noteworthy, he planned to write (although he did not live to do so) a book called *Principles of Economics:* it is significant that political economy was now called economics, and its expositions were becoming texts.

It was not all foolishness, although too much of it was. Economics, after all, does concern the actions of aggregates of people, and human aggregates, like aggregates of atoms, do tend to display statistical regularities and laws of probability. Thus, as the professoriat turned its eyes to the exploration of the idea of *equilibrium*—the state toward which the market would tend as the result of the random collisions of individuals all seeking to maximize their utilities—it did in fact elucidate some tendencies of the social universe. The equations of Léon Walras are still used to depict the attributes of a social system at rest.

The question is, does a system "at rest" actually depict the realities—the fundamental realities—of the social universe? The earlier economists, from Smith through Mill and of course Marx, had a compelling image in their minds of a society that was by its nature *expansive.* True, its expansion might encounter barriers, or might run out of steam, or might develop into economic downturns, but the central force of the economic world was nonetheless inseparable from a political and psychological tendency toward growth.

It was this basic conception that was lacking in the new concentration on equilibrium as the most interesting, most revealing aspect of the system. Suddenly capitalism was no longer seen as an historic social vehicle under constant tension but as a static, rather historyless, mode of organization. The driving propulsion of the system—the propulsion that had fascinated all its prior investigators—was now overlooked, ignored, forgotten. Whatever aspects of a capitalist economy were illumined in the new perspective, its historic mission was not.

And so, as a counterpart to this pale world of equations, an underworld of economics flourished. There had always been such an underworld, a strange limbo of cranks and heretics, whose doctrines had failed to attain the stature of respectability. One such was the irrepressible Bernard Mandeville, who shocked the eighteenth century with a witty demonstration that virtue was vice and vice virtue. Mandeville merely pointed out that the profligate expenditure of the sinful rich gave work to the poor, while the stingy rectitude of the virtuous penny pincher did not; hence, said Mandeville, private immorality may redound to the public welfare, whereas private uprightness may be a social burden. The sophisticated lesson of his *Fable of the Bees* was too much for the eighteenth century to swallow; Mandeville's book was convicted as a public nuisance by a grand jury in Middlesex in 1723, and Mandeville himself was roundly castigated by Adam Smith and everyone else.

But whereas the earlier eccentrics and charlatans were largely banished by the opinions of sturdy thinkers like Smith or Ricardo, now the underworld claimed its recruits for a different reason. There was simply no longer any room in the official world of economics for those who wanted to take the whole gamut of human behavior for their forum, and there was little tolerance in the stuffy world of Victorian correctness for those whose diagnosis of society left room for moral doubtings or seemed to indicate the need for radical reform.

And so the underworld took on new life. Marx went there because his doctrine was unpleasant. Malthus went there because his idea of "general gluts" was an arithmetical absurdity and because his doubts about the benefits of saving were totally at variance with the Victorian admiration for thrift. The Utopians went there because what they were talking about was arrant nonsense and wasn't "economics" anyway, and finally anyone went there whose doctrines failed to accord with the elegant world that the academicians erected in their classrooms and fondly believed existed outside them.

It was a far more interesting place, this underworld, than the serene realms above. It abounded with wonderful personalities, and in it sprouted a weird and luxuriant tangle of ideas. There was, for example, a man who has been almost forgotten in the march of economic ideas. He is Frédéric Bastiat, an eccentric Frenchman, who lived from 1801 to 1850, and who in that short space of time and an even shorter space of literary life—six years—brought to bear on economics that most devastating of all weapons: ridicule. Look at this madhouse of a world, says Bastiat. It goes to enormous efforts to tunnel underneath a mountain in order to connect two countries. And then what does it do? Having labored mightily to facilitate the interchange of goods, it sets up customs guards on both sides of the mountain and makes it as difficult as possible for merchandise to travel through the tunnel!

Bastiat had a gift for pointing out absurdities; his little book *Economic Sophisms* is as close to humor as economics has ever come. When, for example, the Paris-Madrid railroad was being debated in the French Assembly, one M. Simiot argued that it should have a gap at Bordeaux, because a break in the line there would redound greatly to the wealth of the Bordeaux porters, commissionaires, hotelkeepers, bargemen, and the like, and thus, by enriching Bordeaux, would enrich France. Bastiat seized on the idea with avidity. Fine, he said, but let's not stop at Bordeaux alone. "If Bordeaux has a right to profit by a gap . . . than Angoulême, Poitiers, Tours, Orléans . . . should also demand gaps as being for the general interest. . . . In this way we shall succeed in having a railway composed of successive gaps, and which may be denominated a *Negative Railway*."

Bastiat was a wit in the world of economics, but his private life was tragic. Born in Bayonne, he was orphaned at an early age and, worse yet, contracted tuberculosis. He studied at a university, and then tried business, but he had no head for commercial details. He turned to agriculture, but he fared equally badly there; like Tolstoi's well-meaning count, the more he interfered in the running of his family estate, the worse it did. He dreamed of heroism, but his military adventures had a Don Quixote twist: when the Bourbons were run out of France in 1830, Bastiat rounded up six hundred young men and led them to storm a royalist citadel, regardless of cost. Poor Bastiat—the fortress meekly hauled down its flag and invited everyone in for a feast instead.

It seemed that he was doomed to disappointment. But his enforced idleness turned his interests to economics, and he began to read and discuss the topics of the day. A neighboring country gentleman urged him to put his ideas on paper, and Bastiat wrote an article on free trade and sent it in to a Parisian journal. His thoughts were original and his style wonderfully sharp. The article was printed, and overnight this mild scholar of the provinces was famous.

He came to Paris. "He had not had time to call in the assistance of a Parisian hatter and tailor," writes M. de Molinari, "and with his long hair, his tiny hat, his ample frockcoat and his family umbrella, you would have been apt to mistake him for an honest peasant who came to town for the first time to see the metropolis."

But the country scholar had a pen that bit. Every day he read the Paris papers in which the deputies and ministers of France argued for and defended their policies of selfishness and blind self-interest; then he would answer with a rejoinder that rocked Paris with laughter. For example, when the Chamber of Deputies in the 1840s legislated higher duties on all foreign goods in order to benefit French industry, Bastiat turned out this masterpiece of economic satire:

PETITION OF THE MANUFACTURERS OF CANDLES, WAXLIGHTS, LAMPS, CANDLESTICKS, STREET LAMPS, SNUFFERS, EXTINGUISHERS, AND OF THE PRODUCERS OF OIL, TALLOW,

RESIN, ALCOHOL, AND GENERALLY EVERYTHING CONNECTED WITH LIGHTING

To Messieurs the Members of the Chamber of Deputies

Gentlemen,

. . . We are suffering from the intolerable competition of a foreign rival, placed, it would seem, in a condition so far superior to our own for the production of light, that he absolutely *inundates* our *national market* with it at a price fabulously reduced. . . . This rival . . . is no other than the sun.

What we pray for, is, that it may please you to pass a law ordering the shutting up of all windows, skylights, dormer-windows, outside and inside shutters, curtains, blinds, bull's-eyes; in a word of all openings, holes, chinks, and fissures.

. . . If you shut up as much as possible all access to natural light and create a demand for artificial light, which of our French manufacturers will not benefit by it?

. . . If more tallow is consumed, then there must be more oxen and sheep . . . if more oil is consumed, then we shall have extended cultivation of the poppy, of the olive . . . our heaths will be covered with resinous trees.

Make your choice, but be logical; for as long as you exclude, as you do, iron, corn, foreign fabrics, *in proportion* as their prices approximate to zero, what inconsistency it would be to admit the light of the sun, the price of which is already at *zero* during the entire day!

A more dramatic—if fantastic—defense of free trade has never been written. But it was not only against protective tariffs that Bastiat protested: this man laughed at every form of economic double-thinking. In 1848, when the Socialists began to propound their ideas for the salvation of society with more regard for passion than practicability, Bastiat turned against them the same weapons that he had used against the *ancien régime.* "Everyone wants to live at the expense of the state," he wrote. "They forget that the state lives at the expense of everyone."

But his special target, his most hated "sophism," was the rationalization of private greed under the pretentious cover of a protective tariff erected for the "national good." How he loved to demolish the specious thinking that argued for barriers to trade under the guise of liberal economics! When the French ministry proposed to raise the duty on imported cloth to "protect" the French workingman, Bastiat replied with this delicious paradox:

"Pass a law to this effect," wrote Bastiat to the Minister of Commerce. "No one shall henceforth be permitted to employ any beams or rafters but such as are produced and fashioned by blunt hatchets. . . . Whereas at present we give a hundred blows of the axe, we shall then give three hundred. The work which we now do in an hour will then require three hours. What a powerful encouragement will thus be given to labor! . . . Whoever shall henceforth desire to have a roof to cover him must comply with our exactions, just as at present whoever desires clothes to his back must comply with yours."

His criticisms, for all their penetrating mockery, met with little practical success. He went to England to meet the leaders of the free-trade movement there and returned to organize a free-trade association in Paris. It lasted only eighteen months—Bastiat was never any good as an organizer.

But 1848 was now at hand and Bastiat was elected to the National Assembly. By then the danger seemed to him the other extreme—that men would pay too much attention to the imperfections of the system and would blindly choose socialism in its stead. He began a book entitled *Economic Harmonies* in which he was to show that the apparent disorder of the world was a disorder of the surface only; that underneath, the impetus of a thousand different self-seeking agents became transmuted in the marketplace into a higher social good. But his health was now disastrously bad. He could barely breathe, and his face was livid with the ravages of his disease. He moved to Pisa, where he read in the papers of his own death and of the commonplace expressions of regret which accompanied it: regret at the passing of "the great economist," the "illustrious author." He wrote a friend: "Thank God I am not dead. I assure you I should breathe my last without pain and almost with joy if I were certain of leaving to the friends who love me, not poignant regrets, but a gentle, affectionate, somewhat melancholy remembrance of me." He struggled to finish his book before he himself should be finished. But it was too late. In 1850 he passed away, whispering at the end something that the listening priest thought was "Truth, truth . . ."

He is a very small figure in the economic constellation. He was enormously conservative but not influential, even among conservatives. His function, it seems, was to prick the pomposities of his time; but beneath the raillery and the wit lies the more disturbing question: does the system always make sense? Are there paradoxes where the public and private weals collide? Can we trust the automatic mechanism of private interest when it is perverted at every turn by the far from automatic mechanism of the political structure it erects?

The questions were never squarely faced in the Elysian fields above. The official world of economics took little notice of the paradoxes proposed by its jester. Instead it sailed serenely on toward the development of the quantitative niceties of a pleasure-seeking world, and the questions raised by Bastiat remained unanswered. Certainly mathematical psychics was hardly the tool with which to unlock the dilemma of the Negative Railway and the Blunt Hatchet; Stanley Jevons, who with Edgeworth was the great proponent of making economics a "science," admitted, "About politics, I confess myself in a fog." Unfortunately, he was not alone.

And so the underworld continued to prosper. In 1879 it gained an American recruit, a bearded, gentle, fiercely self-sure man, who said that "Political Economy . . . as currently taught *is* hopeless and despairing. But this [is] because she has been degraded and shackled; her truths dislocated; her

THE VICTORIAN WORLD   183

harmonies ignored; the word she would utter gagged in her mouth, and her protest against wrong turned into an indorsement of injustice." And that was not all. For this heretic maintained not only that economics had failed to see the answer to the riddle of poverty although it was clearly laid out before her eyes, but that with his remedy, a whole new world stood ready to unfold: "Words fail the thought! It is the Golden Age of which poets have sung and high-raised seers have told in metaphor! . . . It is the culmination of Christianity—the city of God with its walls of jasper and its gates of pearl!"

The newcomer was Henry George. No wonder he was in the underworld, for his early career must certainly have seemed an uncouth preparation for serious thinking to the cloistered keepers of the true doctrine. Henry George had been everything in life: adventurer, gold prospector, worker, sailor, compositor, journalist, government bureaucrat, and lecturer. He had never even gone to college; at thirteen he had left school to ship out as foremast boy on the 586-ton *Hindoo* bound for Australia and Calcutta. At a time when his contemporaries were learning Latin, he had bought a pet monkey and watched a man fall from the rigging, and become a thin, intense, independent boy with a wanderlust. Back from the East, he tried a job in a printing firm in his hometown of Philadelphia, and then at nineteen, shipped out again, this time to California, with the thought of gold in mind.

Before he left, he rated himself on a phrenological chart:

Amativeness. . . . . large
Philoprogenitiveness . . . . moderate
Adhesiveness . . . . large
Inhabitiveness . . . . large
Concentrativeness. . . . . small

and so on, with a rating of "full" on Alimentativeness, "small" on Acquisitiveness, "large" on Self-esteem, and "small" on Mirthfulness. It was not a bad estimate in some respects—although it is odd to see Caution rated "large," for when George reached San Francisco in 1858 he skipped ashore, although he had signed on for a year, and headed for Victoria and gold. He found gold—but it was fool's gold, and he decided the life at sea was the life for him after all. Instead—his bump of Concentrativeness being small—he became a typesetter in a San Francisco shop, then a weigher in a rice mill, then, in his own words, "a tramp." Another trek to the gold fields was equally unrewarding, and he returned to San Francisco impoverished.

He met Annie Fox, and eloped with her; she was a seventeen-year-old innocent and he a handsome young lad with a Bill Cody mustache and pointed beard. The trusting young Miss Fox took with her a bulky package on her secret marriage flight; the young adventurer thought it might be jewels, but it turned out to be only the *Household Book of Poetry* and other volumes.

There followed years of the most wretched poverty. Henry George was an odd-job printer, and work was hard to come by and ill paid at best. When Annie had her second child, George wrote: "I walked along the street and made up my mind to get money from the first man whose appearance might indicate he had it to give. I stopped a man—a stranger—and told him I wanted $5. He asked me what I wanted it for. I told him my wife was confined and that I had nothing to give her to eat. He gave me the money. If he had not, I think I was desperate enough to have killed him."

Now—at age twenty-six—he began to write. He landed a job in the composing room of the San Francisco *Times* and sent a piece upstairs to Noah Brooks, the editor. Brooks suspected that the boy had copied it, but when nothing resembling it appeared in any of the other newspapers for several days he printed it, and then went downstairs to look for George. He found him, a slight young man, rather undersized, standing on a board to raise himself to the height of his type case. George became a reporter.

Within a few years he left the *Times* to join the San Francisco *Post*, a crusading journal. George began to write about matters of more than routine interest: about the Chinese coolies and their indenture, and about the land grabbing of the railroads and the machinations of the local trusts.

He wrote a long letter to J. S. Mill in France on the immigration question and was graced with a long affirmative reply. And in between his newly found political interests he had time for ventures in the best journalistic tradition: when the ship *Sunrise* came to town with a hushed-up story about a captain and mate who had hounded their crew until two men had leaped overboard to their death, George and the *Post* ferreted out the story and brought the officers to justice.

The newspaper was sold, and Henry George wangled himself a political sinecure—Inspector of Gas Meters. It was not that he wanted a life of leisure; rather, he had begun to read the great economists and his central interest was now clearly formed—already he was a kind of local authority. He needed time to study and to write and to deliver lectures to the working classes on the ideas of the great Mill.

When the University of California established a chair of political economy, he was widely considered as a strong candidate for the post. But to qualify he had to deliver a lecture before faculty and students, and George was rash enough to voice such sentiments as this: "The name of political economy has been constantly invoked against every effort of the working classes to increase their wages," and then to compound the shock he added: "For the study of political economy, you need no special knowledge, no extensive library, no costly laboratory. You do not even need textbooks nor teachers, if you will but think for yourselves."

That was the beginning and the end of his academic career. A more suitable candidate was found for the post, and George went back to pamphleteering and study. And then suddenly, "in daylight and in a city street, there came to me a thought, a vision, a call—give it what name you please. . . . It was that that impelled me to write *Progress and Poverty,* and that sustained me when else I should have failed. And when I had finished the last page, in the dead of night, when I was entirely alone, I flung myself on my knees and wept like a child."

As might be expected, it was a book written from the heart, a cry of mingled protest and hope. And as might also be expected, it suffered from too much passion and too little professional circumspection. But what a contrast to the dull texts of the day—no wonder the guardians of economics could not seriously consider an argument that was couched in such a style as this:

> Take now . . . some hard-headed business man, who has no theories, but knows how to make money. Say to him: "Here is a little village; in ten years it will be a great city—in ten years the railroad will have taken the place of the stage coach, the electric light of the candle; it will abound with all the machinery and improvements that so enormously multiply the effective power of labor. Will, in ten years, interest be any higher?"
>
> He will tell you, "No!"
>
> "Will the wages of common labor be any higher . . . ?"
>
> He will tell you, "No, the wages of common labor will not be any higher. . . ."
>
> "What, then, will be higher?"
>
> "Rent, the value of land. Go, get yourself a piece of ground, and hold possession."
>
> And if, under such circumstances, you take his advice, you need do nothing more. You may sit down and smoke your pipe; you may lie around like the *lazzaroni* of Naples or the *leperos* of Mexico; you may go up in a balloon or down a hole in the ground; and without doing one stroke of work, without adding one iota of wealth to the community, in ten years you will be rich! In the new city you may have a luxurious mansion, but among its public buildings will be an almshouse.

We need not spell out the whole emotionally charged argument; the crux of it lies in this passage. Henry George is outraged at the spectacle of men whose incomes—sometimes fabulous incomes—derive not from the services they have rendered the community, but merely from the fact that they have had the good fortune to hold advantageously situated soil.

Ricardo, of course, saw all this long before him. But at best, Ricardo had only claimed that the tendency of a growing society to enrich the holders of its land would redound to the misfortune of the capitalist. To Henry George, this was only the entering wedge. The injustice of rents not only robbed the capitalist of his honest profit but weighed on the shoulders of the workingman as well. More damaging yet, he found it to be the cause of those industrial "paroxysms," as he called them, that from time to time shook society to its roots.

The argument was not too clearly delineated. Primarily it rested on the fact that since rent was assumed from the start to be a kind of social extortion, naturally it represented an unfair distribution of produce to landlords at the expense of workers and industrialists. And as for paroxysms—well, George was convinced that rent led inevitably to wild speculation in land values (as indeed it did on the West Coast) and just as inevitably to an eventual collapse which would bring the rest of the structure of prices tumbling down beside it.

Having discovered the true causes of poverty and the fundamental check to progress, it was simple for George to propose a remedy—a single massive tax. It would be a tax on land, a tax that would absorb all rents. And then, with the cancer removed from the body of society, the millenium could be allowed to come. The single tax would not only dispense with the need for all other kinds of taxes, but in abolishing rent it would "raise wages, increase the earnings of capital, extirpate pauperism, abolish poverty, give remunerative employment to whoever wishes it, afford free scope to human powers, purify government, and carry civilization to yet nobler heights." It would be—there is no other word— the ultimate panacea.

It is an elusive thesis when we seek to evaluate it. Of course it is naïve, and the equation of rent with sin could have occurred only to someone as messianic as George himself. Similarly, to put the blame for industrial depressions on land speculation is to blow up one small aspect of an expanding economy quite out of proportion to reality: land speculations can be troublesome, but severe depressions have taken place in countries where land values were anything but inflated.

So we need not linger here. But when we come to the central body of the thesis, we must pause. For while George's mechanical diagnosis is superficial and faulty, his basic criticism of society is a moral and not a mechanistic one. Why, asks Henry George, should rent exist? Why should a man benefit merely from the fact of ownership, when he may render no services to the community in exchange? We may justify the rewards of an industrialist by describing his profits as the prize for his foresight and ingenuity, but where is the foresight of a man whose grandfather owned a pasture on which, two generations later, society saw fit to erect a skyscraper?

The question is provocative, but it is not so easy to condemn the institution of rent out of hand. For landlords are not the only passive beneficiaries of the growth of society. The stockholder in an expanding company, the workman whose productivity is enhanced by technical progress, the consumer whose real income rises as the nation prospers, all these are also beneficiaries of communal advancement. The unearned gains that accrue to a well-situated landlord are enjoyed in different forms by all of us. The problem is not just that of land rents, but of all unearned income; and while this is certainly a serious problem, it cannot be adequately approached through land ownership alone.

And then the rent problem is not so drastic as it was viewed by Henry George. A small, but steady flow of rents goes to farmers, homeowners, modest citizens. And even in the monopolistic area of rental incomes—in the real-estate operations of a metropolis—a shifting and fluid market is in operation. Rents are not frozen in archaic feudal patterns, but constantly pass from hand to hand as land is bought and sold, appraised and reappraised. Suffice it to point out that rental income in the United States has shrunk from 6 percent of the national income in 1929 to less than 2 percent today.

But no matter whether the thesis held together logically or whether its moral condemnation was fully justified. The book struck a tremendously responsive chord. *Progress and Poverty* became a best-seller, and overnight Henry George was catapulted into national prominence. "I consider *Progress and Poverty* as *the* book of this half-century," said the reviewer in the San Francisco *Argonaut,* and the New York *Tribune* claimed that it had "no equal since the publication of the *Wealth of Nations* by Adam Smith." Even those publications like the *Examiner* and *Chronicle,* which called it "the most pernicious treatise on political economy that has been published for many a day," only served to enhance its fame.

George went to England; he returned after a lecture tour an international figure. He was drafted to run for mayor of New York, and in a three-cornered race he beat Theodore Roosevelt and only narrowly lost to the Tammany candidate.

The single tax was a religion to him by now. He organized Land and Labor Clubs and lectured to enthusiastic audiences here and in Great Britain. A friend asked him, "Does this mean war? Can you, unless dealing with craven conditions among men, hope to take land away from its owners without war?" "I do not see," said George, "that a musket need be fired. But if necessary, war be it, then. There was never a holier cause. No, never a holier cause!"

"Here was the gentlest and kindest of men," comments his friend, James Russell Taylor, "who would shrink from a gun fired in anger, ready for universal war rather than that his gospel should not be accepted. It was the courage . . . which makes one a majority."

Needless to say, the whole doctrine was anathema to the world of respectable opinion. A Catholic priest who had associated himself with George in his mayoralty fight was temporarily excommunicated; the Pope himself addressed an encyclical to the land question; and when George sent him an elaborately printed and bound reply, it was ignored. "I will not insult my readers by discussing a project so steeped in infamy," wrote General Francis A. Walker, a leading professional economist in the United States; but while officialdom looked at his book with shock or with amused contempt, the man himself struck home to his audience. *Progress and Poverty* sold more copies than all the economic texts previously published in the country; in England, his name became a household word. Not only that, but the import of his ideas—albeit usually in watered form—became part of the heritage of men like Woodrow Wilson, John Dewey, Louis Brandeis. Indeed there is a devoted following of Henry George's still active today.

In 1897, old, unwell, but still indomitable, he permitted himself to be drafted for a second mayoralty race, knowing full well that the strain of the campaign might be too much for his failing heart. It was; he was called "marauder," "assailant of other people's right," "apostle of anarchy and destruction," and he did die, on the eve of the election. His funeral was attended by thousands. He was a religious man; let us hope that his soul went straight to heaven. As for his reputation—that went straight into the underworld of economics, and there he exists today; almost-Messiah, semi-crackpot, and disturbing questioner of the morality of our economic institutions.

But something else was going on in the underworld, something more important than Henry George's fulminations against rent and his ecstatic vision of a City of God to be built on the foundation of the single tax. A new and vigorous spirit was sweeping England and the Continent and even the United States, a spirit that manifested itself in the proliferation of such slogans as "The Anglo-Saxon race is infallibly destined to be the predominant force in the history and civilization of the world." The spirit was not confined to England: across the Channel, Victor Hugo declared, "France is needed by humanity"; in Russia the spokesman for absolutism, Konstantin Pobyedonostsev, proclaimed that Russia's freedom from the taint of Western decadence had given her the accolade of leadership for the East. In Germany the Kaiser was explaining how *der alte Gott* was on their side; and in the New World, Theodore Roosevelt was making himself the American spokesman for a similar philosophy.

The age of imperialism had begun, and the mapmakers were busy changing the colors that denoted ownership of the darker continents. Between 1870 and 1898 Britain added 4 million square miles and 88 million people to its empire; France gained nearly the same area of territory, with 40 million souls attached; Germany won a million miles and 16 million colonials; Belgium took 900,000 miles and 30 million people; even Portugal joined the race, with 800,000 miles of new lands and 9 million inhabitants.

In truth, three generations had changed the face of the earth. But more than that, they had witnessed an equally remarkable change in the attitude with which the West viewed that process of change. In the days of Adam Smith, it will be remembered, the Scots philosopher regarded with scorn the attempts of merchants to play the role of kings, and he urged the independence of the American Colonies. And Smith's contempt for colonies was widely shared: James Mill, the father of John Stuart Mill, called the colonies "a vast system of outdoor relief for the upper classes," and even Disraeli in 1852 had put himself on record as believing that "these wretched colonies are millstones around our necks."

But now all this had changed. Britain had acquired her empire, as it had frequently been remarked, in a fit of absent-mindedness, but absentmindedness was replaced by single-mindedness as the pace of imperialism accelerated. Lord Rosebery epitomized the sentiment of the day when he called the British Empire "the greatest secular agency for good the world has ever known." "Yes," said Mark Twain, watching a Jubilee procession for Queen Victoria which proudly displayed the pomp of England's possessions, "the English are mentioned in Scripture—'Blessed are the meek, for they shall inherit the earth.'"

By most people, the race for empire was approvingly regarded. In England, Kipling was its poet laureate, and the popular sentiment was that of the music-hall song:

We don't want to fight, but by jingo if we do,
We've got the ships, we've got the men, we've got the
money too!

Another, rather different nod of approval came from those who agreed with Sir Charles Crossthwaite that the real question between Britain and Siam was "who was to get the trade with them, and how we could make the most of them, so as to find fresh markets for our goods and also employment for those superfluous articles of the present day, our boys."

And then, too, the process of empire building brought with it prosperity for the empire builders. No small part of the gain in working-class amenities which had so pleased the Committee on Depression was the result of sweated labor overseas: the colonies were now the proletariat's proletariat. No wonder imperialism was a popular policy.

Throughout all of this, the officialdom of economics stood to one side, watching the process of imperial growth with equanimity, and confining its remarks to the effect that new possessions might have on the course of trade. Again it was the critics of the underworld that focused attention on this new phenomenon of history. For, as they looked at the worldwide race for domination, they saw something very different from the mere exciting clash of politics or the inexplicable whims of personalities in power.

They saw a whole new direction to the drift of capitalism; in fact, they saw imperialism as signaling a change in the fundamental character of capitalism itself. Still more significant, they divined in the new restless process of expansion the most dangerous tendency that capitalism had yet revealed—a tendency that led to war.

It was a mild-mannered heretic who first made this charge, the product, as he described himself, of "the middle stratum of the middle class of a middle-sized town of the Midlands." John A. Hobson was a frail little man, much worried over his health and plagued by an impediment in his speech which made him nervous about lecturing. Born in 1858, he prepared for an academic career at Oxford; and by all we know of his background and personality (which is not much, for this shy and retiring man managed successfully to avoid *Who's Who*), he was destined for the cloistered anonymity of English public-school life.

Two factors intervened. He read the works of Ruskin, the British critic and essayist who mocked at the bourgeois Victorian canons of monetary value and who trumpeted, "Wealth is life!" From Ruskin, Hobson acquired an idea of economics as a humanist rather than an impersonal science; and he turned from the refinement of orthodox doctrine to preaching the virtues of a world where cooperative labor guilds would give a higher value to human personality than the crass world of wages and profits. His scheme, Hobson insisted, was "as certain as a proposition in Euclid."

As a Utopian he might have been respectable; the English like eccentrics. It was as a heretic, a trampler on the virtues of tradition, that he became an economic pariah. Chance threw him into the company of a person called A. F. Mummery, an independent thinker, a successful businessman, and an intrepid mountain climber (he was to meet his death in 1895 on the heights of Nanga Parbat). "My intercourse with him, I need hardly say," writes Hobson, "did not lie on this physical plane. But he was a mental climber as well. . . ." Mummery had speculated as to the cause of those periodic slumps in trade which had worried the business community as far back as the early eighteenth century, and he had an idea as to their origin, which was, as Hobson put it, considered by the professordom "as equivalent in rationality to an attempt to prove the flatness of the earth." For Mummery, hearkening back to Malthus, thought that the cause of depression lay in the fact of excessive *saving*, in the chronic inability of the business system to distribute enough purchasing power to buy its own products back.

Hobson argued at first and then became convinced that Mummery was right. The two wrote *The Physiology of Industry*, setting forth their heretical notion that savings might undermine prosperity. This was too much for the official world to swallow. Had not all the great economists, from Adam Smith onward, stressed the fact that saving was only one side of the golden coin of accumulation? Did not every act of saving automatically add to the fund of capital which was used to put more people to work? To say that saving might result in unemployment was not only nonsense of the most arrant kind, but it was positively inimical to one of the legs of social stability—thrift. The economic world was shocked: the London University Extension Lectures found that they could manage to dispense with Mr. Hobson's presence; the Charity Organization Society withdrew an invitation to speak. The scholar had become a heretic and the heretic now became, perforce, an outcast.

All this seems considerably removed from the problem of imperialism. But ideas germinate in devious ways. Hobson's exclusion from the world of respectability led him into the path of social criticism, and the social critic now turned his attention to the great political problem of the day: Africa.

The background of the African problem was complex and emotional. Dutch settlers had set up their independent states in the Transvaal country in 1836, solid communities of "Kaffir-flogging, Bible-reading" farmers. But the land they chose, wide and sunny and exhilarating as it was, hid more wealth than it displayed. In 1869 diamonds were discovered; in 1885 gold. Within a few years the pace of an oxcart settlement was transformed into the frenzied excitement of a community of speculators. Cecil Rhodes appeared on the scene with his projects of railroads and industry; in a moment of madness he sanctioned a raid into the Transvaal and the long-strained tempers of both English and Dutch burst their bonds. The Boer War began.

Hobson had already gone to Africa. This "timidest of God's creatures," as he called himself, traveled to Capetown and Johannesburg, talked with Kruger and Smuts, and finally dined with Rhodes himself on the eve of the Transvaal raid. Rhodes was a complicated and perplexing personality. Two years before his African adventure, a journalist had quoted him as saying:

"I was in the East End of London yesterday and attended a meeting of the unemployed. I listened to the wild speeches, which were just a cry for 'bread,' 'bread,' 'bread,' and on my way home I pondered over the scene. . . . My cherished idea is a solution for the social problems; i.e., in order to save the 40,000,000 inhabitants of the United Kingdom from a bloody civil war, we colonial statesmen must acquire new lands to settle the surplus population, to provide new markets for the goods produced by them in the factories and mines. The Empire, as I have always said, is a bread and butter question."

We do not know whether he expounded the same sentiments to Hobson; the probability is that he did. But it would have made little difference. For what Hobson saw in Africa dovetailed in the most unexpected way with the economic heresy of which he and Mummery had been convicted: the theory of oversaving.

He returned to Britain to write about jingoism and the war in Africa, and then in 1902 he presented the world with a book in which his African observations were strangely melded with his heretical views.

The book was called *Imperialism;* it was a devastating volume. For here was the most important and searing criticism that had ever been levied against the profit system. The worst that Marx had claimed was that the system would destroy itself; what Hobson suggested was that it might destroy the world. He saw the process of imperialism as a relentless and restless tendency of capitalism to rescue itself from a self-imposed dilemma, a tendency that necessarily involved foreign commercial conquest and that thereby inescapably involved a constant risk of war. No more profound moral indictment of capitalism had ever been posed.

What was the substance of Hobson's charge?

It was an argument almost Marxian in its impersonality and inexorable development (although Hobson had no sympathy for the Marxists and their aims). It claimed that capitalism faced an insoluble internal difficulty and that it was forced to turn to imperialism, not out of a pure lust for conquest, but to ensure its own economic survival.

That internal capitalist difficulty was an aspect of the system which had received surprisingly little attention in the past—capitalism's unequal distribution of wealth. The fact that the workings of the profit system very often resulted in a lopsided distribution of wealth had long been a topic for moral concern, but its *economic* consequences were left for Hobson to point out.

The consequence he saw was most surprising. The inequality of incomes led to the strangest of dilemmas—a paradoxical situation in which neither rich nor poor could consume enough goods. The poor could not consume enough because their incomes were too small, and the rich could not consume enough because their incomes were too big! In other words, said Hobson, in order to clear its own market, an economy must consume everything that it makes: each good must have a buyer. Now, if the poor cannot afford to take more than the bare essentials, who is there to take the rest? Obviously, the rich. But while the rich have the money, they lack the physical capacity for *that* much consumption: a man with a million-dollar income would have to consume goods worth a thousand times those bought by a man with only a thousand dollars to spend.

And so, as a consequence of an inequitable division of wealth, the rich were *forced* to save. They saved not only because most of them wished to, anyway, but because they could not very well help themselves—their incomes were simply too large to be consumed.

It was this saving that led to trouble. The automatic savings of the rich strata of society had to be put to use, if the economy was not to suffer from the disastrous effects of an insufficiency of purchasing power. But the question was *how* to put the savings to work. The classical answer was to invest them in ever more factories and more production and thus to ascend to an even higher level of output and productivity: Smith, Ricardo, Mill, all the great economists agreed on this solution to the problem. But Hobson saw a difficulty in the way. For if the mass of the people were *already* having trouble buying all the goods thrown on the market because their incomes were too small, how, he asked, could a sensible capitalist invest in equipment that would throw still more goods on an overcrowded market? What would be gained from investing savings in another shoe factory, let us say, when the market was already swamped with more shoes than could be readily absorbed? What was to be done?

Hobson's answer was devilishly neat. The automatic savings of the rich could be invested in one way that would put them to use without the troublesome accompaniment of more production at home. They could be invested overseas.

And this is the genesis of imperialism. It is, wrote Hobson, "the endeavor of the great controllers of industry to broaden the channel for the flow of their surplus wealth by seeking foreign markets and foreign investments to take off the goods and capital they cannot use at home."

The result is disastrous. For it is not one nation only which is sending its surplus wealth abroad. All nations are in the same boat. Hence there ensues a race to partition the world, with each nation trying to fence off for its investors the richest and most lucrative markets it can seize. Thus Africa becomes a huge market (and a source of cheap raw materials) to be split among the capitalists of England and Germany and Italy and Belgium; Asia becomes a rich pie to be carved up among the Japanese and the Russians and the Dutch. India becomes a dumping ground for British industry, and China becomes an India for Japan.

Imperialism thus paves the way to war—not by swashbuckling adventures or high tragedy, but through a sordid process in which capitalist nations compete for outlets for their unemployed wealth. A less-inspiring cause for bloodshed could hardly be imagined.

Needless to say, such a theory of violence and struggle found little encouragement in the official world of economists. Hobson, it was said, kept "muddling economics up with other things" and since those "other things" were hardly suggestive of a world organized around the pursuit of pleasure, the official world regarded the theory of imperialism as a display of the sort of bad manners one would expect of a man whose economics outraged such common-sense doctrines as the social beneficence of thrift.

But while the doctrine was scrupulously avoided by those who might have subjected it to an intelligent, if critical, scrutiny, it was embraced wholeheartedly by another section of the underworld: the Marxists. The idea, after all, was not entirely original with Hobson; variants of it had been worked out by a German economist named Rodbertus, and by Rosa Luxemburg, a fiery German revolutionist. But Hobson's treatment was broader and deeper, and it was embroidered into the official cloak of Marxist doctrine by none other than their leading theoretician—an exile named Vladimir Ilich Ulyanov, better known as Lenin.

The theory emerged from its baptism somewhat changed. Hobson had puzzled over the question of why capitalist nations so avidly sought colonies after decades of more or less indifference to them. His theory of imperialism was not a dogma, and still less an ironclad prediction of absolutely inescapable war. Indeed, he expressed the hope that rival imperialisms might arrange a kind of final settlement of the world and exist peaceably side by side on a live-and-let-live basis.

But in Marxist garb, the theory took on tones both more menacing and more inexorable. Not only was imperialism placed as the capstone of the Marxist economic arch, but it was broadened and widened beyond Hobson's framework until it accounted for the whole social complexion of latter-day capitalism. And what a frightening picture emerged!

> Imperialism, the highest phase of capitalist development, immensely increases the productive forces of the world economy, shapes the entire world in its own image, and drags all colonies, all races, all peoples into the sphere of finance capitalist exploitation. At the same time the monopolist form of capital increasingly develops elements of parasitic degeneration and decay. . . . Imperialism piles up untold wealth from the immense superprofits it squeezes out of the millions of colonial workers and peasants. In this process, imperialism creates the type of the decaying, parasitically degenerating rentier state and entire strata of parasites who live by coupon clipping. The epoch of imperialism, which completes the process of creating the material prerequisites of socialism (concentration of the means of production, socialization of labour on a gigantic scale, the strengthening of workers' organizations) at the same time makes the contradictions between the "Great Powers" sharper, and provokes wars which result in the breakdown of the

single world economy. Thus imperialism is decaying, dying capitalism. It is the last state of capitalist development as a whole; it is the onset of the socialist world revolution.

The writer is Bukharin; the occasion, the Third International; the date, 1928. Writer, occasion, and date notwithstanding, the voice we hear is that of Lenin. And more disturbing yet, Lenin's conception of a ravaging and ravaged capitalism, internally corrupt and externally predatory, was the formal Soviet explanation of the world in which we live until the demise of the Soviet Union.

Of the fact of imperialism there is no doubt. No one who is familiar with the history of the late nineteenth and early twentieth centuries can fail to mark the line of plunder, territorial aggrandizement, and oppressive colonialism that runs like a telltale thread through the endless incidents of international jealousy, friction, and war. If it is no longer fashionable to regard the First World War as "purely" an imperialist conflict, there is no doubt that imperialist jockeying for position did much to bring it into being.

But conquest and colonies are as old as ancient Egypt, and as the Soviet invasions of Hungary, Czechoslovakia, and Afghanistan have made clear in modern times, they will continue whether capitalism is there to furnish an excuse or not. The question that the *economic* theory of imperialism makes us face is whether the conquests of the last fifty years have been differently motivated from the conquests that came before or may follow after. It is a simple matter to understand the thirst for power of the dynastic state. Imperialism asks us to consider whether the more impersonal forces of the market economy can lead to the same end result.

The apologists for the colonial system claimed that it could not. In 1868, Bismarck himself wrote: "All the advantages claimed for the mother country are for the most part illusions. England is abandoning its colonial policy; she finds it too costly." And other defenders of the system echoed his remarks: they pointed out that colonies "didn't pay"; that colonization was not undertaken gladly, but that it was forced on the great powers by virtue of their civilizing mission in the world; that colonies gained more than the mother country, and so on.

But they simply missed the point. True, some colonies did not pay—in 1865 a Committee of Commons actually recommended the abandonment of all British holdings save on the west coast of Africa on the ground that they were highly unprofitable ventures. But while *all* colonies did not yield a profit, *some* colonies were fabulously rewarding: the tea gardens in Ceylon, for example, would return 50 percent dividends on invested capital in a banner year. And while *all* industry did not benefit from overseas markets, *some* important industries could hardly have existed without them: the classic case in point is the dependence of the British cotton industry on the Indian market. And for England as a whole, foreign investment certainly provided a profitable outlet for savings: between 1870 and 1914, *one-half* of English savings were invested abroad, and the flow of dividends and interest from foreign investments provided 10 percent of the British national income.

To be sure, there were other motives generously mixed in with the purely economic, and the economic compensatory effect of imperialism was not quite so simple as J. A. Hobson had described it. But by and large, one could hardly find an explanation for the thrust of European power into Africa and Asia that did not contain some flavor of economic advantage. In the case of Holland, for example, the huge plantations of Java and Sumatra offered a field for profitable investment of great importance for Dutch capital; in the case of Malaya, invaluable and cheap raw materials provided John Bull with a lucrative international monopoly; in the case of the Middle East, there were oil and the strategic control over shipping through the Suez Canal. "What our industries lack . . . what they lack more and more, is markets," said a French minister in 1885; and in 1926 Dr. Schacht, then president of the German Reichsbank, declared: "The fight for raw materials plays the most important role in world politics, an even greater role than before the war. Germany's only solution is her acquisition of colonies." From country to country the motives might differ, but the common denominator of economic gain was to be found in all.

Does this mean that imperialism is indeed an inseparable part of capitalism? The answer is not a simple one. Certainly capitalism has been an expansive system from its earliest days, a system whose driving force has been the effort to accumulate ever larger amounts of capital itself. Therefore from early on, we find that capitalist firms have looked to foreign lands, both for markets and for cheap raw materials; and equally important, the governments of capitalist nations have usually supported and protected their private enterprisers in these overseas ventures.

This much of the imperialist scenario seems beyond question. But we have come to look on this process of capitalist expansion in a somewhat different fashion from that of Hobson or Lenin. The driving force does not seem to be lodged in a pileup of undigested savings at home that require investment abroad. Rather, the underlying propulsive mechanism appears to be the extraordinary capacity of the capitalist mode of economic organization to displace other modes, and to establish itself in noncapitalist settings. There is something about the technological orientation, the efficiency, the sheer dynamism of capitalist ways of production that makes the expansion of the system "irresistible."

Thus we tend today to see the process of imperialism as part of *the internationalization of capital*, a process that began even before capitalism was fully formed and that has not yet run its course. But here an important distinction must be made between the internationalizations of different eras. Imperialism of the kind that helped bring on World War I was not just the transplantation of capitalist modes of production into Africa and Asia and Latin America. It was this plus undisguised political interference, terrific exploitation, military force, and a general disregard for the interests of the poorer nations. What is so striking about late nineteenth- or early twentieth-century British investment in India, for example, is that it was largely based on and ruled by England's needs, not India's requirements. In the case of the Belgian Congo or the Netherlands Indies, "largely" can be read "entirely."

Some part of this old-fashioned imperialism remains, although its outward manifestations have changed. The Second World War brought a general end to the relationship of colonialism within which the older economic hegemony exerted its sway. Where there were only supine colonies before the war, there emerged independent nations after it; and although many of these nations were (and still are) impoverished and weak, their national status has made it impossible for the European nations to exercise the same cavalier domination that was commonplace in the first half of the century.

Things have been somewhat different in the case of the United States. Here military force has been applied against underdeveloped nations many times since the war—against Cuba, Vietnam, Nicaragua, and Iraq among other instances—so that the United States has inherited the unenviable title of the main imperialist power in the world. But the motives that have prompted our imperialist adventures are not those that sent the Marines into the banana republic or the gunboats into China in the nineteenth century. It is not American property that we have been protecting, but American ideology. Rather like the English during the period of the French Revolution, until the Soviet debacle our government felt itself threatened by an immense revolutionary force—the force of worldwide communism, whose most likely recruits seemed to be the frail and unstable nations of the Third World. As a result, we have reacted to nearly every socialist tendency in those nations as if it were the entering wedge of a foreign-dominated Communist regime, and have supported every reactionary government in those nations as part of the same struggle against communism.

How this defensive-minded, aggressive-oriented policy will end remains to be seen. Perhaps the United States will be able to maintain a world safe for capitalism by bringing economic or military force to bear on socialist governments that appear in the underdeveloped world. Perhaps such a

policy will end in our own frustration and demoralization.
Whatever the outcome, however, this aspect of imperialism
bears more relation to the problem of protecting a great
kingdom from the influence of outsiders—a problem as old
as ancient China or Rome—than to the direct support for
business enterprises that was the frank motive for the imperial thrust of the last century. It is a direct political, rather than
an indirect economic, form of foreign domination.

Meanwhile, there is a second aspect to the changing face
of imperialism that is unmistakably economic. It is the spectacular emergence of the multinational corporation as the
principal agency by which capital moves from its home country overseas.

The multinationals are giant corporations, such as Coca-
Cola, IBM, Microsoft, and Royal Dutch Shell, whose manufacturing or processing operations are located in many
nations. A multinational will drill for oil in the Middle East or
Africa, refine it in Europe or America, and sell it in Japan; or
it may extract ore in Australia, process it in Japan, and ship
the finished beams to the United States.

Multinationals have brought two changes to the overall
internationalization of capital. First, they have changed its
geographic flows. In the days of classic imperialism, as we
have seen, the objective of capitalist expansion was focused
mainly on gaining access to raw materials or to markets for
basic commodities, like textiles. The multinationals have
turned away from these basic commodities toward the sorts
of high-technology goods in which they are world leaders,
such as computers and pharmaceuticals. The result has been
a striking shift in the overseas allocation of capital. In 1897 almost half of American overseas capital was invested in plantations, railways, or mining properties. Today only a small
fraction of our foreign investment is in those fields. Instead,
the bulk of our overseas capital has moved into manufacturing, and three-quarters of the flow of international investment goes to Europe and Canada and other developed
capitalist lands. So, too, the great preponderance of French or
Japanese or German international investment seeks out lo-

cations in the developed world (including the United States), rather than in the old colonial parts of the globe.

A second economic consequence of the rise of the multinationals has been their remarkable ability to combine high technology with cheap and untrained labor. The incredibly complicated mechanisms that underlie modern economic life, such as computer parts or television subassemblies, can be produced in the Hong Kongs and South Koreas and Thailands of the world, using scientific machines operated by men and women just off the paddy fields. From the point of view of imperialism, the upshot of this is a perplexing one. The ability to transplant whole production processes into areas of the world that only yesterday were peasant economies has succeeded to an unprecedented degree in exporting the social institutions of capitalism. Just as the factors of production themselves emerged from a precapitalist social setting during the great economic revolution we witnessed in our opening chapters, so in our times a new economic revolution is bringing the market economy into regions that were formerly only passive, not active forces in the world economy. To that extent, modern imperialism has been a great force for the vitalization of capitalism abroad.

At the same time, the new imperialism has greatly intensified the competitiveness of the system in its developed homelands. This is not only the result of the interpenetration of each other's markets that we discussed above, but because the manufacturing outposts of the multinationals in the underdeveloped regions can fire artillery barrages of low-cost commodities back into their motherlands. As no nation knows better than the United States, TV sets made in Hong Kong or Taiwan, or automobiles made in South Korea or assembled in Mexico, can easily undersell the same products manufactured in California or the Midwest.

It is too soon to foretell the consequences of this internationalization and intensification of competition or what may be the outcome of the financial and political crises that have appeared—not surprisingly—in nearly all the Asian "tigers." What seems beyond doubt is that we have moved in the direction of a global economy in which new world-straddling enterprises coexist uneasily with older national boundaries and prerogatives. It is an ironic ending to our consideration of the problem of imperialism that the movement whose origins were connected with alleviating the pressures on capital has ended up by making them worse.

John Hobson died in 1940; in the London *Times* a properly circumspect obituary duly noted both his prescient ideas and his lack of general recognition.

For unrecognized he was. The most renowned economist of the Victorian world was an economist utterly unlike Hobson: Alfred Marshall—as considered, middle-of-the-road, and "official" as Hobson had been intuitive, extreme, and, so to speak, unauthorized. Yet it is fitting that we conclude this journey through the shadowy regions of the underworld by returning again to Victorian daylight. The economists who worked in that daylight might not have seen the disturbing sights revealed to more adventurous souls, but they did one thing that the heretics did not: they taught their world—and even our world—its "economics."

Merely to look at Alfred Marshall's portrait is already to see the stereotype of the teacher: white mustache, white wispy hair, kind bright eyes—an eminently professorial countenance. At the time of his death in 1924, when the greatest economists in England paid homage to his memory, one of them, Professor C. R. Fay, produced this indelible portrait of the Victorian professor *chez lui:*

> Pigou told me I ought to go and see him about a subject for a Fellowship Dissertation. So one afternoon towards twilight I went to Balliol Croft. "Come in, come in," he said, running in from a little passage; and I went with him upstairs. "Have you any idea what to do?" he asked me. I said "no." "Well, then, listen," he said, producing a small black book. He proceeded to read out a list of subjects having previously ordered me to hold up my hand when he came to one I liked. In my nervousness I tried to close with the first subject, but Marshall took no notice and read on. About halfway through the second

page he arrived at "The Recent German Financial Crisis." Having been to Greifswald for a summer I signaled acquiescence. "It wouldn't suit you at all," he said. I kept quiet for another five minutes, and, catching the word "Argentine" made another noise which stopped him. My only reason was that two of my uncles had been in business there. "Have you been there yourself?" he asked. "No," I replied, and he went on. A few moments later he stopped and said, "Have you found a subject you like?" "I don't know," I began. "No one ever does," he said, "but that's my method. Now, what would you like to do?" I gasped out "a comparison of German and English labour." Upon which (for it was now quite dark), he produced a little lantern with an electric button and began prowling around the shelves, handing out books in English and German—von Nostitz, Kuhlman, about 30 in all. "Now," he said, "I'll leave you to smell; when you've finished, blow down the tube and Sarah will bring you some tea."

It was all very remote from the African strife that had disturbed Hobson or the boisterous American speculation that had formed the cradle of environment for Henry George's ideas. Marshall, like his contemporary Edgeworth, was preeminently the product of a university. Although he voyaged to America and even across America to San Francisco, his life, his point of view—and inevitably his economics—smacked of the quietude and refinement of the Cambridge setting.

But exactly what did he teach? The word to sum up Marshall's basic concern is the term we have already identified as the new Victorian vision of the economy—the term "equilibrium." In contrast with Bastiat, who was drawn to the irrationalities of economic sophistry, or with Henry George, who saw the injustices of life cloaked with economic sanction, or with Hobson, who looked for hidden destructive tendencies in the impersonal processes of capitalist economics, Marshall was primarily interested in the self-adjusting, self-correcting nature of the economic world. As his most brilliant pupil,

J. M. Keynes, would later write, he created "a whole Copernican system, in which all the elements of the economic universe are kept in their places by mutual counterpoise and interaction."

Much of this, of course, had been taught before. Adam Smith, Ricardo, Mill, had all expounded the market system as a feedback mechanism of great complexity and efficiency. Yet between the overall vision and the fine working-out of details, there was much unexplored territory and foggy exposition: the theory of market equilibrium which Marshall inherited was a good deal more imposing at a distance than up close. There were sticky bits even about such basic matters as whether prices were really a reflection of the cost of production of a good, or of the final degree of satisfaction yielded by that good—were diamonds high-priced, in other words, because they were hard to find or because people enjoyed wearing them? Perhaps such questions would not make any but an economist's heart beat faster, and yet as long as they remained obscure it was hard to think clearly about many problems that economics sought to attack.

It was to these fuzzy questions of economic theory that Marshall applied himself. In his famous *Principles of Economics* he combined a mind of mathematical precision with a style that was leisurely, discursive, shot through with homely example, and wonderfully lucid. Even a businessman could understand *this* sort of economics, for all the hard logical proofs were thoughtfully relegated to the footnotes (with the result that Keynes irreverently said that any economist would do better to read the footnotes and forget the text than vice versa). At any rate, the book was a tremendous success; originally published in 1890, it is still prescribed fare for the student who aspires to be an economist.

And what was the great contribution of Marshall to the conceptual tangles of economics? The main contribution— the one to which Marshall himself returned time and again— was the insistence on the importance of *time* as the quintessential element in the working-out of the equilibrium process.

For equilibrium, as Marshall pointed out, changed its

basic meaning according to whether the adjustment process of the economy took place in a short-run or a long-run period. In the short run, buyers and sellers met to higgle on the marketplace, but basically the bargaining process revolved about a fixed quantity of goods—the diamonds that the diamond merchants brought along with them in their suitcases. Over the longer run, however, the quantity of diamonds was not fixed. New mines could be opened if the demand warranted it; old mines could be abandoned if supply was superabundant. Hence in the very short run it was the psychic utility of diamonds—that is, the demand for them—which exercised the more immediate influence on their market price; but over the long run, as the recurring flow of supply was adjusted to consumers' wants, cost of production again asserted its upper hand. Neither cost nor utility, of course, could ever be quite divorced from the determination of price; demand and supply, in Marshall's own words, were like "the blades of a pair of scissors," and it was as fruitless to ask whether supply or demand alone regulated price as to ask whether the upper or lower blade of the scissors did all the cutting. But while both blades cut, one of them, so to speak, was the active and one the passive edge—the utility-demand edge active when the cut took place in the quick time span of the given market; the cost-supply edge active when the cutting extended over the longer period in which scales of output and patterns of production were subject to change.

It was, like everything Marshall touched with his analytic mind, an illuminating insight. And yet more than theoretical brilliance radiated from the *Principles*. If Marshall was the finest intelligence of the "official" world of economics, he was also its most compassionate intelligence. A genuine concern for the laboring poor, for the "cringing wretches" he noted on his trips to the London slums, for economics as a tool for social betterment—all this was inextricably woven into his book. So, too, it should be noted, was an appraisal of the future that cautioned against succumbing to the "beautiful pictures of life, as it might be under institutions which [the imagination] constructs easily," coupled with hopes that the attitudes of the rich were capable of turning toward "chivalry," to "help the tax-gatherer . . . remove the worst evils of poverty from the land."

We smile at these Victorian sentiments, but they do not constitute the aspect of Marshall's vision that made its greatest imprint on economics itself. For that we turn to the front of the Principles, where two declarations meet the eye. The first is a typically charming Marshallian passage describing an individual weighing the pleasures to be received from a purchase against the loss of pleasure that the expenditure will entail:

> A rich man, in doubt whether to spend a shilling on a single cigar, is weighing against one another smaller pleasures than a poor man, who is doubting whether to spend a shilling on a supply of tobacco that will last him for a month. The clerk with £100 a year will walk to work in a much heavier rain than the clerk with £300 a year.

The second statement comes a few pages later, where Marshall is discussing the purpose of economics. It is, he says,

> a study of the economic means and aspects of man's political, social and private life; but more especially of his social life. . . . It shuns many political issues, which the practical man cannot ignore . . . and it is therefore . . . better described by the broad term "Economics" than by the narrower term "Political Economy."

Two things are noteworthy in these seemingly innocuous passages. The first, brilliantly realized in the clerk deciding whether or not to spend the money to take a cab, is nothing less than a new figure who will epitomize the Marshallian vision of the economy as aptly as, if much less dramatically than, the great monarch of the Hobbesian era. The new figure is The Individual, whose calculations not only symbolize the workings of the market system, but are in fact the rock on which the economy itself ultimately rests. Gone is the vision of economics as the study of the social dynamics of Monarchy or of a Smithian Society, not to mention Marxian class warfare. In its place we have economics as explication of the collective life of the individual, which is to say, of everyone for him- or herself.

Intimately tied to this is another change, implicit in the second quotation. It is the disappearance of a theme that was unabashedly a central part of earlier visions—namely, the political content of economics. Marshall sees the purpose of economics as explaining such questions as how equilibrium prices are arrived at, not the underlying question of how the relations of power and obedience that give structure to all stratified societies arise in a social order perceived as just a collection of individuals each seeking his or her "utility."

Why this curious turning away from *political* economy? Two possibilities spring to mind. The first is that the events of 1848, and perhaps the increasing flow of socialistic ideas, made an explicit recognition, much less examination, of power and obedience much more contentious than it would have been in Smith's or Mill's times, when such social relations were taken for granted. A second, quite contrary, possibility is that the gradual acceptance of democratic ideas during the nineteenth century gave the Marshallian vision a plausibility it would not have enjoyed in earlier times.

That is a question we can raise, but not resolve. All we can say with certainty is that Economics now takes the place of Political Economy; and a new chapter of economics begins. All this will become increasingly important as our study moves toward the present. But there is one last matter that deserves a word. It concerns the very element of Marshall's analysis that was his most important gift to economic analysis—the element of time. For time, to Marshall, was abstract time; it was the time in which mathematical curves exfoliate and theoretical experiments may be run and rerun, but it was not the time in which anything ever really *happens*. That is, it was not the irreversible flow of historic time—and, above all, not *the* historic time in which Marshall himself lived. Think for a moment of what he lived to see: a violent anticapitalist revolution in Russia, a world-encompassing war, the first rumblings of anticolonialism. Think of what lay just ahead: the decline of capitalism in much of Europe, a worldwide change in the conception of government, a world-shaking depression in the United States. Yet, of the relevance of economics to all these overwhelming changes, neither Alfred Marshall nor still less his official colleagues had much, if any, understanding. *Natura non facit saltum*—nature makes no sudden leaps—was the motto of the *Principles* in its last edition in 1920, as it had been in its first, in 1890. The fact that history might make sudden leaps, that the world of economics might be inseparably tied to the world of history, that the long and short run of the textbook implied a totally different conception of "time" from that of the relentless ticking of the social clock—all this was far removed from the notions of equilibrium which Marshall made the center of his economic inquiry. For nothing that he said could he be reproached, for he was a man of gentle faith and deeply felt convictions. The trouble was that nothing he said went far enough.

And even this might be condoned in hindsight were it not for one thing. All the while that Marshall and his colleagues were refining their delicate mechanism of equilibrium, a few unorthodox dissenters were insisting that it was not equilibrium but change—violent change—that characterized the real world and properly formed the subject for economic inquiry. War and revolution and depression and social tension were to their minds the basic problems for economic scrutiny—not equilibrium and the nice processes of adjustment of a stable textbook society. But when the heretics and the amateurs pointed this out to Victorian academic officialdom, their interruptions were resented, their warnings shrugged aside, their prescriptions scorned.

The complacency of the official world was not merely a rueful commentary on the times; it was an intellectual tragedy of the first order. For had the academicians paid attention to the underworld, had Alfred Marshall possessed the disturbing vision of a Hobson or Edgeworth, the sense of social wrong of a Henry George, the great catastrophe of the twentieth century might not have burst upon a world utterly unprepared for radical social change. It teaches us, in retro-spect, that ideas, however heretical, cannot safely be ig-nored—least of all by those whose interests are, in the best sense of that misused word, conservative.

viii

The Savage Society
of Thorstein Veblen

One hundred and twenty-five years had now passed since *The Wealth of Nations* appeared in 1776, and in that span of time it seemed as if the great economists had left no aspect of the world unexamined: its magnificence or its squalor, its naïveté or its sometimes sinister overtones, its grandiose achievements in technology or its often mean shortcomings in human values. But this many-sided world, with its dozens of differing interpretations, had nonetheless one common factor. It was European. For all its changing social complexion, this was still the Old World, and as such it insisted on a modicum of punctilio.

Thus it was not without significance that when Dick Arkwright, the barber's apprentice, made his fortune in the spinning jenny he metamorphosed into Sir Richard; the threat to England's traditional reign of gentlemanliness was nicely solved by inducting such parvenus wholesale into the fraternity of gentle blood and manners. The parvenus, it is true, brought with them a train of middle-class attitudes and even a strain of antiaristocratic sentiment, but they brought with them, as well, the sneaking knowledge that there was a higher social stratum than that attainable by wealth alone. As countless comedies of manners testified, there was a difference between the beer baron, with all his millions and his purchased crest, and the impoverished but hereditary baron next door. The successful European money-maker might be rich as Croesus, but the savor of his riches was a trifle dulled by the recognition that this was only one—and by no means the final—step up the social ladder.

All this was vastly different in America. Not only had this country been founded by men who were deeply opposed to gradations of name and birth, but the spirit of individual independence and individual achievement had sunk deep into the national folklore. In America a man was as good as he proved himself, and his success needed no validation from a genealogist. Hence, while there was not too much to differentiate the dark and sweated mills of New England from the gloomy mills of old England, when one looked into the manners and behavior of their masters, the resemblance lessened. For while the European capitalist was still caught in the shadow of a feudal past, the American money-maker basked in the sun—there were no inhibitions on his drive to power or in the exhuberant enjoyment of his wealth. In the bubbling last half of the nineteenth century, money was the stepping-stone to social recognition in the United States, and having acquired a passport of suitable wealth, the American millionaire needed no further visa for his entree into the upper classes.

And so the game of moneymaking in the New World was a rougher and less gentlemanly affair than the competitive struggle abroad. The stakes were higher and the chances for success were greater. The sportsmanship, accordingly, was somewhat less.

In the 1860s, for example, Cornelius Vanderbilt, a fabulous genius of shipping and commerce, found that his own business associates were threatening his interests—a not too uncommon occurrence. He wrote them a letter:

Gentlemen:
You have undertaken to ruin me. I will not sue you, for law takes too long. I will ruin you.

Sincerely,

CORNELIUS VAN DERBILT

And he did. "What do I care about the law? Hain't I got the power?" asked the Commodore. Later J. Pierpont Morgan was to voice much the same sentiment, if in a slightly more polished form. When his associate, Judge Gary, on a rare occasion ventured a legal caveat, Morgan exploded: "Well, I don't know as I want a lawyer to tell me what I cannot do. I hire him to tell me how to do what I want to do."

It was not only in their neglect of the fine processes of the law that the Americans outdid their European contemporaries; when they fought, they abandoned the gentleman's rapier for the roughneck's brass knuckles. An instance in point is the struggle for the control of the Albany-Susquehanna Railroad, a vital link in a system torn between Jim Fisk and the patrician Morgan. Morgan held one end of the line in his own hands, and the other terminal was a Fisk stronghold. The controversy was resolved by each side mounting a locomotive on its end of the track and running the two engines, like gigantic toys, into one another. And even then the losers did not give up, but retired as best they could, ripping up tracks and tearing down trestles as they went.

In this *mêlée* for industrial supremacy no quarter was asked and none given. Even dynamite had its uses, being employed to eliminate one particularly sticky competitor of the Standard Oil group, while less violent means, such as kidnapping, were remarkable more for their ingenuity than for their immorality. In 1881, when a great blizzard blew down the telegraph lines in New York, Jay Gould, the ruthless master of the money markets, was forced to send his orders to his broker by messenger. His enemies saw their chance and acted on it: they kidnapped the boy, substituted another of the same general physiognomy, and for several weeks Gould was dismayed to find that his moves were all somehow known to his adversaries in advance.

Needless to say, the pirates who thus forced one another to walk the plank could scarcely be expected to treat the public with reverence. Gulling and milking the investor were taken as a matter of course, and the stock market was regarded as a kind of private casino for the rich in which the public laid the bets and the financial titans fixed the croupier's wheel. As to what would happen to the general run of bets under such an arrangement—well, that was the public's lookout, an attitude that might have been more commendable had not these same titans done everything in their power to entice the public to enter their preserves.

The public, be it noted, responded with a will; when the news "got around" that Gould or Rockefeller was buying rails or coppers or steels, the public rushed to get in for a free ride. The fact that it took a fleecing for every killing never affected its unbounded faith, and on the strength of this faith a virtual legerdemain of finance was made possible. A head-spinning example was the purchase of the Anaconda Copper Company by Henry Rogers and William Rockefeller without the expenditure of a single dollar of their own. This is how they did it:

1. Rogers and Rockefeller gave a check for $39 million to Marcus Daly for the Anaconda properties, on the condition that he would deposit it in the National City Bank and leave it untouched for a specified period.

2. They then set up a paper organization known as the Amalgamated Copper Company, with their own clerks as dummy directors, and caused Amalgamated to buy Anaconda—not for cash, but for $75 million in Amalgamated stock which was conveniently printed for the purpose.

3. From the National City Bank, Rogers and Rockefeller now borrowed $39 million to cover the check they had given to Marcus Daly, and as collateral for this loan they used the $75 million in Amalgamated stock.

4. They now sold the Amalgamated stock on the market (first having touted it through their brokers) for $75 million.

5. With the proceeds, they retired the $39-million loan from the National City Bank, and pocketed $36 million as their own profit on the deal.

Of course this free-for-all involved staggering dishonesty. A. B. Stickney, president of the Chicago, St. Paul, and Kansas Railway, remarked that as gentlemen he would trust his brother railroad presidents anywhere, but that as rail presidents he wouldn't leave his watch out of sight with them for a moment. There was reason for his cynicism. At one meeting of railroad heads called to agree on a schedule of common freight rates that would rescue the roads from their constant suicidal game of undercutting one another, one railroad president slipped out during an intermission in the proceedings to wire the agreed schedule back to his office so that his line might be the first to undercut the rest. By chance his wire was intercepted, and when the meeting next convened it was faced with the proof positive of the impossibility of honor even among thieves.

It is an age that we are accustomed to look back upon with a blush. Certainly it was grotesque in its trappings (at some parties cigarettes were wrapped in hundred-dollar bills for the thrill of inhaling wealth), and almost medieval in its warrior spirit. But let us not misconstrue the spirit of the times. While the lords of wealth rode roughshod over the public, they trampled equally ruthlessly over each other, and their bold and unprincipled behavior was less a calculated meanness or a conscious flouting of Christian ideals than an unbridled energy that knew no barriers of conscience and nice usage. "I owe the public nothing," Morgan once said, and he meant that remark literally as a credo of his philosophy rather than as a callous *défi* of the world. Business, in this age of barony, was brutal business, and the price of morality was apt to be defeat.

And what did the economists make of all this?

Not very much. The American professionals had followed in the footsteps of their European teachers, and they forced the American world into a mold that was never made for it. The fantastic game of monetary cutthroat was described as the process of "thrift and accumulation"; the outright fraud as "enterprise"; the gilded extravagances of the age as colorless "consumption." Indeed, the world was so

scrubbed as to be unrecognizable. One might read such leading texts as John Bates Clark's *Distribution of Wealth* and
never know that America was a land of millionaires; one
might peruse F. H. Taussig's *Economics* and never come
across a rigged stock market. If one looked into Professor
Laughlin's articles in the *Atlantic Monthly* he would learn
that "sacrifice, exertion, and skill" were responsible for the
great fortunes, and he would be told that every man had a
right "to enjoy the products of his exertion to the exclusion of
everybody else"—presumably this included the right to buy
legislatures as well as diamonds.

Official economics, in a word, was apologist and unper-
ceptive; it turned its eye away from the excesses and exuber-
ance that were the very essence of the American scene and
painted instead a stereotype in formal lines and lusterless
color. While it did not lack honesty or courage or intellectual
competence, it suffered from what Malthus had once called
"the insensible bias of situation and interest." The American
economists were too much bound up in the current of these
enthusiastic times to back away from their subject and view it
coolly and clearly and at a distance.

What was needed was the eye of a stranger—someone
like de Tocqueville or Bryce who could view the scene with
the added clarity and perspective that comes of being foreign
to it. In the person of Thorstein Bunde Veblen—an American by birth but a citizen of nowhere by nature—such an eye
was found.

A very strange man, Thorstein Veblen. He was a peasant
in looks, a Norwegian farmer. A photograph shows his hair,
lank and flat, parted in the middle of a gnomelike head and
falling in an inverted V over a low and sloping forehead.
Peasant eyes, shrewd and speculative, peer out from behind
a blunt nose. An unkempt mustache hides his mouth, and a
short scraggly beard engulfs his chin. He is dressed in a thick
unpressed suit and there is a large safety pin attached to his
vest: it moors his watch. The photograph does not show two
more safety pins hooked into his pants where they suspend
his socks, and it gives us only a suggestion of a thin wiry
frame, and a high-stepping, hunter-like, noiseless gait.

The strange appearance hid a yet stranger personality. Those piercing eyes might hint at an equally piercing mental scrutiny, and that rustic exterior might prepare one for a certain blunt quality of inquiry. But there was no external sign of the keynote to Veblen's life: his alienation from society.

Alienation is often a phenomenon of the sick, and by our standards Veblen must have been neurotic indeed. For he had a quality of nearly hermetic insulation. He walked through life as if he had descended from another world, and the goings-on that appeared so natural to the eyes of his contemporaries appeared to him as piquant, exotic, and curious as the rituals of a savage community to the eye of an anthropologist. Other economists—and this includes both Adam Smith and Karl Marx—were not only in their society, but they were *of* it; sometimes full of admiration for the world about them and sometimes filled with despair and rage at what they saw. Not Thorstein Veblen. In the bustling, boosting, gregarious community in which he lived, he stood apart: uninvolved, unentangled, remote, aloof, disinterested, a stranger.

Because he was a stranger, he was a nonconformist, but not a radical. The world to Veblen was uncomfortable and forbidding; he adapted to it as a missionary might to a land of primitives, refusing to go native, but preserving his integrity at the cost of frightful solitude. Many admired, even loved him, but he had no intimate friends: there was no man he called by his first name, and no woman he could wholly love.

As might be expected, he was a mass of eccentricities. He refused to have a telephone, kept his books stacked along the wall in their original packing cases, and saw no sense in daily making up the beds; the covers were thrown back in the morning and pulled up again at night. Lazy, he allowed the dishes to accumulate until the cupboard was bare and then washed the whole messy heap by turning the hose on them. Taciturn, he would sit for hours in silence when all his visitors were eager to hear his pronouncements. A flouter of convention, he gave all his students the same grade, regardless of their work, but when one student needed a higher mark to qualify for a scholarship, Veblen gladly changed a C to an A. An enfant terrible with an ax to grind for college ad-

ministrations, he would (when the authorities so decreed)
call the roll with exaggerated care, carefully placing to one
side the cards of the students who were absent, and then
when the sheep were weeded from the goats, he would
seemingly by accident mix the two piles together again. Curiously sadistic, he was capable of such meaningless practical
jokes as borrowing a sack from a passing farmer and returning it to him with a hornet's nest inside. Rarely whimsical, he
once told a little girl who inquired what his initials T. B. stood
for that they meant Teddy Bear; she called him that but no
one else dared. Enigmatic, he refused to commit himself on
anything; typically, when someone once asked him his opinion of a certain sociologist's writing in a journal that Veblen
edited, he replied: "The average number of words on a page
is 400. Professor ———'s average 375." And perhaps strangest
of all, this sardonic and unprepossessing man had the inde-
finable quality of being attractive to women. He was always
engaged in one liaison or another, and not always of his own
doing. "What are you to do if the woman moves in on you?"
he once inquired.

A bewildering and complex personality, locked within itself and with only one avenue for expression: he wrote in ra-
zorlike English, in a style much like himself, involuted and
laden with esoteric information and terminology, a kind of
surgical style that left the world raw and exposed but perfectly bloodless, so fine-edged was his blade. He wrote of
philanthropy and called it "essays in pragmatic romance"; of
religion and characterized it as "the fabrication of vendible
imponderables in the nth dimension." He wrote of the main
ecclesiastical organizations as "chain stores" and of the individual church as a "retail outlet"—cruel but telling phrases.
He described a walking stick as "an advertisement that the
bearer's hands are employed otherwise than in useful effort,"
and he noted also that it was a weapon: "The handling of so
tangible and primitive a means of offense is very comforting
to anyone who is gifted with even a moderate share of ferocity." *Gifted* with ferocity! What a savage and yet curiously dry
phrase.

But what had this to do with economics? Nothing, in the

conventional sense of the word. Economics for Veblen had
no relation to the mannerly and precise game of the Victorians in which the ways of the world were justified by the differential calculus, and it bore little kinship with the efforts of
earlier economists to explain how things worked themselves
out. Veblen wanted to know something else: why things were
as they were in the first place. Hence his inquiry began not
with the economic play, but with the players; not with the
plot, but with the whole set of customs and mores which resulted in that particular kind of play called "the business system." In a word, he delved into the nature of economic man
and his economic rites and rituals, and in this almost anthropological approach it was as important for him to notice that
gentlemen carried walking sticks and went to church as that
landlords received something that society called rent. He was
seeking to penetrate to the true nature of the society in which
he lived, and in that search through a maze of deceptions and
conventions he would have to take hints and evidences wherever they revealed themselves: in dress, manners, speech, or
polite usage. Like the psychoanalyst he often fastened on the
smallest of trivia when he believed it to be the projecting
handle of some important but buried reality, and again like
the psychoanalyst he sought for meanings that were often
strange and even repugnant to common sense.

His examination of society, as we shall see, is merciless.
But its biting quality comes not so much from a wish to dis-
parage as from the peculiar coldness with which our fondest
notions are appraised. It is as if nothing were familiar to Veblen, nothing too commonplace to merit his attention, and
therefore nothing beyond judgment. Only a singularly detached mind, after all, would see in a walking stick both a dis-
guised advertisement of leisure and a barbaric weapon.

The detachment seems to have been with him always.
Veblen was born in 1857, a farm boy on the frontier, the
fourth son and sixth child of an immigrant Norwegian family.
His father, Thomas Veblen, was an aloof and distant person,
slow-thinking and independent; Veblen later described him
as the finest mind he ever met. His mother, Kari, was warm,

quick, and passionate; it was she who taught Thorstein the Icelandic lore and Norwegian sagas that fascinated him all his life. But from the beginning he was a queer child, lazy, addicted to reading in the attic instead of doing his chores, given to inventing nicknames that stuck, and precociously bright. A younger brother remarked: "From my earliest recollection I thought he knew everything. I could ask him any question and he would tell me all about it in detail. I have found out since that a good deal he told me was made of whole cloth, but even his lies were good."

To whatever makes an unusual personality was added an upbringing that drove a wedge between himself and the world as a place to be taken at face value. He had a pioneer childhood; simple, austere, sparse. Clothes were homemade, woolens unknown, overcoats fashioned from calfskin. Coffee and sugar were luxuries; so was such a simple garment as an undershirt. But more important, it was a foreign—a stranger's—boyhood. The Norwegians in America formed their own tight-knit and separate communities where Norwegian was the common tongue and Norway the true fatherland. Veblen had to learn English as a foreign tongue, not perfecting it until he went to college, and it is typical of that patriarchal self-enclosed community that the first inkling Veblen had that he was going to college was when he was called in from the fields to find his bags packed and placed waiting in the carriage.

He was then seventeen, and the college of his family's choice was Carleton College Academy, a small outpost of East Coast culture and enlightenment near the Minnesota township where the Veblens farmed. Thorstein had been sent with an eye to his entering the Lutheran ministry, and he found Carleton religious to the core. But there was no hope of taming this already active and iconoclastic intellect or fitting it into a pious atmosphere. At the weekly declamation, rather than a conventional discourse on the necessity of converting the heathen, Veblen threw the faculty into an uproar with "A Plea for Cannibalism" and "An Apology for a Toper." When asked if he was defending these instances of depravity, Veblen blandly replied that he was merely engaged in scientific observations. The faculty recognized his genius but was a bit afraid of him. John Bates Clark, his teacher (who was to become one of the outstanding academic economists in the country), liked him but thought him a "misfit."

This odd and gifted misfit found the unlikeliest of opportunities at Carleton. A romance sprang up between Veblen and the niece of the president of the college, Ellen Rolfe. She was an intellectual and a brilliant personality on her own account, and the two drifted together under a natural gravitation. Veblen read Spencer to Ellen, converted her to agnosticism, and persuaded himself that she was descended from the first Viking hero, Gange Rolfe.

They were married in 1888, but the relationship was to be full of ups and downs. This isolated man who had but little love to bestow seems to have needed the care of a woman, and with few exceptions (one beauty pronounced him a "chimpanzee") he found it in abundance. But the particular woman did not seem so much to matter; Veblen was hardly faithful to Ellen and she was to leave him again and again, sometimes for his indiscretions, sometimes for the cruelty with which he treated her, sometimes out of the sheer frustration of trying to read an inscrutable and walled-off mind. For many years, however, Veblen himself would seek a rapprochement, coming to her house in the woods unannounced, with a black stocking dangling from his hand and inquiring, "Does this garment belong to you, Madam?"

When Veblen left Carleton he had determined on an academic career. There began instead the long, never-ending cumulation of frustrations that would mark his professional life. He was certainly unaggressive about his interests, and yet a kind of ill luck seemed to dog his footsteps: for example, once he was to ask a former student to investigate for him a position with a civic welfare organization in New York, and the student was to comply—only to take the job for himself. But that was to be many years later. Now Veblen obtained a post at tiny Monona Academy in Wisconsin, and then, when Monona closed its doors permanently after a year, he went to Johns Hopkins, hoping for a scholarship to study philosophy.

The scholarship, despite flowery recommendations, failed to materialize. Veblen transferred to Yale, and in 1884 he graduated with a Ph.D. and a broad *a*, but with no future and no prospects.

He returned home, sick from malaria he had contracted in Baltimore and needing a special diet. But he was anything but a grateful invalid. He pestered his family by taking the horse and buggy when they were most needed, and told them they were all tubercular and that they would never be successful because they were not dishonest enough. And he lay around and loafed. "He was lucky enough," wrote a brother, "to come out of a race and family who made of family loyalty and solidarity a religion. . . . Thorstein was the only loafer in a highly respectable community. . . . He read and loafed, and the next day he loafed and read."

Certainly he read everything: political tracts, economics, sociology, Lutheran hymn books, treatises in anthropology. But his idleness aggravated his isolation from society and made it more bitter and still more ingrown. He did occasional odd jobs, puttered with fruitless inventions, commented wryly on the gaudy events of the day, botanized, talked with his father, wrote a few articles, and looked for a job. None came. He had no divinity degree and hence was unacceptable to religious colleges; he lacked the polish and air that might have commended him to others. When he married Ellen, much to the dismay of her family, it was at least partly to find a livelihood; it was hoped that he would secure a position as economist for the Atchison, Topeka, and Santa Fe Railway of which her uncle was president.

But his capricious bad luck intervened. The railway became involved in financial difficulties and was taken over by a committee of bankers, and the position disappeared. Another opened up with the University of Iowa; with his Ph.D., his letters of recommendation, his wife's connections, the appointment seemed sure. It fell through—his lack of forcefulness and his agnosticism counted heavily against him—and then another at St. Olaf's was refused at the eleventh hour. It was as if the fates were conspiring against him, forcing him to remain in his isolation.

The isolation lasted seven years, and in those seven years Veblen did virtually nothing except read. Finally a family council was held. After all, he was thirty-four now and he had never held a respectable position. It was determined that he should take up his graduate studies again and make another attempt to enter the academic world.

He chose Cornell, and in 1891 he walked into the office of J. Laurence Laughlin to announce, "I am Thorstein Veblen." Laughlin, a pillar of conservative economics, must have been taken aback; the speaker wore a coonskin cap and corduroy trousers. But something about him impressed the older man. He went to the president of the university and secured a special grant to take on Veblen as a fellow, and the next year, when the University of Chicago opened its doors and took on Laughlin as the head of its economics department, he brought Veblen along at a salary of $520 a year. It might be added that on Laughlin's death, his principal contribution to economics was adjudged to be that he had secured Veblen for Chicago.

The University of Chicago was not only Veblen's first job—at age thirty-five—but it was an institution that peculiarly mirrored the society he was to dissect. Rockefeller had founded the university, and a popular student jingle went:

John D. Rockefeller,
Wonderful man is he.
Gives all his spare change
To the U. of C.

The university was not, as might have been expected, tied to a policy of unremitting conservatism. Rather, it was the incarnation, in educational circles, of the empire building that had given it birth in the business world. Its president was William Rainey Harper, an ambitious man of only thirty-six, who was admiringly described by Walter Hines Page as a type of captain of industry. He was an entrepreneur college president, who did not hesitate to rob other colleges of their best men by dangling pay before them, and like the Standard Oil group, which was its father, the U. of C. succeeded, by sheer bulk of financial strength, in cornering a large section of the American intellectual capital. All this was later to be caustically described by Veblen's pen, but at the same time it provided him with an adequate milieu of intellectuals. There was Albert Michelson, who was to determine the speed of light with hitherto unknown precision; Jacques Loeb, the physiologist; Lloyd Morgan in sociology; there was a huge library, and a new journal of economics to edit.

Veblen began to be noticed. His immense learning earned him a reputation. "There goes Dr. Veblen who speaks twenty-six languages," said a student. James Hayden Tufts, a noted scholar, came upon him in an examination room and tells, "When I entered the room, the examination had begun and someone I did not know was asking questions. I thought his speech the slowest I had ever heard—it was difficult for me to keep the beginning of the question in mind until the end was reached. But after a while I began to see that here was a subtle mind penetrating to fundamental issues without disclosing its own views except the one determination to get to the bottom of things."

But his isolated personality was impenetrable. No one knew what he thought about anything. People would ask his wife if he was really a Socialist; she had to tell them she herself did not know. He was never without his armor; a polite, controlled objectivity that stripped the world of its emotional content and kept those who would most have liked to pierce his personal shield at arm's length. "Tell me, Professor Veblen," a student once asked him, "do you take anything seriously?" "Yes," he replied in a conspirational whisper, "but don't tell anyone."

In class—this borrows from his later life, but it serves to illumine the man—he would come in gaunt and haggard from a long night over his books and, dropping a bulky German volume on the desk, would begin to turn the pages with nervous fingers yellowed from his sole vanity—a penchant for expensive cigarettes. The Reverend Howard Woolston, a one-time student, has described it thus: "In a low creaking tone, he began a recital of village economy among the early Germans. Presently he came upon some unjust legal fiction imposed by rising nobles and sanctioned by the clergy. A sardonic smile twisted his lips; blue devils leaped to his eyes. With mordant sarcasm, he dissected the torturous assumption that the wish of the aristocrats is the will of God. He showed similar implications in modern institutions. He chuckled quietly. Then returning to history, he continued the exposition."

But not everyone appreciated his teaching methods. His frank feeling about students was the fewer the better, and he made no attempt to liven the discussion; indeed, he delighted in driving his students away. He once asked a religious student the value of her church to her in kegs of beer, and to another who sedulously copied his words and who wanted a sentence repeated, he said he thought it not worth repeating. He mumbled, he rambled, he digressed. His classes dwindled; one ended up with but one student, and later at another university a door card that originally read: "Thorstein Veblen, 10 to 11, Mondays, Wednesdays, and Fridays" was changed by slow degrees to read: "Mondays: 10 to 10:05."

But for the few who listened carefully to that bored droning voice, the idiosyncrasies were worth the reward. One student brought along a guest who later said, "Why, it was creepy. It might have been a dead man's voice slowly speaking on, and if the light had gone out behind those dropped eyelids, would it have made any difference? But," the student added, "we who listened day after day found the unusual manner nicely fitted to convey the detached and slightly sardonic intellect that was moving over the face of things. His detached, free-ranging intellect attracted, and yet it seemed a mutilated personality. The scholarliness of his mind was amazing and delightful. He held in memory detail that would have overwhelmed most minds and become an end in itself, and never lost the magnificent charting of large design. . . . The quiet voice might in one minute make the most adroit use of a bit of current slang or popular doggerel to point out an opinion, and the next might be quoting stanza after stanza of a medieval Latin hymn."

His domestic economy was as tangled as the political

economy that he sought to unravel. He was living at Chicago with his wife, Ellen, but that did not prevent him from carrying on notoriously, to the displeasure of President Harper. When he went so far as to go abroad with another woman, his position on the campus became intolerable. He began casting around for another post.

He had spent fourteen years at Chicago, reaching the magnificent salary of one thousand dollars in 1903. But the years were far from wasted, for his insatiably inquisitive, voraciously acquisitive mind had finally begun to bear fruit. In a series of brilliant essays and two remarkable books he established a national reputation—although more perhaps for oddity than for anything else.

His first book was written when Veblen was forty-two. He was still a lowly instructor, and that year he had gone to President Harper and asked him for the customary few hundred dollars' raise. Harper replied that he did not sufficiently advertise the university, and Veblen replied that he had no intention of doing so. But for the intercession of Laughlin, Veblen would have left; if he had, President Harper would have missed a most signal advertisement. For Veblen was about to publish *The Theory of the Leisure Class*. There is no indication that he expected it to make an especial impression; he had read it to some of his students, dryly remarking that they would find it polysyllabic, and he had had to rewrite it several times before the publishers would accept it. But unexpectedly, it was a sensation. William Dean Howells devoted two long reviews to it, and overnight the book became the *vade mecum* of the intelligentsia of the day: as an eminent sociologist told Veblen, "It fluttered the dovecotes of the East."

No wonder it excited attention, for never was a book of sober analysis written with such pungency. One picked it up at random to chuckle over its wicked insights, its barbed phrases, and its corrosive view of society in which elements of ridiculousness, cruelty, and barbarousness nestled in close juxtaposition with things taken for granted and worn smooth with custom and careless handling. The effect was electric, grotesque, shocking, and amusing, and the choice of words was nothing less than exquisite. A small sample quote:

> ... A certain king of France ... is said to have lost his life through an excess of moral stamina in the observance of good form. In the absence of the functionary whose office it was to shift his master's seat, the king sat uncomplaining before the fire and suffered his royal person to be toasted beyond recovery. But in so doing, he saved his Most Christian Majesty from menial contamination.

For most people the book appeared to be nothing more than just such a satire on the ways of the aristocratic class, and a telling attack on the follies and foibles of the rich. And so, on the surface, it appeared to be. Veblen, in his brocaded prose, embroidered the thesis that the leisure class advertised its superiority through conspicuous expenditure—blatant or subtle—and that its own hallmark—leisure itself—was also enjoyed the more fully by being dangled before the eyes of the public. In a thousand examples it held up to acid examination the attitude that "more expensive" necessarily meant "better." Thus, for example:

> We all feel, sincerely and without misgiving, that we are the more lifted up in spirit for having, even in the privacy of our own household, eaten our daily meal by the help of handwrought silver utensils, from hand-painted china (often of dubious artistic value) laid on high-priced table linen. Any retrogression from the standard of living which we are accustomed to regard as worthy in this respect is felt to be a grievous violation of our human dignity.

Much of the book was concerned with such a scrutiny of the economic psychopathology of our daily lives: the canons of monetary propriety were spelled out as completely and in as quaint a light as if they were a recently exhumed archaeological find. That much of the book was savored with relish by everyone; in a land of advertisement and keeping up with the Joneses, it was impossible to do otherwise than shake one's head and ruefully admire the unmistakable self-portrait.

But the descriptions of our penchant for display, however amusing or to the point, were no more than the illustrative material of the book. For as the title made clear, this was an inquiry into the *theory* of the leisure class. Although Veblen might stop along the route to comment on the more striking local scenery, his interest lay at the terminus of his journey, in such questions as What is the nature of economic man? How does it happen that he so builds his community that it will have a leisure class? What is the economic meaning of leisure itself?

To the classical economists such questions would have been answerable in terms of common sense. They saw the world in terms of individuals who rationally sought to better their own self-interest. Sometimes, as with Malthus's hopelessly multiplying laboring classes, brute human nature got the upper hand, but by and large mankind was depicted as a collection of reasoning beings. In the competitive struggle some rose to the top and some staved at the bottom, and those who were fortunate or sagacious enough to prosper quite naturally took advantage of their fortune to minimize their labors. It was all very simple and quite reasonable.

But such a view of mankind made little sense to Veblen. He was not at all sure that the force that bound society together was the interplay of rationally calculated "self-interest," and he was not even wholly convinced that leisure was in and of itself preferable to work. His readings had introduced him to the ways of little-noticed peoples: the American Indians and the Ainus of Japan, the Todas of the Nilgiri hills and the bushmen of Australia. And these people, in their own simple economies, seemed to lack a leisure class entirely. Even more striking, in such communities where the price of survival was labor, everyone worked, whatever his task, without feeling demeaned by his toil. It was not considerations of profit and loss that provided the positive drive of these economies, but a natural pride of workmanship and a parental feeling of concern for the future generations. Men strove to outdo each other in the performance of their daily stints, and if abstinence from labor—leisure—was condoned at all, it was certainly not respected.

But another kind of community also opened itself to Veblen's gaze. The Polynesians and the ancient Icelanders and the shogunates of feudal Japan were a different kind of preindustrial society: they had well-defined leisure classes. These classes, be it noted, were not idlers. On the contrary, they were among the busiest members of the community. But their "work" was all predatory; they *seized* their riches by force or cunning and took no part in the actual production of wealth by sweat or skill.

But although the leisure classes took without rendering any productive service in return, they did so with the full approval of the community. For these societies were not only rich enough to be able to afford a nonproductive class, but aggressive enough to admire them; far from being regarded as wasters or spoilers, those who rose to the leisured ranks were looked up to as the strong and the able.

As a consequence, a fundamental change in attitudes toward work took place. The activities of the leisure class—the winning of wealth by force—came to be regarded as honorific and dignified. Hence, by contrast, pure labor became tainted with indignity. The irksomeness of work, which the classical economists thought to be inherent in the nature of man himself, Veblen saw as the degradation of a once honored way of life under the impact of a predatory spirit; a community that admires and elevates force and brute prowess cannot beatify human toil.

But what had all this to do with America or Europe? A great deal. For modern man, in Veblen's eyes, was only a shade removed from his barbarian forebears. Poor Edgeworth would have shuddered at the view, for it entailed nothing less than the substitution of warriors, chieftains, medicine men, braves, and an underlying population of humble awestruck common folk in the place of his pleasure machines. "The discipline of savage life," wrote Veblen in a later essay, "has been by far the most protracted and probably the most exacting of any phase of culture in all the life-history of the race; so that by heredity human nature still is, and must indefinitely continue to be, savage human nature."

And so in modern life Veblen saw the heritage of the past. The leisure class had changed its occupation, it had refined its methods, but its aim was still the same—the predatory seizure of goods without work. It did not, of course, any longer seek for booty or women; *that* barbaric it was no more. But it sought for money, and the accumulation of money and its lavish or subtle display became the modern-day counterpart of scalps hanging on one's tepee. Not only was the leisure class still following the old predatory pattern, but it was upheld by the old attitudes of admiration for personal strength. In the eyes of society, the members of the leisure class were still the more warlike and more fearsome members of society and, accordingly, the underlying common folk sought to ape their betters. Everyone, workman and middle-class citizen as well as capitalist, sought through the conspicuous expenditure of money—indeed through its conspicuous waste—to demonstrate his predatory prowess. "In order to stand well in the eyes of the community," explained Veblen, "it is necessary to come up to a certain, somewhat indefinite conventional standard of wealth; just as in the earlier predatory stage it is necessary for the barbarian man to come up to his tribe's standard of physical endurance, cunning, and skill at arms." And similarly, in modern society not only did everyone vie for fierce excellence in the eyes of his fellow man, but as part of the same process, everyone "instinctively" felt the indignity that attached to nonpredatory means of livelihood, such as work.

Does this sound farfetched? We are not accustomed to thinking of ourselves as barbarians, and we writhe under the comparison or scoff at it. But for all its strangeness, there is a core of truth in Veblen's observations. There *is* a social derogation of physical toil as opposed to the more genteel pursuits of office employment. There is the fact that the accumulation of wealth typically proceeds—at least in the case of a successful executive—well beyond the point of rational wants and needs. We need not accept Veblen's anthropological explanation (some of which, such as the supposed "discipline" of "savage life," is weak in the light of contemporary research into primitive communities) to profit by his principal insight—that the motives of economic behavior can be far better understood in terms of deep-buried irrationalities than in terms of the nineteenth-century prettification of behavior into reasonableness and common sense.

Just what these irrationalities are—psychological or anthropological—need not detain us here. Suffice it that when we trace our actions to their source, we find ourselves in a substratum buried far below the nice explanations of sweet reasonability. In their classic study of *Middletown*, for example, Robert and Helen Lynd found that during the Great Depression all but the poorest section of the working class retrenched on food and clothing before it would cut certain "necessary" luxuries; while in contemporary middle- and upper-class behavior, the standard of display for display's sake is amply testified to on the advertising pages of any magazine. No one is exempt from the virus of competitive emulation, and if only in a literary way, the attitudes of Veblen's predatory barbarians help us to understand our own.

And there is still a final conclusion to be drawn. The notion of man as a thinly civilized barbarian does more than explain the presence of a leisure class and the acceptance of display as the norm of expenditure. It gives a clue to the nature of social cohesion itself: For the earlier economists were not too successful in explaining what bound society together in the face of the powerful divergent interests of its component classes. If Marx's view was right, for example, and the proletariat was irreconcilably and diametrically opposed to the capitalist, what prevented the revolution from breaking out at once? Veblen provides an answer. The lower classes are not at swords' points with the upper; they are bound up with them by the intangible but steely bonds of common attitudes. The workers do not seek to displace their managers; they seek to *emulate* them. They themselves acquiesce in the general judgment that the work they do is somehow less "dignified" than the work of their masters, and their goal is not to rid themselves of a superior class but to climb up to it. In the theory of the leisure class lies the kernel of a theory of social stability.

● ●

After the *Leisure Class* appeared in 1899, Veblen had a reputation—although more as a satirist than as an economist. The radicals and intellectuals adored him, but he despised their praise. His fellow economists still questioned whether he was a Socialist, and wondered whether to take him seriously or not. They were justifiably bewildered: he praised Marx in one sentence and criticized him in the next, and his most serious social judgments were often cloaked in a kind of intellectual drollery that might be taken as morbid humor or as a perfectly straightforward sentiment.

But meanwhile, Veblen was working on another book—his own definition of the business system. "The book, I am creditably told," he wrote to an acquaintance, Mrs. Gregory, "is still more 'beyond' or as my friends who have seen it say, beside the point. Its name is *The Theory of Business Enterprise*—a topic on which I am free to theorize with all the abandon that comes of immunity to the facts."

The new book came out in 1904. Factual or not, it was even more coruscating and still more curious than his first. For the point of view that it advocated seemed to fly in the face of common sense itself. Every economist from the days of Adam Smith had made of the capitalist the driving figure in the economic tableau; whether for better or worse, he was generally assumed to be the central generator of economic progress. But with Veblen all this was turned topsy-turvy. The businessman was still the central figure, but no longer the motor force. Now he was portrayed as the *saboteur* of the system!

Needless to say, it was a strange perspective on society that could produce so disconcerting a view. Veblen did not begin, as Ricardo or Marx or the Victorians, with the clash of human interests; he began at a stage below, in the nonhuman substratum of technology. What fascinated him was the machine. He saw society as dominated by the machine, caught up in its standardization, timed to its regular cycle of performance, geared to its insistence on accuracy and precision. More than that, he envisaged the economic process itself as being basically mechanical in character. Economics meant production, and production meant the machinelike meshing of society as it turned out goods. Such a social machine would need tenders, of course—technicians and engineers to make whatever adjustments were necessary to ensure the most efficient cooperation of the parts. But from an overall view, society could best be pictured as a gigantic but purely matter-of-fact mechanism, a highly specialized, highly coordinated human clockwork.

But where would the businessman fit into such a scheme? For the businessman was interested in making money, whereas the machine and its engineer masters knew no end except making goods. If the machine functioned well and fitted together smoothly, where would there be a place for a man whose only aim was profit?

Ideally, there would be none. The machine was not concerned with values and profits; it ground out goods. Hence the businessman would have no function to perform—unless he turned engineer. But as a member of the leisure class he was not interested in engineering; he wanted to accumulate. And this was something the machine was not set up to do at all. So the businessman achieved his end, not by working within the framework of the social machine, but by conspiring against it! His function was not to help make goods, but to cause breakdowns in the regular flow of output so that values would fluctuate and he could capitalize on the confusion to reap a profit. And so, on top of the machinelike dependability of the actual production apparatus in the world, the businessman built a superstructure of credit, loans, and make-believe capitalizations. Below, society turned over in its mechanical routine; above, the structure of finance swayed and shifted. And as the financial counterpart to the real world teetered, opportunities for profit constantly appeared, disappeared, and reappeared. But the price of this profit seeking was high; it was the constant disturbing, undoing, even conscious misdirecting of the efforts of society to provision itself.

It is at first blush a rather shocking thesis. That businessmen should work *against* the interests of production seems worse than heretical. It sounds foolish.

But before we dismiss the theory as the product of a

strangely warped and bitter mind, let us look again at the scene from which Veblen drew his subject. This was, let us remember, the age of American industry that Matthew Josephson has aptly called the time of the robber barons. We have already seen examples of the arrogance, the unaccountable, guiltless power the business titans wielded like so many barbarian chiefs, and we know the bizarre lengths to which they went in the achievement of their often predatory goals. But while all this is grist for Veblen's mill, it does not quite justify his contention of sabotage. For that we must look at one further shortcoming of the robber barons: *these men were uninterested in producing goods.*

We might illustrate with an incident from 1868. At that time Jay Gould was fighting Vanderbilt for control of the Erie Railroad, in a lusty footnote to industrial history in which Gould and his men were forced to flee across the Hudson River in a rowboat, and barricaded themselves in a New Jersey hotel. But it is not their primitive combat that we now stop to remark, but their total unconcern for the actual railroad itself. For while he was fighting Vanderbilt, Gould had a letter from a superintendent telling him:

> The iron rails have broken and laminated and worn out beyond all precedent until there is scarcely a mile of your road, between Jersey City and Salamanca or Buffalo, where it is safe to run a train at the ordinary passenger or train speed, and many portions of the road can only be traversed safely by reducing the speed of all trains to 10 or 15 miles per hour.

When accidents piled up, one vice president of the line said, "The public can take care of itself. It is as much as I can do to take care of the railroad"—by which he meant frantically shoring up its crumbling financial embankments.

And Gould was no exception. Very few of the heroes of the Golden Age of American finance had much interest in the solid realities of what underlay their structure of stocks and bonds and credits. Later on, a Henry Ford might introduce an era of intensely production-minded captains of

industry, but the Harrimans, Morgans, Fricks, and Rocke-
fellers were far more interested in the manipulation of huge
masses of intangible wealth than in the humdrum business of
turning out goods. Henry Villard, for example, was widely
heralded in 1883 as a business hero; in that year he ham-
mered in the Gold Spike that connected his great transconti-
nental Northern Pacific line. Thousands cheered; Chief
Sitting Bull (who was specially let out of jail for the purpose)
formally ceded the hunting lands of his Sioux tribe to the railroad; and the economists declared that Villard's financial
peccadilloes were as nothing compared with his organizing
genius. His admirers might have felt differently had they
known of a letter written by James Hill, a rival railroad man.
He had surveyed the Villard empire with a less enthusiastic
glance and declared: ". . . the lines are located in good country, some of it rich and producing a large tonnage; but the
capitalization is far ahead of what it should be for what there
is to show and the selection of routes and grades is abom-
inable. *Practically it would have to be built over.*"

Or a final example: the founding of the United States
Steel Corporation in 1901. Viewed through Veblen's eyes,
the steel combine was a vast social machine for producing
steel, an assemblage of plants, furnaces, rail lines, and mines
under a common management for their more efficient coor-
dination. But this was only a minor consideration in the eyes
of the men who "made" U.S. Steel. The eventual monster
company had real assets of some $682 million, but against
this had been sold $303 million of bonds, $510 million of preferred stock, and $508 million of common stock. The finan-
cial company, in other words, was twice as "big" as the real
one, and nothing more lay behind its common stock than the
intangible essence of "good will." In the process of creating
these intangibles, however, J. P. Morgan and Company had
earned a fee of $12.5 million, and subscription profits to un-
derlying promoters had come to $50 million. Altogether, it
cost $150 million to float the venture. All this might have
been condoned had the new monopoly been used for the
purpose Veblen had in mind—as an enormously efficient
machine for the provision of steel. It was not. For thirteen

years steel rails were quoted at $28 a ton, whereas it cost less than half of that to make them. In other words, the whole gain in technological unification was subverted to the end of maintaining a structure of make-believe finance.

In the light of the times, Veblen's theory does not seem so farfetched. It stung because it described, almost in the terms of a savage ritual, practices that were recognized as the ultimate of sophistication. But his essential thesis was all too well documented by the facts: the function of the great barons of business was indeed very different from the functions of the men who actually ran the productive mechanism. The bold game of financial chicanery certainly served as much to disturb the flow of goods as to promote it.

Oddly enough, the book created less of a furor than *The Theory of the Leisure Class. Business Enterprise* never leaped the bounds of professional readership to take the country's intelligentsia by storm, as its predecessor had done. It was more difficult; more technical; it even included a few formulas, perhaps to prove to the academicians that he *could* write "technical" economics if he wanted to. But underlying the aloof, unimpassioned prose was an animus impossible to miss. To Veblen, businessmen were essentially predators, however much they or their apologists might drape their activities in the elaborate rationale of supply and demand or marginal utility. Later, in an essay on "The Captain of Industry," Veblen described the businessman as he really saw him; the following passage explains what is meant by the phrase "watchful waiting," which had been used to describe the entrepreneurial function:

> Doubtless this form of words, "watchful waiting" will have been employed in the first place to describe the frame of mind of a toad who has reached years of discretion and has found his appointed place along some frequented run where many flies and spiders pass and repass on their way to complete that destiny to which it has pleased an all-seeing and merciful Providence to call them; but by an easy turn of speech it has also been found suitable to describe that mature order of captains

of industry who are governed by sound business principles. There is a certain bland sufficiency spread across the face of a toad so circumstanced, while his comely bulk gives assurance of a pyramidal stability of principles.

But *The Theory of Business Enterprise* eschewed such rhetoric, for Veblen had a serious purpose in mind—to present a theory of social change. More precisely, it was a theory of the eventual decline of the businessman and of the system that sustained him. Veblen believed that the days of the business leaders were numbered, that despite their power, there was ranged against them a formidable adversary. It was not the proletariat (for the *Leisure Class* had shown how the underlying population looked up to its leaders), but a still more implacable foe: the machine.

For the machine, thought Veblen, "throws out anthropomorphic habits of thought." It forced men to think in terms of matter of fact, in terms precise, measurable, and devoid of superstition and animism. Hence those who came into contact with the machine process found it increasingly difficult to swallow the presumptions of "natural law" and social differentiation which surround the leisure class. And so society divided; not poor against rich, but technician versus businessman, mechanic against war lord, scientist opposed to ritualist.

In a later series of books, principally *The Engineers and the Price System* and *Absentee Ownership and Business Enterprise,* he spelled out the "revolution" in greater detail. Eventually a corps of engineers would be recruited from society to take over the chaos of the business system. Already they held the real power of production in their hands, but they were as yet unaware of the incompatibility of the business system with a system of true industry. But one day they would take counsel among themselves, dispense with the "lieutenants of absentee ownership," and run the economy along the principles of a huge, well-ordered production machine. And if they did not? Then business would increase in predatoriness until it eventually degenerated into a system of naked force, undisguised prerogative, and arbitrary command in which the businessman would give way to a recrudescence of the old warlord. We would call such a system fascism.

But to Veblen, writing in 1921, it was all a long way off. The last sentence of his *Engineers and the Price System* read: "There is nothing in the situation that should reasonably flutter the sensibilities of the Guardians or of that massive body of well-to-do citizens who make up the rank-and-file of absentee owners, just yet." That "just yet" is typical of the man. Despite the studied impersonality of his style, an animus bristles through his writing. And yet, it is not a personal animus, not the rancor of one who is privately affronted, but the amused and ironical detachment of a man apart, a man who sees that all this is transient, and that the ritual and make-believe will in time give way to something else.

This is not the time to make an appraisal of what he said; that will come later. But we might note a curious comparison. Veblen's general approach reminds us of a most un-Veblenesque figure—that strange half-mad Utopian Socialist, Count Henri de Saint-Simon. Remember that Saint-Simon also extolled the producer and mocked the ornamental functionary. Perhaps it will serve to temper our judgment of Veblen's scorn of the business overlord if we reflect that at one time Saint-Simon's jibes at "M. the brother to the King" must have similarly shocked public sentiment.

The year 1906 was Veblen's last at Chicago. He was beginning to be famous abroad; he had attended a banquet at which the King of Norway was present and in an unusual display of sentiment had sent the menu to his mother, who was deeply moved that her son had met a king. But at home things were not so good. His philanderings had gone too far, and despite his books and his newly won rank of assistant professor, his conduct was not such as to advertise the university in the manner advocated by President Harper.

He sought a new position. But his fame was closer to notoriety than repute, and he had much difficulty in finding another post. Eventually he went to Stanford. His reputation had preceded him: his fearsome scholarship, his personal untouchability, his extramarital proclivities. All were amply vindicated. He impressed those few of his colleagues who could endure his maddening refusal to commit himself on anything, and he became known as "the last man who knew everything." But his home economics were unchanged: on one occasion, hoping to be tactful, a friend referred to a young lady staying at his house as his niece. "That was not my niece," said Veblen. And that disposed of that.

His wife divorced him in 1911. He must have been an impossible husband (he would leave the letters from his admirers in his pockets, where she would be sure to find them), and yet, rather pathetically, it was she who hoped that the marriage would eventually right itself. It never did, more than temporarily; once when Ellen thought that she was pregnant, Veblen sent her home in a panic. He considered himself totally unfit to be a father and rationalized his fears with anthropological arguments on the unimportance of the male in the household. Finally a divorce became an inescapable necessity. "Mr. Veblen," wrote Ellen at the end of a long letter of self-commiseration, "though his part of the bargain is to furnish me with $25 a month—probably will not do it." She was right.

The year of his divorce he moved on again, this time to the University of Missouri. He stayed in the house of his friend Davenport, a well-known economist—a lonely and idiosyncratic man writing in the cellar. Yet it was a period of great productivity for Veblen. He looked back on the days at Chicago and summed up the perversion of centers of learning into centers of high-powered public relations and football in the most stinging commentary ever penned on the American university: *The Higher Learning in America*. While it was still in composition Veblen said, half-seriously, that it would be subtitled "A Study in Total Depravity."

But more important, he turned his eyes to Europe, where the threat of war was imminent, and he wrote about Germany, comparing her dynastic and warlike state to a tapeworm, in these vitriolic words: ". . . the tapeworm's relation to his host is not something easy to beautify in words, or even to authenticate in such convincing fashion as will ensure his affectionate retention on grounds of use and wont." The book on *Imperial Germany* suffered an unusual fate; although the propaganda office of the government wanted to use it for war purposes, the Post Office found in it so many remarks uncomplimentary to Britain and the United States that they barred it from the mails.

When war finally came, he offered his services to Washington: this man, to whom patriotism was only another symptom of a barbaric culture, was not devoid of it himself. But in Washington he was juggled about like a hot potato; everybody had heard of him, but no one wanted him. Finally they shelved him in an unimportant post in the Food Administration. There he behaved like himself: he wrote memoranda on how best to get in the crops—but since his suggestions involved a wholesale reorganization of rural social and business ways, they were called "interesting" and ignored. He proposed a steep tax on the employers of domestic servants in order to release manpower; that too was overlooked. It was a typical Veblen proposal: butlers and footmen, he said, "are typically and eminently an able-bodied sort, who will readily qualify as stevedores and freighthandlers as soon as the day's work has somewhat hardened their muscles and reduced their bulk."

In 1918 he came to New York to write for the *Dial*, a liberal magazine. He had recently published *An Inquiry into the Nature of the Peace* in which he boldly stated that the alternatives facing Europe were a perpetuation of the old order with all its barbarous incentives to war or the abandonment of the business system itself. The program was at first talked about and then lost its fashion; Veblen touted it in the *Dial*, but with every issue the circulation dropped. He was asked to lecture at the newly formed New School for Social Research with a bevy of stars: John Dewey, Charles A. Beard, Dean Roscoe Pound. But even that turned sour; he was still a mumbler in the classroom, and his lectures, which were filled to overflowing at first, were reduced to a handful in short order.

It was a strange mixture of fame and failure. H. L. Mencken has written that "Veblenism was shining in full bril-

liance. There were Veblenists, Veblen Clubs, Veblen remedies for all the sorrows of the world. There were, in Chicago,
Veblen Girls—perhaps Gibson Girls grown middle-aged and
despairing." But for the man himself there was nothing. A
bust of himself in the lobby of the New School caused him
such acute embarrassment that it was finally less prominently
displayed in the library. Personally, he was nearly helpless,
nurse-maided through the everyday problems of living by a
few devoted former students including Wesley Mitchell and
Isadore Lubin, already important economists in their own
right. For a while he watched eagerly for a sign of a new
world to come: an age of engineers and technicians, and he
hoped that the Russian Revolution might usher in such an
era. But he was disappointed in what he saw, and as Horace
Kallen of the New School has written, "When the thing failed
to come off, he gave signs of a certain relaxation of will and
interest, of a kind of turning toward death. . . ."

Belatedly he was offered the presidency of the American
Economic Association. He turned it down with the comment,
"They didn't offer it to me when I needed it." Finally he went
back to California. Joseph Dorfman, in a definitive biography, tells of his arriving at his small cabin in the West and
thinking that someone had unjustly seized his plot of land.
"He took a hatchet and methodically broke the windows,
going at the matter with a dull intensity that was like madness, the intensity of a physically lazy person roused into sudden activity by anger." It was all a misunderstanding, and he
settled there, in home-built rustic furniture that must have
reminded him of his boyhood, in coarse workmen's clothes
purchased by mail from Sears, Roebuck, disturbing nothing
of nature, not even a weed, and allowing the rats and skunks
to brush by his legs and explore his cabin as he sat immobile,
wrapped in unhappy distant thoughts.

It was neither a happy nor a successful life on which to
look back. A second wife, whom he had married in 1914, had
had delusions of persecution and had been institutionalized;
his friends were far away; his work had been captured by the
dilettantes and was largely disregarded by the economists
and unknown to the engineers.

He was seventy now and he wrote no more. "I have decided not to break the Sabbath," he declared. "It is such a nice Sabbath." His students came to see him and found him more distant than ever. He was subjected to adulation and received letters from self-appointed disciples. "Can you tell me in what house in Chicago it was that you did your early writings and if possible what room?" inquired one. Another, having finished *The Theory of Business Enterprise,* wrote to him asking his advice on how to make money.

In 1929, a few months before the great crash, he died. He left behind a will and this unsigned penciled injunction: "It is also my wish, in case of death, to be cremated, if it can conveniently be done, as expeditiously and inexpensively as may be, without any ritual or ceremony of any kind; that my ashes be thrown loose into the sea, or into some sizable stream running into the sea; that no tombstone, slab, epitaph, effigy, tablet, inscription or monument of any kind or nature, be set up in my memory or name at any place or at any time; that no obituary, memorial, portrait, or biography of me, nor any letters written to or by me be printed or published, or in any way reproduced, copied, or circulated."

As is always the case, his request was ignored: he was cremated and his ashes strewn out over the Pacific, but his memorialization by the written word began immediately.

What are we to think of this strange figure?

It is hardly necessary to point out that he went to extremes. His characterization of the leisure class, for example, was a masterpiece of portraiture on one page but a caricature on the next. When he picks out the silent component of wealth in our accepted canons of beauty, when he slyly mentions that "the high gloss of a gentleman's hat or of a patent-leather shoe has no more intrinsic beauty than a similarly high gloss on a threadbare sleeve," he is on sound ground and we must meekly accept the judgment of snobbery that has been passed on our taste. But when he writes, "The vulgar suggestion of thrift, which is nearly inseparable from the cow, is a standing objection to the decorative use of the animal," he shades off into the absurd. The irrepressible Mencken picked him up on that one: "Has the genial professor, pondering his great problems, ever taken a walk in the country? And has he, in the course of that walk, ever crossed a pasture inhabited by a cow? And has he, in making that crossing, ever passed astern of the cow herself? And has he, thus passing astern, ever stepped carelessly and—?"

Much the same criticism can be brought against Veblen's characterization of the businessman, or for that matter, the leisure class itself. That the financial titan of the halcyon days of American capitalism was a robber baron there is no doubt, and Veblen's portrait of him, savage though it is, is uncomfortably close to the truth. But, like Marx, Veblen did not seriously inquire into the extent that the institution of business, much as the monarchy of England, might adapt itself to a vastly altered world. More to the point—because it is closer to Veblen's own approach—he did not see that the machine, that wholesale rearranger of life, would change the nature of the entrepreneurial function just as much as it would alter the thought processes of the workman, and that the businessman himself would be forced into a more bureaucratic mold by virtue of his duties as a manager of a vast, ongoing machine.

It is true that Veblen's infatuation with the machine leaves us a little wary; it is a jarring note in a philosopher otherwise so devoid of lyricism. It may be that machines make us think matter-of-factly—but about what? Charlie Chaplin in *Modern Times* was not a happy or well-adjusted man. A corps of engineers might well run our society more efficiently, but whether they would run it more humanely is another question.

Yet Veblen did put his finger on a central process of change, a process that loomed larger than any other in his time and that had been strangely overlooked in all the investigations of his contemporary economists. *That process was the emergence of technology and science as the leading forces of social change in modern times—indeed, as the institutional force whose advent en masse was the identifying element of modern times.* It was thus in many ways a historic vision as much as an economic one. Veblen saw that the watershed of the technological age was as great as any in history and that the introduction of machinery into the finest interstices and over the largest spans of life was accomplishing a revolution comparable with that in which men learned to domesticate animals or to live in cities. Like every great discoverer of that which is obvious but has been unseen, Veblen was far too impatient; processes that would take generations, even centuries, he expected to mature in decades or even years. Yet it is to his credit that he perceived the machine as the primary fact of economic life in his time, and for this single brilliant insight he must be placed in the gallery of the worldly philosophers.

And then, too, he gave economics a new pair of eyes with which to see the world. After Veblen's savage description of the mores of daily life, the neoclassical picture of society as a well-mannered tea party became increasingly difficult to maintain. His scorn of the Victorian school was bitingly expressed when he once wrote: "A gang of Aleutian Islanders, slushing about in the wrack and surf with rakes and magical incantations for the capture of shellfish, are held . . . to be engaged on a feat of hedonistic equilibration in rent, wages, and interest"; and just as he ridiculed the classical attempt to resolve the primitive human struggle by fitting it into a fleshless and bloodless framework, so he highlighted the emptiness of trying to understand the actions of modern man in terms that derived from an incomplete and outmoded set of preconceptions. Man, said Veblen, is not to be comprehended in terms of sophisticated "economic laws" in which both his innate ferocity and creativity are smothered under a cloak of rationalization. He is better dealt with in the less flattering but more fundamental vocabulary of the anthropologist or the psychologist: a creature of strong and irrational drives, credulous, untutored, ritualistic. Leave aside flattering fictions, he asked of the economists, and find out why man actually behaves as he does.

His pupil, Wesley Clair Mitchell, a great economic investigator in his own right, summed him up this way: "There was the disturbing influence of Thorstein Veblen—that visitor from another world who dissected the current commonplaces which the student had unconsciously acquired, as if the most familiar of his daily thoughts were the curious products wrought in him by outside forces. No other such emancipator of the mind from the subtle tyranny of circumstance has been known in social science, and no other such enlarger of the realm of inquiry."

The Heresies
of John Maynard Keynes

A few years before his death, Thorstein Veblen had done something oddly out of character—he had taken a plunge in the stock market. A friend had recommended an oil stock, and Veblen, thinking of the financial problems of old age, had risked a part of his savings. He made a little money on the venture at first, but his inseparable bad luck plagued him—no sooner had the stock gone up than it was cited in the current oil scandals. His investment eventually became worthless.

The incident is unimportant in itself except insofar as it reveals one more tiny chink in Veblen's armor. And yet, in another context, this pathetic misadventure is curiously revealing. For Veblen himself had fallen victim to the same dazzling lure that blinded America: when the most disenchanted of its observers could be tempted to swallow a draught, is there any wonder that the country was drunk with the elixir of prosperity?

Certainly the signs of prosperity were visible at every hand. America in the late 1920s had found jobs for 45 million of its citizens to whom it paid some $77 billion in wages, rents, profits, and interest—a flood of income comparable to nothing the world had ever seen. When Herbert Hoover said with earnest simplicity, "We shall soon with the help of God be within sight of the day when poverty will be banished from the nation," he might have been shortsighted—as who was not?—but he rested his case on the incontrovertible fact that the average American family lived better, ate better, dressed better, and enjoyed more of the amenities of life than any average family thitherto in the history of the world.

The nation was possessed of a new self-image, one a great deal more uplifting than the buccaneering ideals of the robber barons. John J. Raskob, chairman of the Democratic party, gave it precise expression in the title of an article he wrote for the *Ladies' Home Journal:* "Everybody Ought to Be Rich." "If a man saves $15 a week," Raskob wrote, "and invests in good common stocks, at the end of twenty years he will have at least $80,000 and an income from investments of around $400 a month. He will be rich."

That bit of arithmetic merely presupposed that such a man would keep reinvesting his dividends, figured at about 6 percent a year. But there was an even more alluring road to riches. Had a devotee of Raskob's formula *spent* his dividends and merely allowed his money to increase with the trend of stock prices, he would have achieved his goal of wealth just as rapidly and a good deal less painfully. Suppose he had bought stock in 1921 with the $780 he would have saved at $15 a week. By 1922 his money would be worth $1,092. If he then added another $780 yearly he would have found himself worth $4,800 in 1925, $6,900 a year later, $8,800 in 1927, and an incredible $16,000 in 1928. Incredible? By May 1929 he would have figured his worldly wealth at over $21,000—worth ten times that in 1980s values. And when the Great Bull Market had gone on for nearly half a generation in an almost uninterrupted rise, who could be blamed for thinking this the royal road to riches? Barber or bootblack, banker or businessman, everyone gambled and everyone won, and the only question in most people's minds was why they had never thought of it before.

It is hardly necessary to dwell upon the sequel. In the awful last week of October 1929, the market collapsed. To the brokers on the floor of the Stock Exchange it must have been as if Niagara had suddenly burst through the windows, for a cataract of unmanageable selling converged on the marketplace. In sheer exhaustion brokers wept and tore their collars; they watched stupefied as immense fortunes melted like spun sugar; they shouted themselves hoarse trying to attract the attention of a buyer. The grim jokes of the period speak for themselves: it was said that with every share of Goldman Sachs you got a complimentary revolver, and that when you booked a hotel room the clerk inquired, "For sleeping or jumping?"

When the debris was swept away the wreckage was fearful to behold. In two insane months the market lost all the ground it had gained in two manic years; $40 billion of values simply disappeared. By the end of three years our investor's paper fortune of $21,000 had diminished by 80 percent; his original $7,000 of savings was worth barely $4,000. The vision of Every Man a Wealthy Man had been shown up as a hallucination.

In retrospect it was inevitable. The stock market had been built on a honeycomb of loans that could bear just so much strain and no more. And more than that, there were shaky timbers and rotten wood in the foundation which propped up the magnificent show of prosperity. Chairman Raskob's formula for retirement was arithmetically accurate enough, all right, but it never raised the question of how a man was to save $15 out of an average pay envelope that came to only $30.

The national flood of income was indubitably imposing in its bulk, but when one followed its course into its millions of terminal rivulets, it was apparent that the nation as a whole benefited very unevenly from its flow. Some 24,000 families at the apex of the social pyramid received a stream of income three times as large as 6 million families squashed at the bottom—the average income of the fortunate families at the peak was 630 *times* the average income of the families at the base. Nor was this the only shortcoming. Disregarded in the hullabaloo of limitless prosperity were two million citizens out of work, and ignored behind their façade of classical marble, banks had been failing at the rate of two a day for *six years* before the crash. And then there was the fact that the average American had used his prosperity in a suicidal way;

he had mortgaged himself up to his neck, had extended his resources dangerously under the temptation of installment buying, and then had ensured his fate by eagerly buying fantastic quantities of stock—some 300 million shares, it is estimated—not outright, but on margin, that is, on borrowed money.

Inevitable or not, it was far from visible at the time. It was a rare day that did not carry the news of some typical figure assuring the nation of its basic health. Even so eminent an economist as Irving Fisher of Yale was lulled by the superficial evidences of prosperity into announcing that we were marching along a "permanently high plateau"—a figure of speech given a macabre humor by the fact that stocks fell off the brink of that plateau one week to the day after he made his statement.

Dramatic as it was, it was not the wild decline of the stock market which most damaged the faith of a generation firmly wedded to the conviction of never-ending prosperity. It was what happened at home. A few items from those dreary years may serve to illustrate. In Muncie, Indiana—the city made famous by its selection as "Middletown"—every fourth factory worker lost his job by the end of 1930. In Chicago the majority of working women were earning less than twenty-five cents an hour, and a quarter of them made less than ten cents. In New York's Bowery alone, two thousand jobless crowded into bread lines every day. In the nation as a whole, residential construction fell by 95 percent. Nine million savings accounts were lost. Eighty-five thousand businesses failed. The national volume of salaries dwindled 40 percent; dividends 56 percent; wages 60 percent.

And the worst of it, the most depressing aspect of the Great Depression, was that there seemed to be no end to it, no turning point, no relief. In 1930, the nation manfully whistled "Happy Days Are Here Again," but the national income precipitously fell from $87 billion to $75 billion. In 1931 the country sang "I've Got Five Dollars"; meanwhile its income plummeted to $59 billion. In 1932 the song was grimmer: "Brother, Can You Spare a Dime?"—national income had dwindled to a miserable $42 billion.

By 1933 the nation was virtually prostrate. The income of the country was down to $39 billion. Over half the prosperity of only four years back had vanished without a trace; the average standard of living was back where it had been twenty years before. On street corners, in homes, in Hoovervilles, 14 million unemployed sat, haunting the land. It seemed as if the proud spirit of hope had been permanently crushed out of America.

It was the unemployment that was hardest to bear. The jobless millions were like an embolism in the nation's vital circulation; and while their indisputable existence argued more forcibly than any text that something was wrong with the system, the economists wrung their hands and racked their brains and called upon the spirit of Adam Smith, but could offer neither diagnosis nor remedy. Unemployment—this kind of unemployment—was simply not listed among the possible ills of the system; it was absurd, unreasonable, and therefore impossible. But it was there.

It would seem logical that the man who would seek to solve this paradox of not enough production existing side by side with men fruitlessly seeking work would be a Left-Winger, an economist with strong sympathies for the proletariat, an angry man. Nothing could be further from the fact. The man who tackled it was almost a dilettante with nothing like a chip on his shoulder. The simple truth was that his talents inclined in every direction. He had, for example, written a most recondite book on mathematical probability, a book that Bertrand Russell had declared "impossible to praise too highly"; then he had gone on to match his skill in abstruse logic with a flair for making money—he accumulated a fortune of £500,000 by way of the most treacherous of all roads to riches: dealing in international currencies and commodities. More impressive yet, he had written much of his mathematics treatise on the side, as it were, while engaged in government service, and he piled up his private wealth by applying himself for only half an hour a day while still abed.

But this is only a sample of his many-sidedness. He was an economist, of course—a Cambridge don with all the dignity and erudition that go with such an appointment; but when it came to choosing a wife he eschewed the ladies of learning and picked the leading ballerina from Diaghilev's famous company. He managed to be simultaneously the darling of the Bloomsbury set, the cluster of Britain's most avant-garde intellectual brilliants, and also the chairman of a life insurance company, a niche in life rarely noted for its intellectual abandon. He was a pillar of stability in delicate matters of international diplomacy, but his official correctness did not prevent him from acquiring a knowledge of other European politicians that included their mistresses, neuroses, and financial prejudices. He collected modern art before it was fashionable to do so, but at the same time he was a classicist with the finest private collection of Newton's writings in the world. He ran a theater, and he came to be a Director of the Bank of England. He knew Roosevelt and Churchill and also Bernard Shaw and Pablo Picasso. He played bridge like a speculator, preferring a spectacular play to a sound contract, and solitaire like a statistician, noting how long it took for the game to come out twice running. And he once claimed that he had but one regret in life—he wished he had drunk more champagne.

His name was John Maynard Keynes, an old British name (pronounced to rhyme with "rains") that could be traced back to one William de Cahagnes and 1066. Keynes was a traditionalist; he liked to think that greatness ran in families, and it is true that his own father was John Neville Keynes, a well-known economist in his own right. But it took more than the ordinary gifts of heritage to account for the son; it was as if the talents that would have sufficed half a dozen men were by happy accident crowded into one person.

He was born in 1883, in the very year that Karl Marx died. But the two economists who thus touched each other in time, and who were each to exert the profoundest influence on the philosophy of the capitalist system, could hardly have differed more. Marx was bitter, at bay, heavy and disappointed; as we know, he was the draftsman of Capitalism

Doomed. Keynes loved life and sailed through it buoyant, at ease, and consummately successful, to become the architect of Capitalism Viable. Perhaps we can trace Marx's passionate prophecy of collapse to the thread of neurotic failure that marked his practical life; if so, we can surely credit Keynes's persuasive salesmanship of reconstruction to the exhilaration and achievement that marked his.

His boyhood was Victorian, Old School, and premonitory of brilliance. At age four and a half he was already puzzling out for himself the economic meaning of interest; at six he was wondering about how his brain worked; at seven his father found him a "thoroughly delightful companion." He went to a Mr. Goodchild's preparatory school, where he gave evidence of his flair for handling his fellows: he had a "slave" who obediently trailed him with his schoolbooks, a service rendered in exchange for assistance with the knottier problems of homework, and a "commercial treaty" with another boy whom he disliked: Keynes agreed to get the boy one book a week out of the library in exchange for which the party of the second part agreed never to approach within fifteen yards of the party of the first.

At fourteen he applied for and won a scholarship to Eton. Horror stories on English public schools to the contrary, he was neither sadistically abused nor intellectually quashed. He bloomed; his marks were superlative; he won prizes by the score; bought himself a lavender waistcoat; acquired a taste for champagne; grew tall and rather stooped and cultivated a mustache; rowed; became a formidable debater; and without turning into a snob became an Eton enthusiast. Yet a letter to his father when he was only seventeen shows a discernment unusual for that age. The Boer War had come to a climax and the headmaster made a speech; Keynes described it perfectly in five phrases: "It was the usual stuff. Ought to show our thankfulness; remember dignity of school; if anything done must be of best; as always before."

Eton was a vast success; King's College at Cambridge was to be a triumph. Alfred Marshall begged him to become a fulltime economist; Professor Pigou—Marshall's heir-to-be—had him to breakfast once a week. He was elected Secretary of the Union, a post automatically carrying an eventual presidency of one of the most famous nongovernmental debating societies in the world; he was sought out by Leonard Woolf and Lytton Strachey (whose lover he became), and the nucleus of what was to be known as the Bloomsbury group came into being; he climbed mountains (Strachey complained at the "multitudes of imbecile mountains") ; bought books; stayed up in the small hours arguing; shone. He was a phenomenon.

But even phenomena must eat and there came the question of what to do. He had very little money, and the prospect of an academic career offered less. And he had larger visions: "I want to manage a railway or organize a Trust or at least swindle the investing public," he wrote to Strachey; "it is so easy and fascinating to master the principles of these things."

No one offered him a railway or a trust, and the "swindling" showed only an impious side to Keynes's imagination. He chose instead to try the public route to success. He took the civil service examinations with an apparent indifference that made Strachey's sister ask if his insouciance was a pose. No, he had it all figured out and so what was the use of fretting; he was sure to land in the top ten. Of course he did; he was second, and his lowest mark was in the economics section of the examination. "I evidently knew more about Economy than my examiners," he explained later, a remark that would be unforgivably presumptuous if it were not, in this case, entirely true.

Hence, in 1907 to the India Office. Keynes hated it. He was spending his freshest energies at home on an early draft of his mathematical treatise, and he found the post of a minor official in public office a far cry from running a railway. After two years he had had enough. His efforts, he declared, consisted in having one pedigreed bull shipped to Bombay, and all that he had found in government work was that an ill-considered remark might result in your being "snubbed." He resigned and went back to Cambridge. But his years could not have been so utterly useless. From what he had learned of Indian affairs he wrote a book in 1913 on *Indian Currency and Finance*, which everyone admitted to be a small masterpiece, and when a Royal Commission was formed that same year to look into the Indian currency problem Keynes at twenty-nine was asked to be a member—a remarkable honor.

Cambridge was more to his liking. He was an immediate success, and as a mark of the esteem in which he was held, he was given the editorship of the *Economic Journal*, Britain's most influential economic publication—a post he was to hold for thirty-three years.

Even more pleasant than Cambridge was Bloomsbury. Bloomsbury was both a place and a state of mind; the little group of intellectuals to whom Keynes had belonged as an undergraduate had now acquired a home, a philosophy, and a reputation. Perhaps not more than twenty or thirty people ever belonged to that charmed circle, but their opinions set the artistic standards of England—after all, it included Leonard and Virginia Woolf, E. M. Forster, Clive Bell, Roger Fry, Lytton Strachey. If Bloomsbury smiled, a poet's name was made; if it frowned, he was dropped. It is said that the Bloomsbury group could use the word "really" in a dozen different intonations, of which sophisticated boredom was by no means the least. It was a group at once idealistic and cynical, courageous and fragile. And slightly mad; there was the incident known as the Dreadnought Hoax in which Virginia Woolf (then Stephen) and a few co-conspirators dressed up as the Emperor of Abyssinia and entourage, and were escorted with honors aboard one of His Majesty's most closely guarded battleships.

In all of this, Keynes was a central figure—adviser, councillor, referee. He could talk about anything with complete assurance: William Walton the composer, Frederick Ashton the choreographer, and many another artist or professional was used to Keynes's "No, no, you're absolutely wrong about that. . . ." His nickname, it might be added, was Pozzo, a sobriquet pinned on him after a Corsican diplomat known for his multifarious interests and his scheming mind.

It was a rather dilettantish beginning for one who was to set the capitalist world on its ears.

● ●

The war years somewhat disrupted Bloomsbury. Keynes was called to the Treasury and assigned to work on Britain's overseas finances. He must have been something of a phenomenon there, too. An anecdote in point was later recounted by an old associate: "There was an urgent need for Spanish *pesetas*. With difficulty a smallish sum was raked up. Keynes duly reported this to a relieved Secretary to the Treasury, who remarked that at any rate for a short time we had a supply of *pesetas*. 'Oh no!' said Keynes. 'What!' said his horrified chief. 'I've sold them all; I'm going to break the market.' And he did."

He was soon a key figure in the Treasury. His first biographer and fellow economist, Roy Harrod, tells us that men of ripe judgment have declared that Keynes contributed more to winning the war than any other person in civil life. Be that as it may, he managed to find time for other things. On a financial mission to France he was seized with the idea that it would help balance the French accounts with the British if they sold some of their pictures to the National Gallery. He thus casually acquired a hundred thousand dollars' worth of Corot, Delacroix, Forain, Gauguin, Ingres, and Manet for the British, and managed to get a Cézanne for himself: Big Bertha was shelling Paris and prices were pleasantly depressed. Back in London he attended the ballet; Lydia Lopokova was dancing the part of the beauty in "The Good-Humored Ladies," and she was the rage. The Sitwells had her to a party, where she and Keynes met. One can imagine Keynes with his classic English and Lydia with her classic struggles with English—"I dislike being in the country in August," she said, "because my legs get so bitten by barristers."

But all this was tangential to the main thing—the settlement of Europe after the war. Keynes was now an important personage—one of those unidentified men one sees standing behind the chair of a head of state ready to whisper a guiding word. He went to Paris as Deputy for the Chancellor of the Exchequer on the Supreme Economic Council with full power to make decisions and as representative of the Treasury at the Peace Conference itself. But he was only second echelon; he had a grandstand seat but no power to interfere directly in the game. It must have been an agony of frustration and impotence, for at close quarters he watched while Wilson was outmaneuvered by Clemenceau and the ambition of a humane peace replaced by the achievement of a vindictive one.

"It must be weeks since I've written anyone," he wrote to his mother in 1919, "but I've been utterly worn out, partly by work, partly by depression at the evil around me. I've never been so miserable as for the last two or three weeks; the Peace is outrageous and impossible and can bring nothing but misfortune behind it."

He dragged himself from the sickbed to protest against what he called the "murder of Vienna," but he could not stop the tide. The peace was to be a Carthaginian one, and Germany was to pay a sum of reparations so huge that it would force her into the most vicious practices of international trade in order to earn the pounds and francs and dollars. This was not the popular opinion, of course, but Keynes saw that in the Versailles Treaty lay the unwitting goad for an even more formidable resurgence of German autarchy and militarism.

He resigned in despair; then three days before the treaty was signed he began his polemic against it. He called it *The Economic Consequences of the Peace;* when it appeared that December (he wrote it at top speed and fury), it made his name.

It was brilliantly written and crushing. Keynes had seen the protagonists at work, and his descriptions of them combined the skill of a novelist with the cutting insight of a Bloomsbury critic. He wrote of Clemenceau that "He had only one illusion—France, and one disillusion—mankind, including his own colleagues not least"; and of Wilson, ". . . like Odysseus, he looked wiser when seated." But while his portraits sparkled, it was his analysis of the harm that had been done that was unforgettable. For Keynes saw the Conference as a reckless settlement of political grudge in utter disregard of the pressing problem of the moment—the resuscitation of Europe into an integrating and functioning whole:

The Council of Four paid no attention to these issues, being preoccupied with others,—Clemenceau to crush the economic life of his enemy, Lloyd George to do a deal and bring home something that would pass muster for a week, the President to do nothing that was not just and right. It is an extraordinary fact that the fundamental problems of a Europe starving and disintegrating before their eyes, was the one question in which it was impossible to arouse the interest of the Four. Reparation was their main excursion into the economic field, and they settled it as a problem of theology, of politics, of electoral chicane, from every point of view except that of the economic future of the States whose destiny they were handling.

And he went on to deliver this solemn warning:

The danger confronting us, therefore, is the rapid depression of the standard of life of the European populations to a point which will mean actual starvation for some (a point already reached in Russia and approximately reached in Austria). Men will not always die quietly. For starvation, which brings to some lethargy and a helpless despair, drives other temperaments to the nervous instability of hysteria and to a mad despair. And these in their distress may overturn the remnants of organization, and submerge civilization itself in their attempts to satisfy desperately the overwhelming needs of the individual. This is the danger against which all our resources and courage and idealism must now cooperate.

The book was an immense success. The unworkability of the treaty was manifest almost from the moment of its signing, but Keynes was the first to see it, to say it, and to suggest an outright revision. He became known as an economist of extraordinary foresight, and when the Dawes Plan in 1924 began the long process of undoing the impasse of 1919, his gift for prophecy was confirmed.

He was famous now, but there remained the question of

what to do. He chose business, the riskiest possible business, and with a capital of a few thousand pounds he began to speculate in the international markets. He nearly lost it all, was helped with a loan from a banker who had never met him but who was impressed by his work during the war, recouped, and went on to roll up a fortune worth then $2 million. It was all done in the most casual way. Keynes disdained inside information—in fact, he once declared that Wall Street traders could make huge fortunes if only they would disregard their "inside" information—and his own oracles were nothing but his minute scrutiny of balance sheets, his encyclopedic knowledge of finance, his intuition into personalities, and a certain flair for trading. Abed in the morning he would study his items of financial intelligence, make his decisions, phone his orders, and that was that; the day was now free for more important things, like economic theory. He would have gotten along famously with David Ricardo.

He made money, by the way, not only for himself. He became the Bursar of King's College and turned a fund of £30,000 into one of £380,000. He managed an investment trust and guided the finances of a life insurance company.

Meanwhile—there was always more than one thing going on at a time with Keynes—he wrote for the *Manchester Guardian,* gave regular classes in Cambridge, in which he spiced dry theory with an intimate account of the goings-on and personalities of the international commodity marts, bought more pictures, acquired more books, and, after a tumultuous love life with Lytton Strachey, Duncan Grant, and a score of other male lovers, married Lydia Lopokova. The ballerina became the wife of the Cambridge don, a new role, which somewhat to the surprise (and relief) of Keynes's friends she filled to perfection. She gave up her professional career, of course, but a visiting friend later reported hearing alarming thumps and crashes from above: Lydia was still practicing her art.

She was extremely beautiful; he was altogether the proper admirer, not handsome but tall and dignified. His large, somewhat gawky frame provided a suitable pedestal for a longish, triangular, inquisitive face: a straight nose, a clipped mustache held over from Eton days, full, mobile lips, and a rather disappointing chin. The eyes were most revealing; under arching brows they could be grave, icy, sparkling, or "soft as bees' bottoms in blue flowers," as one editor wrote, depending, perhaps, on whether he was acting as government emissary, speculator, Bloomsbury brilliant, or balletomane.

There was one odd mannerism: Keynes liked to sit like an English variant of a Chinese mandarin, with his hands tucked out of sight in the opposing sleeves of his coat. It was a gesture of concealment made all the more curious because of his inordinate interest in other people's hands and his pride in his own. Indeed, he even went to the extent of having casts made of his and his wife's hands and talked of making a collection of casts of his friends'; and when he met a man the first thing he noticed was the character of his palms and fingers and nails. Later, when he first talked with Franklin Roosevelt, he noted down this description of the President:

> . . . But at first, of course, I did not look closely at these things. For naturally my concentrated attention was on his hands. Firm and fairly strong, but not clever or with finesse, shortish round nails like those at the end of a business man's fingers. I cannot draw them right, yet while not distinguished (to my eye) they are not of a common type. All the same, they were oddly familiar. Where had I seen them before? I spent ten minutes at least searching my memory as for a forgotten name, hardly knowing what I was saying about silver and balanced budgets and public works. At last it came to me. Sir Edward Grey. A more solid and Americanized Sir Edward Grey.

It is doubtful whether Roosevelt would have written as he did to Felix Frankfurter—"I had a grand talk with K. and liked him immensely"—had he known that he was being summed up in the eyes of the other as a businessman's version of an English Foreign Secretary.

• •

By 1935 it was already a brilliantly established career.
The book on *Indian Currency and Finance* had been a tour
de force, albeit a small one; *The Economic Consequences of
the Peace* had made an éclat; and the *Treatise on Probability*
was an equal triumph, although far more specialized. An
amusing incident in regard to this last book: Keynes was having dinner with Max Planck, the mathematical genius who
was responsible for the development of quantum mechanics,
one of the more bewildering achievements of the human
mind. Planck turned to Keynes and told him that he had once
considered going into economics himself. But he had decided against it—it was too hard. Keynes repeated the story
with relish to a friend back at Cambridge. "Why, that's odd,"
said the friend. "Bertrand Russell was telling me just the
other day that he'd also thought about going into economics.
But he decided it was too easy."

But mathematics was only a sideline, as we know; in
1923 a *Tract on Monetary Reform* again raised the eyebrows
of the world. Now Keynes was inveighing against the
fetishism of gold, against the peculiar passivity evidenced by
men's abdication of conscious control of their own currencies
and their transfer of this responsibility to the impersonal
mechanism of an international gold standard. It was a technical book, of course, but like all of Keynes's works, lit up with
telling phrases. One thrust will surely be added to the stock
of English aphorisms: talking of the "long run" consequences
of some venerable economic axiom, Keynes dryly wrote: "In
the long run we are all dead."

Then to top it off, in 1930 he published a *Treatise on
Money*—a long, difficult, uneven, sometimes brilliant and
sometimes baffling attempt to account for the behavior of the
whole economy. The *Treatise* was a fascinating book, for it
took as its central problem the question of what made the
economy operate so unevenly—now bustling with prosperity,
now sluggish with depression.

The question, of course, had absorbed the attention of
economists for decades. Great speculative crashes aside—
like the 1929 bust and its predecessors in history (we saw one

such in eighteenth-century France when the Mississippi Company collapsed)—the normal course of trade seemed to evidence a wavelike succession of expansions and contractions, not unlike a kind of economic breathing. In England, for example, business had been bad in 1801, good in 1802, bad in 1808, good in 1810, bad in 1815, and so on for over a hundred years; in America the pattern was the same, although the dates were slightly different.

What lay behind this alternation of prosperity and depression? At first the cycles of business were thought to be a sort of mass nervous disorder: "These periodic collapses are really mental in their nature, depending on variations of despondency, hopefulness, excitement, disappointment, and panic," wrote an observer in 1867. But although such a statement was undoubtedly a good description of the state of mind in Wall Street or Lombard Street, Lancaster or New England, it left unanswered the basic question: What causes such a widespread nervous hysteria?

Some early explanations looked *outside* the economic process for an answer. W. Stanley Jevons, whom we have briefly met before, ventured an explanation that pinned the blame on *sunspots*—not quite so farfetched an idea as it might at first appear. For Jevons was impressed by the fact that business cycles from 1721 to 1878 had had an average duration, from boom to boom, of 10.46 years, and that sunspots (which had been discovered in 1801 by Sir William Herschel) showed a periodicity of 10.45 years. The correlation, Jevons was convinced, was too close to be purely accidental. Sunspots, he thought, caused weather cycles, which caused rainfall cycles, which caused crop cycles, which caused business cycles.

It was not a bad theory—except for one thing. A more careful calculation of the sunspot cycles lengthened their periodicity to eleven years and the neat correspondence between celestial mechanics and the vagaries of business broke down. Sunspots went the way of astronomy, and the quest for the motivating factors of business cycles returned to more earthbound considerations.

It returned, in fact, to an area first bumblingly but intuitively pointed out by Malthus a century before—the area of saving. Perhaps we remember Mathus's doubts—his ill-articulated feeling that saving could somehow result in a "general glut." Ricardo had scoffed; Mill had pooh-poohed; and the idea had become part of the disreputable and dangerous nonsense of the underworld. To say that saving might be a source of trouble—why, that was impugning thrift itself! It was almost immoral: had not Adam Smith written, "What is prudence in the conduct of every private family can scarce be folly in that of a great nation?"

But when the early economists refused to consider that saving might be a stumbling block for an economy, they were not indulging in moral proselytizing; they were only observing the facts of the real world.

For in the early 1800s, by and large those who saved were the very same people as those who put savings to use. In the hard-pressed world of Ricardo or Mill, virtually the only people who could afford to save were wealthy landlords and capitalists, and any sums they put together were usually employed in productive investments of one kind or another. Hence saving was rightly called "accumulation," for it represented a two-sided coin; on the one hand the amassing of a sum of money, and on the other hand its immediate employment in purchasing the tools or buildings or land to make still more money.

But toward the middle of the nineteenth century, the structure of the economy changed. The distribution of wealth improved, and along with it the possibility of saving became open to more and more members of society. And at the same time, business became larger and more institutionalized; increasingly it looked for new capital not just in the pockets of its individual manager-owners but also in the anonymous pocketbooks of savers all over the country. Hence saving and investing became divorced from one another—they became separate operations carried out by separate groups of people.

And this did introduce trouble into the economy. Malthus was right after all, although for reasons he had never foreseen.

• •

The trouble is so important—so central to the problem of depression—that we must take a moment to make it clear.

We must start out by understanding how we measure the prosperity of a nation. It is not by its gold—poverty-stricken Africa for years was rich in gold. Nor is it by its physical assets—buildings, mines, factories, and forests did not evaporate in 1932. Prosperity and depression are not so much matters of past glories but of present accomplishments; therefore they are measured by the *incomes* that we earn. When most of us individually (and therefore all of us collectively) enjoy high incomes, the nation is well off; when our total individual (or national) income drops, we are in depression.

But income—national income—is not a static concept. Indeed the central characteristic of an economy is the *flow* of incomes from hand to hand. With every purchase that we make, we transfer a part of our incomes into someone else's pocket. Similarly every penny of our own incomes, be it wages, salaries, rents, profits, or interest, ultimately derives from money that someone else has spent. Consider any portion of the income that you enjoy and it will be clear that it has originated from someone else's pocket: when he or she engaged your services, or patronized your store, or bought the output of the corporation in which you own bonds or stock.

It is by this process of handing money around—taking in each other's wash, it has been described—that the economy is constantly revitalized.

Now to a large extent this process of handing income around takes place quite naturally and without hindrance. All of us spend the bulk of our incomes on goods for our own use and enjoyment—on consumption goods, so-called—and since we go on buying consumption goods with fairly consistent regularity, the handing around of a large portion of our national income is assured. The fact that we must eat and clothe ourselves, and that we crave enjoyment, ensures a regular and steady spending on the part of all of us.

So far everything is quite simple and direct. But there is

one portion of our incomes which does *not* go directly out onto the marketplace to become another's income: that is the money we save. If we tucked these savings into mattresses or hoarded them in cash, we should obviously break the circular flow of income. For then we should be returning to society less than it gave to us. If such a freezing process were widespread and continued, there would soon be a cumulative fall in everybody's money income, as less and less was handed around at each turn. We should be suffering from a depression.

But this dangerous break in the income flow does not normally take place. For we do not freeze our savings. We put them into stocks or bonds or banks and in this way make it possible for them to be used again. Thus, if we buy new stock we give our savings directly to business; if we put our savings in a bank, they can be used on loan by businessmen who seek capital. Whether we bank our savings or use them to buy insurance or securities, the channels exist for those savings to go back into circulation via the activities of business. For when our savings are taken and spent by business, they again turn up as someone's wages, someone's salary, or someone's profit.

But—and notice this vital fact—there is nothing *automatic* about this savings-investment channel. Business does not need savings to carry on its everyday operations; it pays its expenses from the proceeds of its sales. Business needs savings only if it is *expanding* its operation, for its regular receipts will not usually provide it with enough capital to build a new factory or to add substantially to its equipment.

And here is where the trouble enters. A thrifty community will always attempt to save some part of its income. But business is not always in a position to expand its operations. When the business outlook is poor, whether because of "gluts" in particular markets, or because the international situation is alarming, or because businessmen are nervous about inflation, or for any other reason, the impetus to invest will wane. Why should businessmen expand their facilities when they look to the future with trepidation?

And therein lies the possibility of depression. *If our*

savings do not become invested by expanding business firms, our incomes must decline. We should be in the same spiral of contraction as if we had frozen our savings by hoarding them.

Can such an eventuality come to pass? We shall see. But note meanwhile that this is a strange and passionless tug of war. Here are no greedy landlords, no avaricious capitalists. There are only perfectly virtuous citizens prudently attempting to save some of their incomes, and perfectly virtuous businessmen who are just as prudently making up their minds whether the business situation warrants taking the risk of buying a new machine or building a new plant. And yet, on the outcome of those two sensible decisions the fate of the economy hangs. For if the decisions are out of joint—if the businessmen invest less than the community tries to save, for example—then the economy will have to adjust to the crimp of depression. The vital question of boom or slump depends more than anything else on this.

The vulnerability of our fate to the interplay of savings and investment is, in a sense, the price we pay for economic freedom. There was no such problem in Soviet Russia, nor was there such in the Egypt of the Pharaohs. For in economies of edict both savings and investment are determined from above, and a total control over the nation's entire economic life ensures that the nation's savings will be used to finance its pyramids or power plants. But not so in a capitalist world. For there both the decision to save and the impetus to invest are left to the free decisions of the economic actors themselves. And because those decisions are free, they can be out of joint. There can be too little investment to absorb our savings or too little savings to support our investment. Economic freedom is a highly desirable state—but in bust and boom we must be prepared to face its possible consequences.

We have almost lost sight of John Maynard Keynes and the *Treatise on Money.* But not quite. For the *Treatise* was a sparkling exposition of this seesaw of savings and investment. The idea was not original with Keynes, for a long list of important economists had already pointed to the critical roles of these two factors in the business cycle. But, as with every-thing that Keynes touched, the bare abstractions of econom-ics took on a new luster in his prose. Thus:

> It has been usual to think of the accumulated wealth of the world as having been painfully built up out of that voluntary abstinence of individuals from the immediate enjoyment of consumption, which we call Thrift. But it should be obvious that mere abstinence is not enough by itself to build cities or drain fens.
>
> . . . It is Enterprise which builds and improves the world's possessions. . . . If Enterprise is afoot, wealth ac-cumulates whatever may be happening to Thrift; and if Enterprise is asleep, wealth decays whatever Thrift may be doing.

Yet, for all its masterful analysis, no sooner had Keynes written the *Treatise* than, figuratively, he tore it up. For his theory of a seesaw of savings and investment failed at one central point: it did not explain how an economy could re-main in a state of prolonged depression. Indeed, as the very analogy of the seesaw indicates, it seemed as if an economy that was weighted down by surplus savings must, in fairly short order, right itself and swing the other way.

For savings and investment—Thrift and Enterprise—were not utterly unconnected economic activities. On the contrary, they were tied together in the market where busi-nessmen "bought" savings, or at least borrowed them: the money market. Savings, like any other commodity, had its price: the rate of interest. Therefore (so it seemed), at the bottom of a slump when there was a flood of savings, its price should decline—exactly as, when there was a glut of shoes, the price of shoes declined. And as the price of savings cheapened—as the rate of interest went down—the *incentive* to invest appeared very likely to increase: if a new factory was too expensive to build when the money for it would cost 10 percent, might it not look much more profitable when the money could be had for a payment of only 5 percent?

Hence the seesaw theory seemed to promise that there would be an automatic safety switch built right into the business cycle itself; that when savings became too abundant, they would become cheaper to borrow, and that thereby business would be encouraged to invest. The economy might contract, said the theory, but it seemed certain to rebound.

But this was exactly what failed to happen in the Great Depression. The rate of interest declined, but nothing happened. The old nostrums were trotted out—a pinch of local relief and a large dose of hopeful waiting—and still the patient failed to improve. For all its logic, something was patently missing from the neat formulation of the rate of interest always hovering over the seesaw of savings and investment to keep it in balance. Something else must be holding the economy back.

Keynes's master book had been brewing for some time. "To understand *my* state of mind," he had written to George Bernard Shaw in 1935—he had just reread Marx and Engels at Shaw's suggestion and found them little to his liking— ". . . you have to know that I believe myself to be writing a book on economic theory which will largely revolutionize— not, I suppose at once, but in the course of the next ten years —the way the world thinks about economic problems. . . . I can't expect you or anyone else to believe this at the present stage. But for myself I don't merely hope what I say—in my own mind, I'm quite sure."

He was, as usual, quite right. The book was to be a bombshell. Yet it is very doubtful whether Shaw would have recognized it as such had he attempted to digest it. It had a forbidding title, *The General Theory of Employment, Interest and Money,* and a still more forbidding interior: one can imagine Shaw goggling on page 25 at "Let Z be the aggregate supply price of the output from employing N men, the relationship between Z and N being written $Z = \phi(N)$, which can be called the Aggregate Supply Function." And if this were not enough to frighten off almost anyone, there was a great dearth of that panorama of social action which the layman

had come to expect from a perusal of Smith or Mill or Marx.
Here and there were wonderful passages—there is a famous
one comparing the choosing of stocks and the picking of
beauty contest winners—but the passages came as oases between deserts of algebra and abstract analysis.

And yet the book was revolutionary: no other word will
quite do. It stood economics on its head, very much as *The
Wealth of Nations* and *Capital* had done.

For *The General Theory* had a startling and dismaying
conclusion. There was no automatic safety mechanism after
all! Rather than a seesaw that would always right itself, the
economy resembled an elevator: it could be going up or
down, but it could also be standing perfectly still. And it was
just as capable of standing still on the ground floor as at the
top of the shaft. A depression, in other words, might not cure
itself at all; the economy could lie stagnant indefinitely, like a
ship becalmed.

But how could this be? Would not the flood of savings at
the bottom of the slump push down the rate of interest, and
would this not in turn induce business to use cheap money to
expand its plant?

Keynes found the flaw in this argument in the simplest
and most obvious (once it had been pointed out) fact of economic life: *there would be no flood of savings at the bottom of
the trough.* For what happened when an economy went into
an economic tailspin was that its income contracted, and
what happened as its income contracted was that its savings
were squeezed out. How could a community be expected to
save as much when everyone was hard up as when everyone
was prosperous? asked Keynes. Quite obviously, it could not.
The result of a depression would not be a glut of savings but a
drying-up of savings; not a flood of saving, but a trickle.

And so it was, in fact. In 1929 the American private citi-
zenry put aside $3.7 billion out of its income; by 1932 and
1933 it was saving *nothing*—in fact, it was even drawing
down its old savings made in the years before. Corporations,
which had tucked away $2.6 billion at the top of the boom
after paying out taxes and dividends, found themselves losing
nearly $6 billion three years later. Quite obviously Keynes

was right: saving was a kind of luxury that could not withstand hard times.

But the larger consequence of this decline in saving was of greater significance than even the loss of individual security that the decline brought about. The larger consequence was that the economy found itself in a condition of paralysis just when it most needed to be dynamic. For if there was *no* surplus of saving, there would be *no* pressure on interest rates to encourage businessmen to borrow. And if there were no borrowing and investment spending, there would be *no* impetus for expansion. The economy would not budge an inch: it would remain in a condition of "equilibrium" despite the presence of unemployed men and women and underutilized plant and equipment.

Thus the paradox of poverty amidst plenty and the anomaly of idle men and idle machines. At the bottom of a slump there was a heartless contradiction between a crying need for goods and an insufficiency of production. But the contradiction was purely a moral one. For the economy did not operate to satisfy human *wants*—wants are always as large as dreams. It turned out goods to satisfy *demand*—and demand is as small as a person's pocketbook. Hence the unemployed were little more than economic zeros; they might as well have been on the moon for all the economic influence they exerted on the marketplace.

To be sure, once investment declined and the economy shrank in size, social misery appeared. But not—as Keynes points out—*effective* social misery: the nation's conscience would not do as an effective substitute for enough investment. Rather, since savings declined along with investment, the economic flow turned over evenly, quite unaffected by the fact that it was smaller than it used to be.

A peculiar state of affairs, indeed a tragedy without a villain. No one can blame society for saving, when saving is so apparently a private virtue. It is equally impossible to chastise businessmen for not investing when no one would be so happy to comply as they—if they saw a reasonable chance for success. The difficulty is no longer a moral one—a question of justice, exploitation, or even human foolishness. It is a technical difficulty, almost a mechanical fault. But its price is no less high for all of that. For the price of inactivity is unemployment.

And here was the most indigestible fact of all. The willingness to invest could not go on indefinitely. Sooner or later, investment was likely to contract.

For, at any time, an industry is limited by the size of the market to which it caters. Let us take the example of the railroads in the 1860s—a time of vast investment in new railroad lines. The early railway magnates were not building for the markets of the 1960s; had they proceeded to lay the trackage the economy would need a hundred years later, they would have been building lines to nonexistent cities in uninhabited territory. So they built what could be used—and then they stopped. Similarly with the auto industry. Even if Henry Ford had been able to find the capital to build the 1950 River Rouge plant in 1910, he would have gone bankrupt in a hurry; the roads, the gas stations, the *demand* for that many cars were simply lacking. Or to bring the matter a little closer, by the late 1990s American business was spending just over $1 trillion a year for new equipment, but it was not spending $2 trillion. Someday it might well have to, but as the century drew to its end, that day had not yet arrived.

And so investment has its typical pattern: at first eagerness to take advantage of a new opportunity; then, caution lest enthusiasm lead to overbuilding; then inactivity when the market has been satisfied for the time being.

If, as each separate investment project came to a halt, another immediately appeared, there need never be a slump. But such is not likely to be the case. The mere fact that human wants are vast does not mean that *any* investment will pay for itself; the economy is littered with businesses that have died of rash and foolhardy overexpansion. Most investment needs more than the stimulus of sanguine expectations; it needs something more concrete, some new invention, some better way of doing things, some intriguing product to catch the public eye. And such opportunities, as any businessman will tell you, are not always there.

Hence, when one investment project dies, there may not

be another ready to step into the breach. If there is—if investment maintains its size, although it changes its composition—the economy will sail smoothly along. But if there is no ready substitute for each investment casualty, contraction will begin.

Looking at this intrinsic vulnerability of the system, Keynes wrote:

> Ancient Egypt was doubly fortunate and doubtless owed to this its fabled wealth, in that it possessed *two* activities, namely pyramid-building and the search for the precious metals, the fruits of which, since they could not serve the needs of man by being consumed, did not stale with abundance. The Middle Ages built cathedrals and sang dirges. Two pyramids, two masses for the dead are twice as good as one; but not so two railways from London to York.

Here, then, was the gloomy diagnosis of *The General Theory:*

> First, an economy in depression could stay there. There was nothing inherent in the economic mechanism to pull it out. One could have "equilibrium" with unemployment, even massive unemployment.
>
> Second, prosperity depended on investment. If business spending for capital equipment fell, a spiral of contraction would begin. Only if business investment rose would a spiral of expansion follow.
>
> And third, investment was an undependable drive wheel for the economy. Uncertainty, not assurance, lay at the very core of capitalism. Through no fault of the businessman it was constantly threatened with satiety, and satiety spelled economic decline.

Certainly it was an unsettling outlook. But it would have been utterly unlike Keynes to content himself with making a diagnosis of gloom and letting it go at that. With all its prophecy of danger, *The General Theory* was never meant to be a book of doom. On the contrary, it held out a promise and it proposed a cure.

As a matter of fact, the cure had begun before its actual prescription was written; the medicine was being applied before the doctors were precisely sure what it was supposed to do. The Hundred Days of the New Deal had enacted a flood of social legislation that had been backing up for twenty years behind a dam of governmental apathy. These laws were meant to improve the social tone, the morale, of a discontented nation. But it was not social legislation that was designed to revitalize the patient. That tonic was something else: the deliberate undertaking of government spending to stimulate the economy.

It began as makeshift work-relief. Unemployment had reached the point at which some sort of action was dictated by pure political necessity—after all, this was a time when there were riots in Dearborn and a ragged march on Washington, when families huddled for warmth in municipal incinerator buildings and even scrabbled for food in garbage trucks. Relief was essential and began under Hoover; then, under Roosevelt, relief turned into leaf-raking, and leaf-raking turned into constructive enterprise. The government was suddenly a major economic investor: roads, dams, auditoriums, airfields, harbors, and housing projects blossomed forth.

Keynes came to Washington in 1934—this was when he made his notes on the impression of President Roosevelt's hands—and urged that the program be extended further. The statistics showed that the bottom had fallen out of private investment activity: business expansion, which had pumped out $15 billion in wages and salaries and profits in 1929, had fallen to the appalling figure of $886 *million* in 1932—a drop of 94 percent. Something had to start up the investment motor that hoisted the economic car up the shaft, and he hoped that government spending would act as such a stimulus by bolstering the nation's general buying power— "priming the pump," it was called in those days.

Hence when *The General Theory* came out in 1936,

what it offered was not so much a new and radical program as a defense of a course of action that was already being applied. A defense and an explanation. For *The General Theory* pointed out that the catastrophe facing America and, indeed, the whole Western world, was only the consequence of a lack of sufficient investment on the part of business. And so the remedy was perfectly logical: if business was not able to expand, the government must take up the slack.

With his tongue only partly in his cheek Keynes had written:

> If the Treasury were to fill old bottles with bank notes, bury them at suitable depths in disused coal mines which are then filled up to the surface with town rubbish, and leave it to private enterprise on well tried principles of *laissez-faire* to dig the notes up again . . . there need be no more unemployment and with the help of the repercussions, the real income of the community would probably become a good deal larger than it is. It would, indeed, be more sensible to build houses and the like; but if there are practical difficulties in the way of doing this, the above would be better than nothing.

To some it no doubt appeared that many of the more unorthodox government projects were no more sane than Keynes's whimsical proposal. But now, at least, they had a rationale behind them if private enterprise found itself unable to carry forward with a big enough program of investment, then the government must fill in as best it could—the need for stimulation of some sort was so imperative that almost anything was better than nothing.

And if investment could not be directly stimulated, why then, at least consumption could. While investment was the capricious element in the system, consumption provided the great floor of economic activity; hence public works projects were thought to attack the problem with a two-edged sword: by directly helping to sustain the buying power of the otherwise unemployed, and by leading the way for a resumption of private business expansion.

Keynes himself in a letter to *The New York Times* in 1934 wrote, "I see the problem of recovery in the following light: How soon will normal business enterprise come to the rescue? On what scale, by which expedients, and for how long is abnormal government expenditure advisable in the meantime?"

Note "abnormal." Keynes did not see the government program as a permanent interference with the course of business. He saw it as lending a helping hand to a system that had slipped and was struggling to regain its balance.

It seemed the essence of common sense; in fact it *was* the essence of common sense. And yet the pump-priming program never brought the results that the planners had hoped for. Total government spending, which had hovered at the $10-billion level from 1929 until 1933, rose to $12 billion, to $13 billion, then to $15 billion by 1936. Private investment picked itself up from the floor and recovered two-thirds of its loss: private firms invested $10 billion by 1936. The national income and national consumption rose by 50 percent after three years of government injections. And yet unemployment lingered on; it was manageable now, but there were still at least 9 million out of work—hardly the mark of a new economic era.

There were two reasons why the cure did not work better. First, the program of government spending was never carried out to the full extent that would have been necessary to bring the economy up to full employment. Later, in the Second World War, government spending rose to the then monumental figure of $103 billion: this brought not only full employment, but inflation. But within the framework of a peacetime economy in the thirties, such all-out spending was quite impossible; indeed, even a modest program of government expenditure soon brought murmurs that federal power was overstepping its traditional bounds. To make matters worse, the Federal Reserve Board was more afraid of inflation (at the bottom of a depression!) than of unemployment, so that policies were established that *discouraged* bank lending.

The second reason was closely allied with the first. Neither Keynes nor the government spenders had taken into account that the beneficiaries of the new medicine might consider it worse than the disease. Government spending was *meant* as a helping hand for business. It was *interpreted* by business as a threatening gesture.

Nor is this surprising. The New Deal had swept in on a wave of antibusiness sentiment; values and standards that had become virtually sacrosanct were suddenly held up to skeptical scrutiny and criticism. The whole conception of "business rights," "property rights," and "the role of government" was rudely shaken; within a few years business was asked to forget its traditions of unquestioned preeminence and to adopt a new philosophy of cooperation with labor unions, acceptance of new rules and regulations, reform of many of its practices. Little wonder that it regarded the government in Washington as inimical, biased, and downright radical. And no wonder, in such an atmosphere, that its eagerness to undertake large-scale investment was dampened by the uneasiness it felt in this unfamiliar climate.

Hence every effort of the government to undertake a program of sufficient magnitude to mop up all the unemployed—probably a program at least twice as large as it did in fact undertake—was assailed as further evidence of Socialist design. And at the same time, the halfway measures the government did employ were just enough to frighten business away from undertaking a full-scale effort by itself. It was a situation not unlike that found in medicine; the medicine cured the patient of one illness, only to weaken him with its side effects. Government spending never truly cured the economy—not because it was economically unsound, but because it was ideologically upsetting.

It was not meant to be upsetting; it was a policy born of desperation rather than design. Had the government not begun to open the valve of public spending, in all likelihood private business would eventually again have led the way: it always had done so in the past, and despite the severity of the Great Depression, it would in time unquestionably have found new avenues of adventure. But it was impossible to wait. The American people had waited for four long years, and they were in no mood to wait much longer. Economists began to speak of *stagnation* as the chronic condition of capitalism. The voice of Marx rang louder than it ever had rung in the past; many pointed to the unemployed as prima facie evidence that Marx was right. The mumble of Veblen was discernible in the faddish vogue of the technocrats, who wanted to call out not the proletariat but the engineers. And there was the still more chilling voice that never wearied of pointing out that Hitler and Mussolini knew what to do with *their* unemployed. In this welter of remedies and advocacy of desperate action, the message of *The General Theory*, the civilized voice of Keynes, was certainly moderate and reassuring.

For while Keynes espoused a policy of managing capitalism, he was no opponent of private enterprise. "It is better that a man should tyrannize over his bank-balance than over his fellow citizens," he had written in *The General Theory*, and he went on to state that if the government would only concern itself with providing enough public investment, the working of the vast bulk of the economy could and should be left to private initiative. In review, *The General Theory* was not a radical solution; it was, rather, an explanation of why an inescapable remedy should work. If an economy in the doldrums could drift indefinitely, the price of government inaction might be graver by far than the consequences of bold unorthodoxy.

The real question was a moral, not an economic one. During the Second World War, Professor Hayek wrote a book, *The Road to Serfdom*, which, for all its exaggerations, contained a deeply felt and cogent indictment of the overplanned economy. Keynes sympathized with and liked the book. But while praising it, he wrote to Hayek:

> I should . . . conclude rather differently. I should say that what we want is not no planning, or even less planning, indeed I should say we almost certainly want more. But the planning should take place in a community in which as many people as possible, both leaders and followers, wholly share your own moral position. Moderate planning will be safe enough if those carrying it out are

rightly oriented in their own minds and hearts to the moral issue. This is in fact already true of some of them. But the curse is that there is also an important section who could be said to want planning not in order to enjoy its fruits, but because morally they hold ideas exactly the opposite of yours, and wish to serve not God but the devil.

Is this perhaps a naïve hope? Can capitalism be managed—in the sense that government planners will turn the faucet of spending on and *off* in such a way as to supplement, but never to displace, private investment? The issue is still with us; still unresolved.

But we will postpone discussion of it to the coming chapter. For here we are dealing with the man Keynes and his beliefs, however misguided we may judge them to be. And it would be a grave error in judgment to place this man, whose aim was to rescue capitalism, in the camp of those who wanted to submerge it. True, he urged the "socialization" of investment, although he was never very clear about what that meant; but if he sacrificed the part, it was to save the whole.

For at heart he was a conservative—long an admirer of Edmund Burke and of the tradition of limited government for which Burke stood. "How can I accept the [Communistic] doctrine," he had written in 1931—when the view was by no means shared by many others—"which sets up as its bible, above and beyond criticism, an obsolete textbook which I know not only to be scientifically erroneous but without interest or application to the modern world? How can I adopt a creed which, preferring the mud to the fish, exalts the boorish proletariat above the bourgeoisie and the intelligentsia, who with all their faults, are the quality of life and surely carry the seeds of all human achievement?"

One might quibble with Keynes's theories, with his diagnosis, and with his cure—although, in justice, it must be said that no more thoughtful theory, no profounder diagnosis, and no more convincing cure was propounded by those who insisted that Keynes was only a mischievous meddler with a system that worked well enough. But no one could gainsay his aim: the creation of a capitalist economy in which unemployment—the greatest and gravest threat to its continuance—would be largely eliminated.

He was a man incapable of doing only one thing at a time. While he was constructing *The General Theory* in his mind, he was building a theater in Cambridge with his pocketbook. It was a typically Keynesian venture. Starting at a loss, the theater was in the black in two years, and its artistic success was immense. Keynes was everywhere at the same time: financial backer, ticket taker (on one occasion when the clerk failed to materialize), husband of the leading lady (Lydia acted in Shakespeare, with extremely good notices), even concessionaire. He attached a restaurant to the theater and jealously watched its receipts, graphing them against different types of entertainment to ascertain how food consumption varied with the state of one's humor. There was a bar, too, where champagne was sold at a specially low discount to promote its wider consumption. It was probably the most pleasant interlude in his pleasant life.

But it did not go on for long. In 1937 his success story was cut short; he suffered a heart attack and was forced into idleness. Well—comparative idleness. He continued to do an active trading business and to edit the *Economic Journal* and to write a few brilliant articles in defense of *The General Theory*. One academician had said, upon its appearance, "Einstein has actually done for Physics what Mr. Keynes believes himself to have done for Economics," and Keynes was not a man to let someone get away with *that*. When he wanted to, he could wield an acid pen, and he now set to work systematically to demolish his critics, singly and en masse; sometimes with sarcasm, occasionally with brilliance, and not infrequently with petulance: "Mr. X *refuses* to understand me," seemed to rise like a sigh of despair from many of his brief communications.

But the war was approaching; Munich was followed by worse. Keynes watched in indignation the pusillanimous letters of some Left-Wingers to the *New Statesman and Nation,* on whose board he managed to find time to serve. He wrote to its columns: "Surely it is impossible to believe that there can really be such a person as 'A Socialist'! I disbelieve in his existence," and then, "When it comes to a showdown, scarce four weeks have passed before they remember that they are pacifists and write defeatist letters to your columns, leaving the defence of freedom and civilization to Colonel Blimp and the Old School Tie, for whom Three Cheers."

When the war came, Keynes was too ill to be a permanent member of the government. They gave him a room in the Treasury and picked his brains. He had already written another book, *How to Pay for the War,* a daring plan that urged "deferred savings" as the principal means of financing the war. The plan was simple—a portion of every wage earner's pay would automatically be invested in government bonds that would not be available for redemption until after the war. Then, just when consumer buying would again be needed, the savings certificates could be cashed.

Compulsory saving—what a change from his earlier efforts to achieve a kind of compulsory investment! But the change was in the times and not in Keynes's thinking. The old problem had been too little investment, and its symptom had been unemployment. The new problem was too much investment—an all-out armament effort—and its symptom was inflation. But the framework of *The General Theory* was as useful in understanding inflation as it had been in understanding inflation's opposite—unemployment. Only it was upside down. Now more and more incomes were being handed out with each turn of the wheel, instead of less and less. Accordingly, the cure was the opposite of the depression tonic. Then Keynes had urged that investment be bolstered by every possible means; now he urged that savings must be increased.

The point is important because many have mistakenly judged Keynes as an economist who favored inflation. He did favor "reflation" (a pumping-up of incomes and not prices) from the depths of the depression. But to think that he favored inflation for inflation's sake was to disregard such a passage as this from *The Economic Consequences of the Peace:*

Lenin is said to have declared that the best way to destroy the Capitalist System was to debauch the currency. By a continuing process of inflation, governments can confiscate, secretly and unobserved, an important part of the wealth of their citizens. By this method they not only confiscate, but they confiscate *arbitrarily*. . . . Lenin was certainly right. There is no subtler, no surer means of overturning the existing basis of society than to debauch the currency. The process engages all the hidden forces of economic law on the side of destruction, and does it in a manner which not one man in a million is able to diagnose.

But despite its logic and its appeal—Keynes made much of the fact that his deferred-savings plan would serve to widen the distribution of wealth by making everyone an owner of government bonds—the plan failed to arouse much support. It was too new; the old methods of taxation and rationing and voluntary-savings drives were tried and trusty weapons of war finance. A deferred-credit scheme was tacked on as an ornamental flourish, but it was never given the central place Keynes had envisaged for it.

But he had no time to lament its cool reception; he was now fully embroiled in the British war effort. In 1941 he flew via Lisbon to the United States. It was to be the first of six such trips; Lydia went with him as his nurse and guardian. Ever since his first heart attack she had assumed the role of timekeeper for her indefatigable husband, and many a dignitary had been politely but firmly ushered out at the expiration of his allotted stay. "Time, gentlemen," said Lydia, and business stopped.

His trips to the United States involved the precarious problems of Britain's war finance and the overhanging question of what was to happen in the terrible postwar interim. Britain was not the only one concerned; the United States, as well, wanted to lay the foundation for a flow of international trade that would avoid the desperate financial warfare that had too often led to actual warfare. An International Bank and an International Monetary Fund were to be established to act as guardians of the international flow of money; in place of the old dog-eat-dog world where each nation sought to undercut everyone else, there would be a new cooperative effort to help out a nation that found itself in monetary difficulties.

The final conference was held at Bretton Woods, New Hampshire. Keynes, despite his illness and fatigue, clearly dominated the conference; not when it came to winning all his points, for the final plan was far closer to the American proposals than to the British, but by virtue of his personality. One of the delegates gives us an insight into the man in this entry in his journal:

> This evening, I participated in a particularly *recherché* celebration. Today is the 500th anniversary of the Concordat between King's College, Cambridge, and New College, Oxford, and to commemorate the occasion, Keynes gave a small banquet in his room. . . . Keynes, who had been looking forward to the event for weeks as excitedly as a schoolboy, was at his most charming. He delivered an exquisite allocution. . . . It was an interesting example of the curiously complex nature of this extraordinary man. So radical in outlook in matters purely intellectual, in matters of culture he is a true Burkean conservative. It was all very pianissimo, as befitting the occasion, but his emotion when he spoke of our debt to the past was truly moving.

When Keynes made his final speech at the conclusion of the conference—"If we can continue in a larger task, as we have begun in this limited task, there is hope for the world"—the delegates rose and cheered him.

As always, his major efforts did not preclude a few minor ones. He was made a Director of the Bank of England ("Which will make an honest woman of the other is anyone's guess," he had declared) and chairman of a new government committee that concerned itself with music and the arts. Thus, while he was carrying the weight of presenting Britain's point of view to an international economic council, he was also keeping up a stream of correspondence on music travelers, the Vic-Wells Ballet, poetry reading, and library exhibits. And of course he kept on collecting; he scooped the Folger Library on a rare volume of Spenser and explained a little guiltily to the librarian that he had used the Foreign Office bag to have the catalogue sent over to him.

And the honors started to pour in. He was elevated to the peerage: he was now Lord Keynes, Baron of Tilton, an estate he had bought in middle life only to discover to his delight that one of the branches of the Keynes line had once owned these lands. There were honorary degrees to be accepted at Edinburgh, at the Sorbonne, and from his own university. There was an appointment to the Board of Trustees of the National Gallery. And still there was work: the first loan to Britain had to be negotiated, and Keynes, of course, was given the task of presenting Britain's viewpoint. When he returned from that trip and a reporter asked him if it were true that England was now to be the forty-ninth state, Keynes's reply was succinct: "No such luck."

In 1946 the ordeal was over. He went back to Sussex to read and relax and prepare for a resumption of teaching at Cambridge. One morning there was a fit of coughing; Lydia flew to his side; he was dead.

The services were held in Westminster Abbey. His father, John Neville Keynes, aged ninety-three, and his mother, Florence, walked up the aisle. The country mourned the loss of a great leader, gone just at a time when his acumen and wisdom were most needed; as the *Times* said in a lengthy obituary on April 22, "By his death the country has lost a great Englishman."

He was not an angel by any means. This most sparkling of the great economists was only a human being, albeit a remarkable one, with all the faults and foibles of any person. He could win twenty-two pounds from two countesses and a duke at bridge and crow delightedly; he could also undertip a bootblack in Algiers and refuse to rectify his error, saying, of all things, "I will not be a party to debasing the currency." He could be extraordinarily kind to a slow-thinking student (economists, he said, should be humble, like dentists) and obnoxiously cutting to a businessman or high official to whom he happened to take an intuitive dislike. Sir Harry Goschen, the chairman of the National Provincial Bank, once rubbed Keynes wrong by urging that "we let matters take their natural course." Keynes replied, "Is it more appropriate to smile or rage at these artless sentiments? Best of all, perhaps, just to let Sir Harry take *his* natural course."

Keynes himself gave the clue to his own genius—although he was not at the time writing about himself. Discussing his old teacher Alfred Marshall (whom he both loved and rather lovingly derided as "an absurd old man"), Keynes spelled out the qualifications for an economist:

> The study of economics does not seem to require any specialized gifts of an unusually high order. Is it not, intellectually regarded, a very easy subject compared with the higher branches of philosophy or pure science? An easy subject, at which very few excel! The paradox finds its explanation, perhaps, in that the master-economist must possess a rare *combination* of gifts. He must be mathematician, historian, statesman, philosopher—in some degree. He must understand symbols and speak in words. He must contemplate the particular in terms of the general, and touch abstract and concrete in the same flight of thought. He must study the present in the light of the past for the purposes of the future. No part of man's nature or his institutions must lie entirely outside his regard. He must be purposeful and disinterested in a simultaneous mood; as aloof and incorruptible as an artist, yet sometimes as near the earth as a politician.

Marshall—as Keynes says—only approximated that ideal, for, Victorian that he was, he lacked the necessary iconoclasm to give his economics deep social penetration. Keynes came closer: the Bloomsbury attitude of "nothing sacred" spilled over into the sacred precincts of economic orthodoxy; once again the world was put into focus by a man not so blind as to fail to see its sickness, and not so emotionally and intellectually dispossessed as to wish not to cure it. If he was an economic sophisticate, he was politically devout, and it is this combination of an engineering mind and a hopeful heart that his vision reveals.

And what of his analysis? There lies a more complex tale. "Keynesian" economics dominated the field in the United States from 1940 until the 1960s. Then began a slipping away, until by 1980, in the words of Alan Blinder, a staunch supporter, "It was hard to find an American economist under the age of forty who professed to be a Keynesian."

What was the cause of this dramatic shift? In part it was a failure to find a satisfactory way of reconciling Keynes's "macro" view of the economy, dominated by massive flows of expenditure often determined by the unpredictable "animal spirits" of investors, with the Marshallian "micro" view that emphasized the centrality of individual markets ruled by the rational considerations of buyers and sellers. From another angle, Keynesianism was weakened by a resurgence of interest in inflation-related questions of money. From yet other quarters came a growing disenchantment with the activist role of government explicit in Keynes, and a return to a belief in individual behavior as a steering as well as driving force that could not be outwitted by Keynesian policies.

Thus Keynesianism withered—but it did not die. Instead, beginning in the 1980s we entered a new period of economic thought in which there was no clear agreement as to how to perceive the economy. The result was—and as of this writing, still is—a crisis of vision, with its inescapable correlate, an absence of any clear-cut analytic prescription. Curiously—perhaps significantly—this hiatus affected the United States, and to some extent Great Britain, much more than Europe. European economists had never been devotees of Marshall and they kept a certain distance from Keynes. Instead there arose in Scandinavia, Germany, the Netherlands, and France a kind of pragmatic fusion of micro and macro. Its vision could perhaps be summed up in the conception of capitalism as the only workable system at hand, but one that could not function satisfactorily without a strong government presence aware of both the needs to compete in an ever more globalized world, and of the necessity to provide generous programs of both welfare and education for those who were casualties of that process. The outcome is a very pragmatic "worldly" philosophy, for which our country has yet to find a workable counterpart. This is a matter to which we will return before we are done.

X

The Contradictions of Joseph Schumpeter

In 1930, while most people were occupied with the darkening depression, Keynes was toying with an idea of a very different hue. In disregard of his own dictum that in the long run we are all dead, he had just taken a glimpse into the future—the long-term future—and he had come up with a prophecy quite in contrast with the contemporary rumblings of stagnation. For what Keynes saw ahead, barring such catastrophes as an uncontrollable flood of population or a totally destructive war, was not a continuation of the current state of misery and doubt, but a prospect so fair as to be almost unbelievable—nothing less than Adam Smith's heralded land of universal plenty.

Keynes called his little excursion into the future *Economic Possibilities for Our Grandchildren* (of whom, it might be added, he himself had none). And what were these possibilities? Well, not to wax too lyrical, they hinted at something like a modest millennium: by the year 2030, Keynes thought, the economic problem might be solved—not just the immediate crimp of depression, but the economic problem itself, the age-old fact of Not Enough to Go Around. For the first time in history, mankind—British mankind, at any rate—would have emerged from a struggle against want into a new milieu in which everybody could with ease be given a generous helping at the communal table.

It was a typically Keynesian thrust in an unexpected direction. After the First World War, when the world was basking in a glow of self-congratulation, it was Keynes who had rattled the skeleton in the closet; now in the thirties, when the world turned to self-commiseration, it was the same Keynes who bravely talked of an impending end to its travail. But he was not merely whistling in the dark. On the contrary, he was only taking up a strand of economics which had absorbed all the master planners of the past—the tendency of capitalism to grow.

In times of depression that tendency was apt to be overlooked. And yet, looking backward over two hundred years of capitalism, it was not merely a meaningless succession of exhilarating booms and frustrating busts that·characterized the system, but a steady, albeit highly irregular, upward climb. The forty million Englishmen of Keynes's day most certainly did not consider themselves the benefactors of a bountiful providence, but, for all the hardship of the times, they unquestionably enjoyed a far better seat at Nature's table than the ten million Englishmen of Malthus's time.

It was not that Nature herself had become more generous. On the contrary, as the famous Law of Diminishing Returns made clear, Nature yielded up her wealth more grudgingly as she was more intensively cultivated. The secret to economic growth lay in the fact that each generation attacked·Nature not only with its own energies and resources, but with the heritage of equipment accumulated by its forebears. And as that heritage grew—as each generation added its quota of new knowledge, factories, tools, and techniques to the wealth of the past—human productivity increased with astonishing rapidity. A factory worker in the 1960s in the United States worked with technological powers that made him a Superman compared with his post–Civil War grandfather. If only this process of steadily enhancing productivity would continue for another century—a mere three generations—then capitalism would have done the trick. For another hundred years of amassing wealth, Keynes calculated, at the same pace as the last hundred years, would multiply England's real productive wealth by *seven and one-half* times. By the year 2030, every worker would have at his elbow enough machinery to make *him* a Superman in terms of his grandfather who lived in 1930.

And such a vast increase in productiveness could make all the difference. It could relegate economics as a science of scarcity to the history books. The new problem of society would be not how to find leisure, but how to cope with unprecedented quantities of it. With a grin Keynes quoted the traditional epitaph of the old charwoman:

> Don't mourn for me, friends, don't weep for me never,
> For I'm going to do nothing for ever and ever.
> With psalms and sweet music the heavens'll be ringing,
> But I shall have nothing to do with the singing.

It was, of course, only a theoretical jaunt into the future and no one took it very seriously. The machinery was clanking too alarmingly in 1930 for anyone to regard such a prospectus as much more than a pleasant fantasy, and Keynes himself soon lost sight of it in the immediate problem of analyzing the nature of the unemployment that was paralyzing the world.

But wishful or sober, Keynes's vista is important for us. For with *Economic Possibilities for Our Grandchildren* we are for the first time confronted with the question of our own futures. Everything we have considered heretofore is, after all, only history. The evolution of the regulated and codified world of the seventeenth century into the atomistic market capitalism described by Adam Smith; the near escape of that capitalism from the landlord-dominated economy anticipated by Ricardo or the overpopulated subsistence society feared by Malthus; its presumptive self-destruction forecast by Marx; its chronic depressive tendency dissected by Keynes—all these adventures and misadventures of capitalism, however interesting, nevertheless lacked a certain element of suspense. For we knew at each juncture of history what the outcome would finally be. Now we are placed in a more uncomfortable position. As we turn to the modern economists, we are no longer discussing the ideas that helped shape our past: it is our own society, our own fate, our children's inheritance that lie in the balance.

And so we must turn from a study of our past to an appraisal of the future. Where does capitalism stand today? What signposts point to the years ahead? These are the great questions of the modern world, to which we must now bend our attention.

Thus we move to a worldly philosopher who, perhaps even more than Keynes, speaks to us with a voice that is unmistakably contemporary. The voice belongs to a small, dark, aristocratic man with a taste for portentous prose and theatrical gestures. When he lectured on the economy at Harvard in the midst of the depression, Joseph Schumpeter strode into the lecture hall, and divesting himself of his European cloak, announced to the startled class in his Viennese accent, "Chentlemen, you are vorried about the depression. You should not be. For capitalism, a depression is a good cold *douche*." Having been one of those startled listeners, I can testify that the great majority of us did not know that a *douche* was a shower, but we did grasp that this was a very strange and certainly un-Keynesian message.

Schumpeter himself would have been the first to emphasize that his view of economic life was at odds with that of Keynes. The two men shared many social views—above all their admiration for cultivated bourgeois life and their belief in the general values of capitalism—and yet came out with diametrically differing views as to the future. For Keynes, as we have seen, capitalism was intrinsically threatened with the possibility of stagnation; the optimistic outlook for our grandchildren really hinged on appropriate government support. For Schumpeter, capitalism was intrinsically dynamic and growth-oriented; he saw no need for government spending as a permanent auxiliary engine, although he agreed that it might be used to alleviate social distress when a depression occurred.

Yet, for all his faith in the inherent buoyancy of capitalism, Schumpeter's long-term outlook was the very opposite of Keynes's. In his almost perversely teasing way he first maintained that in the "short run" capitalism would indeed trace a long climbing trajectory, adding that "in these things, a century is a 'short run.' " But then came the disconcerting final judgment: "Can capitalism survive? No. I do not think it can." We shall have to learn more about this curiously contradictory man.

Joseph Alois Schumpeter was born in Austria in 1883— the same year as Keynes's birth—of solid but undistinguished stock. His father died when he was four; seven years later his mother married a distinguished general and young Schumpeter was sent to the Theresianum, an exclusive school for the sons of the aristocracy. The exposure of the youngster to an entirely different stratum of society was, by general account, of decisive importance in shaping his outlook. Schumpeter soon adopted the manners and tastes of his schoolmates, acquiring aristocratic airs that clung to him all his life. He irritated his colleagues at more than one university by appearing in faculty meetings in riding habit, and he liked to maintain that he had always had three wishes—to be a great lover, a great horseman, and a great economist—but that, alas, life had granted him only two of the three. For all the aristocratic airs, however, we shall see that in the end Schumpeter awards the laurel of history to another group. But that is a twist to the story that will have to wait until the end of this chapter.

He entered the University of Vienna, a great center of economic learning at the time, and was immediately a star student—"never a beginner," in the opinion of the famous economist Arthur Spiethof—but also immediately an enfant terrible, risking his fate by disagreeing openly with his even more famous teacher, Eugen von Bohm-Bauwerk. After Vienna there was a sojourn in England that led to a brief and unhappy marriage, and then a lucrative position as financial adviser to a princess in Egypt. There Schumpeter performed the miracle of cutting in half the rents on the princess's estates while doubling her income—simply by taking no more for his personal income than he was legally entitled to. More important, while in Egypt he published his first book on the nature of economic theorizing, a book that landed him a professorship in Austria, and three years later, at age twenty-seven, he published *The Theory of Economic Development,* instantly recognized as a small masterpiece.

The Theory of Economic Development sounds like an analysis of what we have come to call the underdeveloped world. But in 1912 the special economic status and problems of that "world" had not yet come into existence—this was still the age of unabashed colonialism. Schumpeter's book was about another kind of development—the way in which capitalism develops its propensities for growth. Scholarly in tone and tedious in style (although lit from time to time with lightning flashes), the book would not strike the casual reader as being of much political importance. Yet this academic treatise was destined to become the basis for one of the most influential interpretations of capitalism ever written.

The exposition begins in Schumpeter's contradictory way. It is a book about capitalist growth and dynamics, but it opens with a depiction of a capitalist economy in which growth is totally absent. Schumpeter's initial portrait describes a capitalism that lacks the very ingredient that brought growth into the worlds of Smith and Mill and Marx and Keynes—namely, the accumulation of capital. Schumpeter describes instead a capitalism sans accumulation—a capitalism whose flow of production is perfectly static and changeless, reproducing itself in a "circular flow" that never alters or expands its creation of wealth.

The model resembles the stationary state envisaged by Ricardo and Mill, with the difference that the stationary state seemed the end of capitalism to the earlier writers, whereas for Schumpeter it was the setting for the beginning of capitalism. Therefore we must examine the characteristics of the circular flow a little more carefully. Because the system has no momentum, inertia is the rule of its economic life: "All knowledge and habit, once acquired," writes Schumpeter, "becomes as firmly rooted in ourselves as a railway embankment in the earth." Thus having found by trial and error the economic course that is most advantageous for ourselves, we repeat it by routine. Economic life may have originally been a challenge; it becomes a habit.

More important, in this changeless flow competition will have removed all earnings that exceed the value of anyone's contribution to output. This means that competition among employers will force them to pay their workers the full value of the product they create, and that owners of land or other natural wealth will likewise receive as rents whatever value their resources contribute. So workers and landowners will get their shares in the circular flow. And capitalists? Another surprise. Capitalists will receive nothing, except their wages as management. That is because any contribution to the value of output that was derived from capital goods they owned would be entirely absorbed by the value of the labor that went into making those goods plus the value of the resources they contained. Thus, exactly as Ricardo or Mill foresaw, *in a static economy there is no place for profit!*

Why does Schumpeter present us with such a strange— not to say strained—image of the system? Perhaps we have already divined the purpose behind his method: the model of a static capitalism is an attempt to answer the question of where profits come from.

The source of profits is a question that has been gingerly handled by most economists. Smith wavered between viewing profit as a deduction from the value created by labor and as a kind of independent return located in capital itself. If profits *were* a deduction, of course, the explanation implied that labor was shortchanged; and if they were a contribution of capital, one would have to explain why the profits went to the *owner* of the machine, not to its inventor or user. Mill suggested that profits were the reward for the "abstinence" of capitalists, but he did not explain why capitalists were entitled to a reward for an activity that was clearly in their own interest. Still other economists described profits as the earnings of "capital," speaking as if the shovel itself were paid for its contribution to output. Marx, of course, said that Smith was right in the first place though he didn't know it—that profits *were* a deduction from the actual value created by the workingman. But that was part of the labor theory of value which everyone knew to be wrong and therefore did not have to be reckoned with.

Schumpeter now came forward with a brilliant answer to this vexing question. Profits, he said, did not arise from the exploitation of labor or from the earnings of capital. They were the result of quite another process. Profits appeared in a static economy when the circular flow failed to follow its routinized course.

Now we can see why the wildly unrealistic circular flow is so brilliant a starting point. For of all the forces leading to disruptions in routine, one stands out. This is the introduction of technological or organizational innovations into the circular flow—new or cheaper ways of making things, or ways of making wholly new things. *As a result of these innovations a flow of income arises that cannot be traced either to the contribution of labor or of resource owners.* A new process enables an innovating capitalist to produce the same goods as his competitors, but at a cheaper cost, exactly as a favorably located piece of land enables its owner to produce crops more cheaply than less well-situated fellow landlords. Again, exactly like the fortunate landlord, the innovating capitalist now receives a "rent" from the differential in his cost. But this rent is not derived from God-given advantages in location or fertility. It springs from the will and intelligence of the innovator, and it will disappear as soon as other capitalists learn the tricks of the pioneer. The new flow is not therefore a more or less permanent rent. It is a wholly transient profit.

An innovation implies an innovator—someone who is responsible for combining the factors of production in new ways. This is obviously not a "normal" businessman, following established routines. The person who introduces change into economic life is a representative of another class—or more accurately, another group, because innovators do not necessarily come from any social class. Schumpeter took an old word from the economic lexicon and used it to describe these revolutionists of production. He called them *entrepreneurs*. Entrepreneurs and their innovating activity were thus the source of profit in the capitalist system.

• •

There is much more to *The Theory of Economic Development* than a paean to the entrepreneur. From Schumpeter's analysis of the impact of innovations on the circular flow there emerges not only a theory of the origin of profits, but of interest and credit, and beyond that an explanation of the business cycle. Innovations were usually the work of pioneers, said Schumpeter, but whereas leadership is rare and difficult, followership is easy. On the heels of the innovator comes a swarm—the word is Schumpeter's—of imitators. The original improvement is thereby generalized throughout the industry, and a rash of bank borrowing and investment spending gives rise to a boom. But the very generalization of the innovation removes its differential advantage. Competition forces prices down to the new cost of production; profits disappear as routine takes over. As profits decline, so does investment. Indeed, contraction may set in as some of the swarm turns out to have made ill-timed or ill-engineered investments.

We will come back to Schumpeter's explanation of the cycle, but right now it is his emphasis on the functions of the entrepreneur that interests us. Note that the entrepreneur is not himself necessarily a profit receiver, even though he is *the* profit generator. Profits go to the owner of the enterprise, just as rent goes to the owner of land. Even more than Ricardo's capitalist, Schumpeter's entrepreneur is squeezed out of his share of income by the very dynamics of the process that he has set in motion.

Moreover, entrepreneurship is not a profession, or a position that can be handed down from one generation to the next. It is a special kind of leadership—not the glamorous kind that creates generals or statesmen, but a much less socially esteemed talent for perceiving and seizing business advantage.

> We shall understand, therefore, [Schumpeter writes] that we do not observe [in the entrepreneur's position] the emergence of all those affective traits which are the glory of all other kinds of social leadership. Add to this

the precariousness of the economic position both of the individual entrepreneur and of the group, and the fact that when his economic success raises him up socially he has no cultural tradition or attitude to fall back on, but moves about in society as an upstart, whose ways are readily laughed at, and we shall understand why this type has never been popular . . .

Why, then, does the entrepreneur carry out his precarious, often thankless task? "First," says Schumpeter, "there is the dream and the will to found a private kingdom, usually, although not necessarily, also a dynasty. . . . Then there is the will to conquer: the impulse to fight, to prove oneself superior to others, to succeed for the sake, not of the fruits of success, but of success itself. . . . Finally, there is the joy of creating, of getting things done, or simply of exercising one's energy and imagination."

It is a strange portrait, a mixture of someone driven by the instinct of workmanship celebrated by Veblen and by the predatory drive he so despised. Certainly there is nothing of the desire for public esteem that motivates Smith's accumulating capitalist, and none of the complicated pressures that force Marx's magnates to expand their capital. Schumpeter's entrepreneur is closer to a romantic figure, a kind of knight errant of the system. Not himself a bourgeois by necessity, the entrepreneur aspires to become one, and by seeking to realize his aspiration, breathes life into a society that would otherwise be as tame as the God-fearing merchantdom in Thomas Mann's *Buddenbrooks*. Moreover, as we shall later see, the entrepreneur plays a role that has even larger implications than those that Schumpeter himself explicitly spelled out. But that too will have to await the final explication of Schumpeter's vision.

The Theory of Economic Development launched Schumpeter on an academic career that was to be interrupted only briefly just after the First World War by a foray into government and business. In 1919 he agreed to join a commission on the nationalization of industry established by the new so-

cialist German government. A young economist asked him
how someone who had so extolled enterprise could take part
in a commission whose aim was to nationalize it. "If somebody wants to commit suicide," Schumpeter replied, "it is
a good thing if a doctor is present." In that same year he
was asked to become finance minister in the newly formed
center-socialist government of Austria. He worked out an
ambitious plan to stabilize the Austrian currency, but con-
flicts and disagreements forced his resignation before the
plan could be approved. It would probably have failed—
nothing could have arrested the inflationary juggernaut gathering momentum at that time. There followed a brief stint as
president of the Biedermann bank, a private bank in Vienna,
but that was pulled down by the storm (as well as by the dishonesty of some of his associates). When the bank went
under, its new president found himself personally in considerable debt. It is characteristic of the would-be aristocrat that
he paid his creditors in full rather than hiding behind the
bankruptcy laws, although it cost him his capital, and that he
continued to pay his debts from his income over the next ten
years. To add to his personal misfortune, he now married the
charming twenty-one-year-old daughter of the superintendent of his mother's apartment house—with whom he had
been in love for five years, and within a year she died in
childbirth, a loss that further darkened Schumpeter's already
saturnine personality. Because it is so revelatory, a near-
comic story must accompany this genuine tragedy. Schumpeter could not bring himself to tell his friends of Annie's
humble background—when she was away for a year before
their marriage, he explained that she was being properly educated in French and Swiss schools. In fact she was earning
her living in Paris as a maid.

Thereafter, his real career began, first as a visiting professor in Japan, then in Germany, soon thereafter at Harvard,
where his manner and his cloak quickly made him into a
campus figure. It was there also that he married Elizabeth
Boody, herself an economist; and finally, it was there that he
declared the depression to be a good cold douche, a remark
that at least one young student never forgot.

The depression was, in fact, a test of Schumpeter's ideas. If capitalism derived its energy from the innovations of entrepreneurs, why was their stimulus missing in the grim years of the 1930s? Keynes had said that depressions reflected the state of expectations of businessmen, but his theory did not require him to account for the reason *why* their "animal spirits" were low. Schumpeter had a more demanding task because he explained boom and bust by the bunching of innovations and the swarming of businessmen. The endless depression therefore cried out for reasons why the new innovations were failing to arrive on time.

Schumpeter leaned on two explanations in *Business Cycles*, a thousand-page, two-volume work published in 1939. Partly he attributed the severity of the depression to the fact that there were not one but three different kinds of business cycles—one of quite short duration, a second with a rhythm of seven to eleven years, and a third with a vast fifty-year pulse associated with epochal inventions like the steam locomotive or the automobile—and that all three cycles were touching their respective bottoms at the same time. A second reason was the negative impact of external factors, ranging from the Russian Revolution to generally inept government policy. These latter were "outside" the reach of business cycle theory, but they contributed nonetheless to the gravity of the situation.

It was by no means an unintelligent assessment of the crisis, although the phenomenon of swarming as the cause of business cycles was never well established. But Schumpeter's book interests us for quite another reason. It is that capitalism, like any other social system, does not live by bread alone. It requires a faith—in its case, faith in the values and virtues of the civilization that capitalism produces and that in turn reproduces capitalism. *And despite the economic success of the system, this faith was losing its mobilizing force.*

Thus the book ends—once again!—on a contradictory note. Judging purely on an economic basis, capitalism still had a long run for its money; indeed, as Schumpeter says in the next to last sentence, if his schema of three interacting investment cycles was correct, the next three decades ought to be much more buoyant than the last two. Then comes the disconcerting last sentence: "But the sociological drift cannot be expected to change."

We already find hints of the argument in his *Theory of Capitalist Development* and more than hints in *Business Cycles*. But the fully developed vision of the future of capitalism does not emerge until 1942, when Schumpeter published *Capitalism, Socialism and Democracy*, a book that changed the way we think about the system.

The book begins with Marx. Oddly, Schumpeter, who was the most self-involved person, defined his intellectual life not so much for himself as against others. Keynes was his immediate bête noire, for Schumpeter was not only philosophically opposed to the Keynesian vision but personally irked that Keynes attracted the attention and admiration of the whole world, while he had to content himself with the recognition of his academic peers. Rather uncharacteristically, he could never bring himself to award to Keynes the credit that was his due: when the *General Theory* appeared, Schumpeter reviewed it with scrapings and bowings to the master ("one of the most brilliant men who ever bent their energies to economic problems"), but with an unbecoming and, worse, uncomprehending dismissal of the book ("the less said about [it] the better").

But the real antagonist in Schumpeter's intellectual life was not Keynes but Marx. Schumpeter had studied Marx in his student days and had participated in seminar discussions with scholars such as Rudolph Hilferding and Otto Bauer, two of the most brilliant young Marxist scholars of their day. He was more deeply familiar than any Western economist with Marx's work as it was then understood—much of that work did not appear in the Anglo-American world until the 1950s. During his Harvard years he was always ready to discuss Marx with his younger colleagues; indeed he was more open-minded about Marx than about Keynes! So it is little wonder that *Capitalism, Socialism and Democracy* begins with Marx, as the only opponent truly worthy of his steel.

Marx the Prophet, Marx the Sociologist, Marx the Economist, Marx the Teacher: those are the four chapters with which the book starts. Perhaps it is already evident where the two men will agree and disagree. For Marx the very essence of capitalism is dialectical change and self-created disequilibrium. All this is grist for Schumpeter's mill—indeed, Marx's conception of capitalism's immanent development is undoubtedly the source of Schumpeter's view. But Marx places the cause of this dynamism in the struggle between the working class and the owning class—a struggle that continually squeezes out surplus value and thereby motivates all capitalists (not just pioneers) to rescue their profits by labor-saving innovations.

Here is where Schumpeter departs from Marx. He offers another view of the system—one that stresses the "bourgeois" side of capitalism, not its insatiable and rapacious aspects. For Schumpeter this bourgeois component was the cultural expression of the rational, hedonist businessman whom he viewed as the very antithesis of the swashbuckling, glory-minded warrior. "The evolution of the bourgeois style of life," he writes, "could be easily—and perhaps most tellingly—described in terms of the genesis of the lounge suit," a remark worthy of Veblen. Thus, in Schumpeter's view, capitalism does *not* achieve its all-important thrust from its central figure, the bourgeois capitalist, but from an outsider, an interloper—the upstart entrepreneur. Marx or Veblen would have doubted the difference, but it is crucial to Schumpeter's interpretation of the system.

We need not linger over other differences with Marx. Schumpeter may not have an exact measure of his opponent, but it is clear that he has outlined a formidable intellect, who must be met and bested on his own ground. And that is precisely what he sets out to do. For we turn the page after the chapter on Marx the Teacher to read: "Can capitalism survive?" Now the answer comes with a double shock: "No. I do not think it can."

But if capitalism is doomed, it cannot be for the reasons that Marx sets forth. And so we embark on a tour de force description of what Schumpeter calls "plausible capitalism." What is plausible capitalism? It is much like a carefully reasoned scenario of the very prospect that Keynes has already laid before us, a scenario of the possibilities for a century of growth. Here is Schumpeter at his absolute best. The fears of the stagnationists as to vanishing investment opportunities are set aside with an airy wave: the conquest of the air, he said, will be as great as that of India. The worries of other economists about the sclerosis of spreading monopolization are similarly sent flying with a description of capitalist innovation as a "perennial gale of creative destruction" in which the agents for innovatory change are the "monopolies" themselves. The stage is thus set for what appears to be a direct refutation of Marx. Plausible capitalism is a reasoned model of an economic system that is caught up in a process of continuous self-renewing growth.

But now comes the Schumpeterian contradiction: capitalism may be an *economic* success, but it is not a *sociological* success. This is because, as we have already seen, the economic base of capitalism creates its ideological superstructure—rational rather than romantic, critical rather than heroic, designed for men in lounge suits, not armor. In the end it is this capitalist frame of mind, this capitalist *mentality*, that brings down the system:

> Capitalism creates a critical frame of mind which, after having destroyed the moral authority of so many other institutions, in the end turns against its own; the bourgeois finds to his amazement that the rationalist attitude does not stop at the credentials of kings and popes but goes on to attack private property and the whole scheme of bourgeois values.

And so the great entrepreneurial adventure comes to an end, not because the working class has risen up or because the system has finally been unable to master a worsening succession of crises, but simply because the atmosphere has changed. Personality and force of character count for less; bureaucratic management for more. Innovation itself becomes institutionalized and reduced to routine. The bourgeois family, the great transmission belt of capitalist values, becomes infected with the disease of rationalism. The bourgeois class loses faith in itself. Thus, while things are going well at the surface, "there is a tendency toward another civilization that slowly works deep down below."

Once again we turn the page: "Can socialism work? Of course it can." It is a very Schumpeterian kind of socialism, a benign, bureaucratic, planned economy. We will talk about it briefly later. But notice the remarkable thing about Schumpeter's argument. He has beaten Marx on his own ground. He surrenders to Marx in what seems to be the crucial point of contention, namely whether capitalism can survive. But he has bested Marx by demonstrating—or at least arguing—that capitalism will give way to socialism for Schumpeter's reasons, not for Marx's! Marx is accorded every honor, but Schumpeter's view nonetheless carries the day.

Does it? The question is of huge importance, not merely to appraise Schumpeter but because the prognosis affects ourselves as residents of the system about whose fate Schumpeter is writing.

We begin with a sense of dazzled admiration mixed with irritation. Schumpeter cannot resist attitudinizing, whether he is tweaking the noses of good bourgeois conservatives or of Marxist zealots. He uses his book to air a great many pet ideas: Marx is a great conservative (!); monopolies "increase the sphere of influence of the better, and decrease the sphere of influence of the inferior, brains"; the more "completely capitalist" a nation is, the less likely it is to be aggressive—a judgment that will interest students of nineteenth-century British imperialism and twentieth-century American foreign policy.

But these characteristic flourishes must be set in perspective by reflecting on the argument as a whole. Does not that argument have a certain ring of authority? Does not the prospect of an immense unexplored technological frontier, of a drift toward bureaucratization in business as well as government, of a waning of the bourgeois ethic strike us as uncannily prescient? Remember now that the book was published in 1942. As a seer, Schumpeter is without equal in his time, at once putting to shame the heady expectations of the contemporary Left, who thought that capitalism was on the way out, the naïve hopes of the contemporary middle, who believed that a modest application of government spending would fix things up once and for all, and the black forebodings of the Right, who saw us headed down the road to serfdom.

Nonetheless, the Schumpeterian prognosis is an uneven one, less impressive on close examination than at first sight. There is no doubt that Schumpeter was right in foreseeing a wide-open technological future, but he did not foresee that the quality of that technology, from nuclear arms and energy to computerization, might pose considerable dangers for capitalism as well as fields for investment. There is no denying his prescience when he spoke of the impending growth of bureaucracy in big business, but it is by no means correct that the rise of lumbering giants would result in a decline in their aggressive behavior: the spectacle of vast multinationals, contending for shares in world markets, does not accord with Schumpeter's prediction of a dwindling capitalist drive for expansion.

And is it really the case that a kind of ennui, a loss of belief, would overtake the capitalist world? If we were writing in the late 1960s, the prognosis would indeed seem farsighted, for Western capitalism then seemed clearly moving toward a kind of planned economy. Thirty-odd years later, the prognosis is less convincing. Not just in the United States but throughout Europe we have witnessed a revival of belief in capitalism, as the movement toward a more planned system produced first growth, then inflation, finally a loss of faith in the planning process itself, to which the collapse of the Soviet system provided the coup de grace.

Of course, Schumpeter is writing about the long run, and we are criticizing him within the time frame of a short run. The revivalist spirit may well prove to be short-lived, and the drift into a kind of mildly socialistic capitalism may resume. Perhaps the movement into bureaucratization will eventually take priority over the drive for business dominance, and the great multinationals will settle down into a kind of giant cartel, dividing up the world into private economic kingdoms, like the imperialism of a century ago.

These are no more than speculations. But Schumpeter's vision is also a speculation—one kind of plausible capitalism, but not the only kind. His scenario may be brilliantly illumining, but it does not emerge from the preceding development of the system with the same logic as we find in the case of Ricardo or Smith or Marx. *This is because Schumpeter's prognosis is not ultimately an economic one at all.* It is, rather, a set of often shrewd assertions about social and political matters that cannot be predicted with the assurance that enabled Smith or Marx to erect their formidable theories. The disaffected intellectual who plays so large a part in spoiling the outlook for Schumpeter's capitalism cannot be said to obey the same imperative as does the accumulating capitalist or the competitive merchant; the businessman who decides that the game is not worth the candle is bowing to cultural, not economic, pressures. Indeed, is it not Schumpeter's triumphant final conclusion that the processes of economics are not sufficient in themselves to determine how the system goes?

His vision, then, cannot be judged by quite the same criteria as those of the other worldly philosophers. His is not so much an economic prognosis as a social one, a judgment about the direction from which the winds of cultural change would blow. With his aristocratic taste, his aloof scholarly stance, his hard experiences in real politics and enterprise, Schumpeter may have been better placed to pass judgment about the drift of things than Keynes, to whom worldly success came too easily, or Marx, to whom it came not at all. Yet the cutting edge of his insight was gained at the expense of the strict economic logic that gave such power to the visions of the classical seers.

The implications of Schumpeter's thesis are disquieting—not merely for capitalism but for economics. Was not the great achievement of the worldly philosophers their ability to deduce the direction in which society was moving? Is not economics built on the capacity to predict—in the large if not in the small? And does not the Schumpeterian scenario mean that all that is now past—that whatever the predictive capability of economics, it no longer matters? We will turn back to this decisive question in our last chapter. But we are not quite finished with the quixotic figure of Schumpeter himself. There remains that last twist to his story. We shall see that it adds more than just an insight into Schumpeter's biography.

Let us begin by reflecting again on the central contradiction in Schumpeter's depiction of capitalism. It lies in the juxtaposition we find in his Theory of Economic Development—capitalism portrayed as a static, inert, changeless "circular flow" and as a system caught up in a dynamic of change, a dynamic that would later be called the gale of creative destruction. How could Schumpeter have allowed himself to depict the system in such inconsistent terms? What possible sense does it make to speak of a changeless circular flow as representing the quintessence of a system that could also be characterized as a continuous process of self-created transformation?

We know Schumpeter's explanation: the circular flow allows us to appreciate the impact of entrepreneurship—not merely as the driving force within capitalism, but as the source of its unique flow of profit income. But there is another way of interpreting Schumpeter's odd juxtaposition. Schumpeter's entrepreneurs, let us recall, do not come from any particular class—they are simply the possessors of a talent for innovation. Capitalist "development" is not therefore intrinsic to capitalism as such. It is the dynamization of society at the hands of a noncapitalist elite!

There is no doubt that Schumpeter himself was a believer in the importance of "elites" in history—minorities of individuals with unusual gifts. Let us read what he has to say about them in his *Theory of Economic Development*, where he takes the case of musical ability:

We can assume that every healthy man can sing if he will. Perhaps half the individuals in an ethnically homogeneous group have the capacity for it to an average degree, a quarter in a progressively diminishing measure, and let us say, a quarter in a measure above the average; and within this quarter, through a series of continually increasing singing ability and continually diminishing number of people who possess it, we come finally to the Carusos.

As it is with singing ability, so it is with the capacity for leadership, including economic leadership. About a quarter of the population, says Schumpeter, is so deficient in this quality that it is consigned to the most routine aspects of economic life—the clerks and functionaries of the business world. Then comes the next half, the possessors of a normal amount of innovating capacity: here we find "practically all business people," who rely mainly on the comfortable ruts of experience but are capable of adapting themselves to the normal range of daily challenges. From there, we reach the true elite—"people who are a type characterised by supernormal qualities of intellect and will."

So history, as a narrative of change and development, is the story of the impact of elites on the inert mass of society. In different social settings the qualities needed to exercise influence will change—military talent has its place in a feudal society, economic talent in a market society—but the driving force of an elite of one kind or another is always there. Thus the echelon of leaders constitutes a special group. As such it assumes its rightful place at the apex of society. There the leaders may change, but not leadership. "The upper strata of society," Schumpeter writes, "are like hotels which are indeed always full of people, but people who are forever changing."

What we have here is yet another thrust at Marx—directed at the Marxian idea of the revolutionary force of the proletariat. All wrong, says Schumpeter. The proletariat cannot be the force for change because by virtue of its sheer numbers it must mainly lie in the normal range of humankind. Individual proletarians may possess leadership capabilities, but leadership itself can be possessed only by a tiny minority.

Perhaps this is why Schumpeter is so philosophical about the advent of socialism. For who will run the managerial economy that he envisages as the end product of capitalism's decline? It will be the possessers of ability, of course, the bourgeoisie. "Here is a class," he writes, "which, by virtue of the selective process of which it is the result, harbors human material of a supernormal quality and hence it is a national asset which it is rational for any social organization to use." So there is no reason for the managerial class to fear socialism. The skills needed to direct a socialist system are sufficiently like those needed to run an advanced capitalist one that the bourgeois elite will find its natural position at the top.

Is this economics? Not by any of the conventional conceptions. It is better described as historical sociology. It is not classes, but elites, that seize the commanding heights. Economics describes the results in societies that reward skills exercised in the marketplace, rather than on the battlefield or in the pulpit or in the managerial office, but be it one elite or another, it is always the Carusos who run the show.

Thus Schumpeter employs his economic model to flesh out a larger social vision. The word itself, we recall from our early pages, is Schumpeter's. In his magisterial survey of economic thought, on which he was working at his death in 1950, "vision" lies at the center of things. Analysis may be the great glory of economics, but analysis does not spring full-blown from the mind of an economist, any more than Minerva from the brow of Jupiter. There is a "preanalytic" process that precedes our logical scenarios, a process from which we cannot escape, and which is inescapably colored with our innermost values and preferences. "Analytic work," writes Schumpeter, ". . . embodies in the picture of things as we see them, and wherever there is any possible motive for wishing to see them in a given rather than another light, the way in which we see things can hardly be distinguished from the way in which we wish to see them."

It is a brilliant insight, which deserves an illustration of which Schumpeter himself was almost certainly unaware. It is why Marshall, the most careful and thoroughgoing economist, did not anticipate Keynes's discovery of the vital difference between the two flows of consumption and investment. We find the answer in Marshall's *Principles* when he discusses the nature of *consumers' goods,* compared with what he called *producers' goods.* He notes that "a distinction to which some prominence has been given" lies between these two types of output. We hold our breath, for we can see Keynes's crucial insight just around the corner. But no. Marshall calls the distinction, "vague and perhaps of not much practical use." Why? Because his vision of the economy emphasizes the process by which goods are *priced,* not the consequences of production for future growth. Moreover, from this perspective, Marshall is right: there is no fundamental difference between pricing shirts and machines. He does not see the difference between producing one and the other.

Was there ever a more dramatic example of the analytical difference that vision makes? If Marshall's eyes, like Keynes's, had been focused on the path of total output, he would have seen what Keynes saw; but looking, as he was, only at pricing, he missed the Keyensian boat. One suspects he would not have boarded it.

Is economics, then, an analysis of that which we wish to see or cannot help ourselves from seeing, rather than a detached and objective dissection of a world that is unambiguously "there"? We will come back to this question in our next chapter when we try to weigh up the accomplishment of the worldly philosophers—and the prospects for worldly philosophy as a whole.

One last knot remains in the string. We recall the young Schumpeter thrust into the milieu of an aristocratic school in Vienna, where he absorbed the values that were to become so important in his own life. Are we mistaken in seeing those values transferred to his own vision of history in which an elite becomes the central moving force? Certainly this elite is an aristocracy, embodying the belief in the natural superiority of the chosen few that lies at the core of all aristocratic views of society. But notice that the Schumpeterian few are chosen not by blood but by "intellect and will." It is thus an aristocracy *of talent.* This is the elite to which Schumpeter belongs. The drama of history, as Schumpeter envisions it, thereby justifies not only capitalism, but a group—Schumpeter's own group!—as resting on something more durable and worthy than mere name or birth. Thus there is a final congruence between personal experience and historic vision that unravels many contradictions.

This is perhaps not an assessment that Schumpeter himself would have welcomed. But neither would he likely have denied it. He aspired to be a great economist—whether that was the wish that life had denied him is not clear. It is interesting that Schumpeter would never lecture on his own theories despite entreaties from his students and colleagues; one scholar has suggested that it was because he felt that in the last analysis his formulations were inadequate. We do not know whether he aspired to be a great visionary—that he certainly was. As analyst or visionary, everyone interested in economics must come to grips with him, not only because of what he accomplished within the discipline, but because in his very achievements he demonstrated its limitations.

xi

The End of the
Worldly Philosophy?

Our preface warned of a possibly diconcerting finale, which the title of this chapter may seem to confirm. But I would remind my readers that "end" has two meanings: *termination* and *purpose,* a dual significance we must bear in mind as we go on to consider both the future and the usefulness of the subject whose name was so happily given to me many years ago, when I had finished this book and was trying to decide what to call it.

How to begin this demanding task? I think it best to go back to beginnings, by reminding ourselves of what economics is ultimately about. Needless to say, it is not merely a discussion of the figures, forecasts, and government pronouncements that are the stuff of the daily economic news. Neither is it the supply and demand diagrams and equations familiar to every economics student. At its core, economics is an explanation system whose purpose is to enlighten us as to the workings, and therefore to the problems and prospects, of that complex social entity we call the economy.

So far, what we have mainly stressed with respect to these explanatory visions and analyses is their extraordinary variety. To go from the Mercantilist monarch to the Marshallian clerk, or from the Smithian Society of Perfect Liberty to the Veblenian society of business sabotage is to run a gamut that seems to defy any possibility of a unifiying object of study. In this final chapter, however, I suggest we look at this array from another perspective—not so much emphasizing surface differences as searching for a common structural core.

To answer that question we must reflect back on the considerations of Chapter II. These began with a look at how humanity survived the first 99 percent of its presence on earth by relying on traditions that governed its hunting and gathering activities, but we would hardly call these complex rules and taboos "economics." The same can be said for the much more complex and inventive systems that appeared around the fourth and third millennia B.C., in the social orders that built cities, irrigation systems, and great pyramids. As we saw, the material life of humankind was now governed not only by remnants of Tradition but by a powerful new force of Command.

There is, perhaps, no more dramatic epoch than the rise of these societies, but do we need the ideas of "economics" to explain or understand the revolution brought by Command? I think not. Just as an example, price changes have always been a major part of the explanation systems of economics, but there were no prices for the blocks that the Pharoah's workmen cut, and certainly not for the pyramids themselves. Command altered society in spectacular ways; it did not bring about an organization of production and distribution for which we would require a wholly new understanding we could call economics.

What, then, finally set the stage for this new means of comprehending society's workings? As we also saw in Chapter II, it was the slow displacement of medieval tradition and feudal command with a social order that did indeed require a new mode of clarification. The social order would in time be called *capitalism;* its means of organizing material life an *economy,* and its new explanation system *economics.*

I can be brief in describing the changes brought by capitalism. The first was a dependency on the acquisitive drive as the principal means of organizing the production and distribution of society's material needs. I ask the reader only to remember that never before, in any society, had the pursuit of wealth been legitimated, much less celebrated, for everyone. Kings, of course; adventurers, perhaps; the lower classes— never.

Second, capitalism consigned both the guidance of production and its pattern of distribution to the encouragements and discouragements of the market. There was no such process in hunting and gathering or command systems: the provision of the very stuff of life by competitive buying and selling is an arrangement that has no parallel in any other social order.

Third, capitalism is the first society to place its overall guidance under two authorities, one public, one private, each with its powers and its boundaries to power. The public authority—government—wields force and establishes law, but does not set itself up to carry on the everyday tasks of production and distribution. This is largely the prerogative of profit-seeking individuals, who produce what they wish, hire those willing to accept the wages and conditions they offer and let go those who do not, but who cannot themselves dragoon labor power, as did the pyramid builders, or physically punish inefficient workers, as could the feudal lord.

These three historic innovations set the stage for the visions of all the great economists. Their descriptions and prescriptions change as the new economy responds with quickened pace to losing the drag of Tradition and the arbitrariness of Command, but for all the changes from Smith to Keynes and Schumpeter there is no mistaking the social formation that is their common source. The worldly philosophy is the child of capitalism and could not exist without it.

Now, what has all this to do with the two meanings of the title of this chapter—the possible end to, and the ultimate purpose of economics itself? The answer to the first question lies in a far-reaching change that has increasingly become the vision of economists. We see its first appearance in the growing disposition to depict the activities of buying and selling in abstract terms, beginning perhaps with the depictions of pleasure and pain in terms of Edgeworth's Felicific Calculus and the "just wage" of labor in von Thünen's formula, both noted in Chapter VII. By Marshall's time beautiful diagrams decorate many chapters, and Keynes, as we have noted, uses algebra to depict his analytic findings.

Curiously enough, however, it is not the ever-growing presence of mathematics that is the crucial change in the economics of our time. Numbers abound in any social order that relies on modern technology. All industrial systems generate and require a mass of quantitative information that would have been unimaginable before the advent of high-speed production and near instantaneous communication. Today's economies are more interdependent than were the workers in Adam Smith's pin factory, and as this interdependency grows, so do both the quantity of, and the demand for, information on a wholly new scale. Here is where statistics and mathematics enter modern economics. Without them how could one reduce the outputs of millions of establishments to a number called Gross Domestic Product, or compute another number called the Price Level to express the average price of uncountable millions of goods and services? This is not to say that mathematical models reveal how best to act on the information that bombards us: the predictive capability of econometrics—the modern combination of statistics and economic theory—is by no means notable for its accuracy. The point, rather, is that there is no alternative to using mathematics in its various forms to elucidate many of the analytical purposes for which economics exists.

For all its prominence, however, mathematization is not the all-important change with which our chapter is concerned. Mathematics today pervades economics, formalizes it, and becomes its favored mode of expression, but no one actually confuses mathematics with economics. The deeper and, to my mind, more significant change is the increasing appearance of a new concept as the vision—indeed, the essence—of economics, and the corresponding disappearance of another much older one. The new vision is Science; the disappearing one, Capitalism.

Let me give greater specificity to this charge by citing from two recent textbooks. *Principles of Economics* by N. Gregory Mankiw and *Economics* by Joseph Stiglitz. Both authors enjoy the highest professional esteem, and have written texts that are models of clarity, intelligence, and accessibility. Let us now see if they illustrate my points. I cite first from the Introduction of the Mankiw book:

> Economists try to address their subject with a scientist's objectivity. They approach the subject of the economy in much the same way as a physicist approaches the study of matter and a biologist approaches the study of life: They devise theories, collect data, and then analyze these data in an attempt to verify their theories.

We shall consider the implications of that central placement of science in a moment, but what of my assertion regarding the abandonment of the description of the economy as capitalist? I turn now to Stiglitz's two-volume text to see what he has to say about the matter. The answer is simple: the word does not appear in its 997 pages of text. For all intents and purposes, Capitalism does not exist in this two-volume introduction to economics.

Selective citations are, quite properly, regarded with suspicion. I could, perhaps, ask skeptical readers to repair to the nearest public library and compare a random selection of volumes of the *American Economic Review*, the flagship journal of the American Economic Association, or its British counterpart, *The Economic Journal*, for any ten years prior to the 1950s, and a like number from the last decade. I think I can guarantee that the skeptic will discover in the second group a pronounced increase of references to the methods of science and a precipitous decrease in the presence of the word *capitalism*. At whatever risk to my plausibility, I must therefore venture suggestions as to why these changes have taken place.

Let us look first at science. There is more than one reason why one might expect the concept of science to become a more and more explicit part of the vision of economists. The first, and by no means the least cogent of these reasons, is that students of the workings of the economy, like students of the workings of nature, seek regularities of behavior as a first clue to the discovery of the "laws" that are perhaps the most important achievement of science. Without knowledge of the laws of gravity we could neither explain (or predict) the orbits of the planets or the trajectory of an airplane. The question, then, is whether there are not also lawlike aspects to economic behavior?

I say "lawlike" because individuals' behaviors are obviously more complex than that of objects moving through space. When the price of clothing goes up, the quantity of clothing we buy is likely to go down; but it may not, if our fancy is caught by an advertising campaign. Nonetheless, no one would deny there is a *general* relationship between the prices of goods and the quantities bought by buyers—as prices change, quantities bought usually change in the opposite direction.

Moreover, this same kind of generally predictable stimulus-response relationship can be found between changes in our incomes and our spending on consumers goods, or changes in the rate of interest and business spending on investment. Thus, economic behavior is marked by a degree of predictability for which it is difficult, or even impossible, to find similar examples in other areas of social life, such as politics. Equally remarkable is that changes in economic stimuli normally bring about movements in opposing directions, depending on our roles—namely, whether we are buyers or sellers. This is another property that marks off economic from non-economic life. Indeed, it is this bipolar effect of price stimuli on behavior that makes markets a means for imposing social order, not disorder, a unique stabilizing effect that again relates economic behavior to some self-balancing natural processes.

Thus it is not surprising that the realization early dawned that a market system bore a certain resemblance to the natural processes to which science directed its attention. There is no doubt wherein lay the attraction of this resemblance. If economics could become a true branch of science, it would enormously increase our capacity to predict the course of events, as well as the outcome of attempts to change that course. To be sure, economic science would no more give us complete control over our future than physical science gives us control over the course of gravity, but unquestionably it would increase our ability to foresee the consequences of changing the workings of the economic system, and thereby to choose the most favorable course of action. Why, then, should we not applaud the increasing tendency to envision economics as a science?

There are two reasons. Marshall himself noted one. Although beguiled by the sciencelike aspects of economics, he warned that "economics cannot be compared with the exact physical sciences) for it deals with the ever-changing and subtle forces of human nature." We speak of the laws of physics or chemistry as describing the behavior of the electrons and mesons that the scientist studies, but there is an unbridgeable gap between the "behavior" of these elements of nature and those of the human beings who constitute the objects of study of social science. When scientists explain the phenomenon of, say, light, with reference to the behavior of electrons, no one supposes that each electron has "decided" whether or where it is to move. In contrast, when econmists explain the phenomenon of price changes by the behavior of buyers and sellers, they cannot describe their object of study without assuming that each individual person has decided to act as he or she did. In a word, aside from pure physical reflexes, human behavior cannot be understood without the concept of volition—the unpredictable capacity to change our minds up to the very last moment. By way of contrast, the elements of nature "behave" as they do for reasons of which we know only one thing: the particles of physics do not "choose" to behave as they do.

Hence a careless usage of the word "behavior" can easily conflate two utterly different things, one of them the quintessential element of conscious existence, the other having nothing whatever to do with it. If economics were in fact a science, we humans would be mere robots, no more capable of choosing what was to be our response to a price rise than is a particle of iron to the presence of a magnet.

A second objection seems quite different, but is actually

the other side of the same coin. It is that the social life of humankind is by its very nature *political*. That is, all societies, once they move from the level of hunting and gathering to that of Command, create categories of privilege and disprivilege, ranging from aristocracy to slavery, from class to caste, from the rights of property to the disadvantages of penury. As those last words make clear, capitalism is no exception to this general statement. Are such crucial economic matters as the distribution of wealth or income determined by the social counterpart of gravity? Are taxes, the rights of inheritance, or the existence of sweatshops expressions of immutable laws of nature? Or are they the highly mutable determinations of the sociopolitical order in which we live?

The question bears on Mankiw's statement that economists "try to address their subject with a scientist's objectivity." But what does it mean to be "objective" about such things as inherited wealth or immiserating poverty? Does it mean that those arrangements reflect some properties of society that must be accepted, just as the scientist accepts the arrangements studied through a telescope or under a microscope? Or does it mean that if we were scrupulously aware of our own private endorsements or rejections of society's arrangements we could, by applying an appropriate discount, arrive at a truly neutral view? In that case, could one use the word "scientific" to describe our findings, even though the object of study was not a product of nature but of society?

The answer is that we cannot. There is, of course, ample room for scientific method in analyzing many problems that economics seeks to clarify, including the requirement that economists report the data they observe as scrupulously as possible. But when it comes to policy recommendations, it is impossible to present economic analyses as if they stemmed unchallengeably from the givens of society. This is because there are no such givens comparable to those of nature. Moreover, to admit to the presence of power and obedience in the arrangements of all stratified societies does not thereby allow us to attribute to our explanations the objectivity we seek in our clarifications of nature. It only applies the language by which we describe nature's workings to those of society. If such a pseudoscientific view were to become the aim of economics, it would indeed spell its termination as a worldly philosophy.

And so our discussion leads us to consider the second of the larger questions I posed at the outset of this chapter—namely, the "end" of our subject in terms of its purpose, its aim. If economics is not to be a science of society, what is to be its ultimate social usefulness?

My answer is that its purpose is to help us better understand the capitalist setting in which we will most likely have to shape our collective destiny for the foreseeable future. Having for many years endorsed the ideas and objectives of democratic socialism, that is not an easy assertion for me to make. But given the experience of socialism in its twentieth-century forms, it is difficult to expect its benign rebirth in the century to come. Indeed, taking into account the strains and stresses clearly visible in the decades ahead, it is all too likely that any prospective socialism, especially in the less developed areas where its advent is most likely, will again develop tendencies for political megalomania, bureaucratic inertia, and ideological intolerance.

To be sure, these strains and stresses will exert their destructive force on capitalist societies as well. Ecological dangers, foremost among them global warming, will bring not only the need to contain the damage of climatic change in the poor nations, but the even more difficult challenge of reducing climate-warming emissions in the richer nations that are their source. Add to this the alarming spread of nuclear weaponry on the one hand, and ethnic, racial, and religious hatreds on the other, and the stage is surely set for problems and tensions from which the capitalist powers cannot be insulated. Finally, there is the fast-growing problem of a globalized economy that arises largely within individual capitalisms, but then escapes their control to become a supranational presence that threatens the sovereignty of the wealthiest of them. In sum, here is a prospect as threatening, if not as desperate, for the rich capitalist world as that which confronts the poor precapitalist or presocialist one.

● ●

What could be the purpose of vision and analysis under these conditions? It must be evident that there is little for economics to offer with respect to the political leadership, the diplomatic skills, and the social inspiration that must play crucial roles in preventing these strains from undoing the workability of capitalist societies. Nonetheless, a worldly philosophy has a unique potential to provide the visionary guidance that will help at least some capitalisms make their way as safely as possible through the coming decades.

Let me stress *some* capitalisms. To say it one last time, the distinctive properties of all capitalisms are the drive for capital, the guidance and constraints of a market system, and the blessings—admittedly, often mixed—of a bifurcation of power into two interpenetrative but still independent sectors. To this, however, must be added a capacity for adaptation and innovation that results in a spectrum of capitalist performances, a spectrum that is visible in the intensity of the drive for capital, the degree of freedom accorded to market dispensations, and the location of the boundary between the public and private realms. Thus we have a considerable variety of capitalist *societies* despite the general similarity of their economies—witness the gulf between the socially, if not always economically, successful capitalisms of Scandanavia and Europe, and the economically successful but socially disastrous capitalism of the United States: consider, for example, that executive compensation in the top corporations in the United States is twice that of France or Germany, whereas the upward mobility of the American poor is half that of those countries and but a third that of Sweden. The first comparison points to a culture of greed; the second to one of social indifference. The combination hardly suggests the institutional adaptability that will be needed by any nation seeking to minimize the strains of the decades ahead, much less serve as a model for world leadership.

It is with respect to these social aspects of capitalism that a reborn worldly philosophy can play its most useful role. Economic analysis, by itself, cannot provide a torch that lights our way into the future, but economic vision could become the source of an awareness of ways by which a capitalist structure can broaden its motivations, increase its flexibility, and develop its social responsibility. In a word, in this time of foreseeable stress, the purposeful end of the worldly philosophy should be to develop a new awareness of the need for, and the possibilities of, socially as well as economically successful capitalisms.

No doubt it will be objected that the realization of such a far-reaching program would require prodigies of political leadership, and that much of the learning needed to give substance to such a vision belongs properly within the boundaries of other fields of knowledge, from psychology and sociology through political science.

All true, all true. Economics alone will not guide a country that has no vital leadership, but leadership will lack for clear directions without the inspiration of an enlightened as well as an enlarged self-definition of economics. Assuredly such a new economics will incorporate knowledge from the domains of other branches of social inquiry, but if the usefulness of the worldly philosophy of the twenty-first century is to match that of the nineteenth and early twentieth, it will need to be both deepened and enlarged, above all compared to the desiccated residue with which we are left today. Bearing in mind the two meanings of "end" in our title, it is to this hopeful vision of tomorrow's worldly philosophy that this book is dedicated.

A Guide
to Further Reading

Economic reading, by popular hearşay, is a veritable desert of dusty prose. In all honesty, much of it is. The student of economics must be prepared for long journeys without a single refreshing sentence; it takes the endurance of a camel and the patience of a saint to finish some of the great texts.

But not all economics falls into this category. There is much that is alive, provocative, and stimulating even to the novice, and much more that is sufficiently interesting, persuasive, or important to warrant a certain amount of heavy going. These are the books I am recommending here. They are by no means an exploration of all of economics—no short list could possibly do that. These are merely good jumping-off points from which to reconnoiter one area of the whole field. There are difficult books here, but no impossible ones and no unrewarding ones. For one reason or another I enjoyed or profited from them all. And incidentally, many of the books mentioned below are available in paperback.*

The reader might want to begin by taking a chance on an economic textbook to see what economics is really "about." It is well worth a try, provided he or she is prepared to go through it at leisure, with education rather than entertain-

---

* Paperback reprints appear so fast it is hard to keep up with them. I have put an asterisk next to all titles that I know to be paperback editions.

ment as his or her aim. Out of a dozen good texts, I would suggest *Economics* by Paul A. Samuelson (McGraw-Hill, New York), certainly the most famous economic text of our times. Samuelson's book is bright, broad-ranging, and demanding—it must be studied, not just read. For a reader who wants a simpler introduction, let me suggest *Economics Explained** by Lester Thurow and myself (Touchstone Books, published by Simon & Schuster, Inc., New York, 1998.)

It is less simple to suggest reading in the history of economic doctrines—to suggest, that is, a book that covers the scope of this one, but in greater detail and with more attention to the full range of economic ideas. Mark Blaug's *Economic Theory in Retrospect* (Cambridge University Press, 1978) is superb but demands a considerable knowledge of economic theory. The famous *Lecture Notes* of Wesley Mitchell have been published by Augustus Kelley under the title *Types of Economic Theory.* They are marvelous reading, but alas, expensive; and their pleasure has been partly spoiled by an editing that has crammed every last variant into the texts so that endless repetition spoils the sweep of Mitchell's extraordinary knowledge. Joseph Schumpeter's posthumous *History of Economic Analysis* (Oxford University Press, New York, 1954) is a masterpiece of its kind, a truly encyclopedic survey of economic analysis, as brilliant and as opinionated as its author. It is apt to be slow going for the nonprofessional; I suspect that most academic economists have never read it through. Finally, I might mention my own *Teachings from the Worldly Philosophy** (New York, W.W. Norton, 1996), which offers selections from the main figures, interspersed with my own comments.

The subject of the rise of capitalism itself has been fascinatingly dealt with in Karl Polanyi's *The Great Transformation** (Farrar & Rinehart, New York, 1944). Polanyi's book is mainly a study of the difficulty of imposing the market idea in the eighteenth century on a nonmarket-oriented world, but it also deals with contemporary aspects of this same problem. It is wholly absorbing. On much the same subject, but focused on a different aspect of the rise of capitalism, R. H. Tawney's *Religion and the Rise of Capitalism** (New York, 1937, recently reissued by Harcourt, Brace) is in a class by itself, a profound work written in an unsurpassable style by a great historian. Max Weber, *The Protestant Ethic and the Spirit of Capitalism** (G. Allen & Unwin, London, 1930) is another classic in the field, but somewhat more demanding of the reader. The person who wants a less specialized overview of the history of capitalist evolution might look into *The Making of Economic Society** (Prentice-Hall, Englewood Cliffs, N.J., 1998) by William Milberg and myself.

For further historical background, the reader can turn to H. Pirenne, *Economic and Social History of Medieval Europe** (Harcourt, Brace, New York, 1937). Or there is the *Cambridge Economic History of Europe* in two volumes with fascinating essays by various economic historians (Cambridge University Press, London, 1952). For enjoyment I would suggest *The Unbound Prometheus,** by David Landes (Cambridge University Press, Cambridge, 1969) and his much praised *The Wealth and Poverty of Nations* (W.W. Norton, New York, 1998), or Paul Mantoux, *The Industrial Revolution in the Eighteenth Century** (Harcourt, Brace, New York, 1928), a venerable classic.

Anyone who would like to sample pre-Smith economic writing has a number of enjoyable possibilities. For pleasure one might read Bernard Mandeville, *The Fable of the Bees* (Penguin Classics, New York, 1970). For a systematic survey of the rise of economic science, there is William Letwin, *The Origins of Scientific Economics* (Doubleday, New York, 1964), and Ronald Meek's marvelous (although specialized) book *The Economics of Physiocracy* (Harvard University Press, 1963). And somehow I should mention C. B. MacPherson's *The Political Theory of Possessive Individualism* (Oxford University Press, New York, 1962). As its title betrays, this is not "economics," but as the reader will discover, it is immensely illumining about economic matters. Let me conclude with a multivolume masterpiece by the French historian Fernand Braudel (Harper & Row, New York, 1967–1979), a "must."

Adam Smith presents a problem. The University of Glasgow has celebrated the bicentennial of *The Wealth of Na-*

tions with a vast, comprehensive, and terribly expensive Collected Works. Someone who wants to become a Smith scholar should certainly read its volume of *Essays* (ed. A. Skinner and E. Wilson, Clarendon Press, Oxford, 1975). Otherwise I would suggest buying the Modern Library *Wealth,* or if one wants to sample large portions of it, plus the "best parts" of *The Theory of Moral Sentiments* and still other writings of Smith, I have put together *The Essential Adam Smith** (W. W. Norton, New York, 1985).

As with Adam Smith, so with Malthus and Ricardo. The nonprofessional reader has slim pickings. Keynes has a nice short sketch of Malthus in his *Essays in Biography* (Horizon Press, New York, 1951), and Mitchell's treatment of Ricardo in the aforementioned *Lecture Notes* is wholly absorbing. The whole of Ricardo's writing is now available in a multivolume edition edited under the scrupulous eye of Piero Sraffa, *Works of David Ricardo* (Cambridge University Press, London, 1951), and the last volume contains a good deal of not terribly interesting biographical material. But the reader is not advised to hurl himself into Ricardo unless he is prepared for intellectual bruises: it is all abstract argument and no easy going at all. If curious nonetheless, try the second volume of Sraffa's work, in which Malthus's *Principles* is reproduced with Ricardo's annihilatory comments affixed to every paragraph. Here are the two friendly adversaries at their best. And for Malthus proper and the population dilemma, read *On Population* (Modern Library, New York, 1960), with a most interesting introduction by the historian Gertrude Himmelfarb. Better yet, any one of a number of modern books on the population problem. Recently, Samuel Huntington has produced a 1,000-page majestic *Malthus* (University of Toronto Press, Toronto, 1997), essential for every would-be scholar in the field.

There is no use trying to read the Utopians. Try instead *The Prophets of Paris* by Frank Manuel (Harvard University Press, 1962), or Alexander Gray's *The Socialist Tradition* (Longmans, Green, London, 1946), on which I have leaned heavily for Saint-Simon and Fourier. Gray's style is a trifle arch, but some of the quainter figures can bear this, and the book is heavily and avowedly biased in favor of Utopian as opposed to "scientific" socialism. If the immersion takes, the library will give one access to the originals—warning, however: they are all intolerably verbose. There is a nice old-fashioned biography of *Robert Owen* by F. Podmore (Appleton, New York, 1907) and a more factual but less readable one by G. D. H. Cole (E. Benn, London, 1925). Neither, however, does adequate justice to this astounding man; perhaps his own story, *The Life of Robert Owen* (Knopf, New York, 1920), is best for that.

Then, of course, there is John Stuart Mill. His *Autobiography* (Columbia University Press, New York, 1944) is classic—and tedious—but there is an excellent biography by Michael Packe (Macmillan, New York, 1954). If Mill interests one, Friedrich A. Hayek has published the correspondence between Mill and Harriet Taylor, *John Stuart Mill and Harriet Taylor* (University of Chicago Press, Chicago, 1951), which sheds a new light on the man. For another and very enlightening view of Mill and his relationship with the redoubtable Harriet, see Gertrude Himmelfarb's *On Liberty and Liberalism* (Knopf, New York, 1974). And as far as economics is concerned, Mill repays the effort. *Principles of Political Economy* (University of Toronto Press, Toronto, 1965) is beautifully written and with liberal skipping, still of interest to the modern reader. A Bantam paperback, *The Essential Works of John Stuart Mill*, contains the *Autobiography* and the justly famous *Essay on Liberty.**

The literature on Marx is voluminous. The reader might tackle a number of excellent recent biographies: the best, to my taste, is David McLellan's *Karl Marx* (Harper & Row, New York, 1973) and his very good shorter book on Marx for the Modern Masters series put out by Viking (New York, 1975). But I would like to tout an older book, *To the Finland Station** (Harcourt, Brace, New York, 1940) by Edmund Wilson. This is, among other things, a biography of Marx and Engels, a review of their work, and a critique of historical writing in general, the excellence of all of which is enhanced by a superlative style. It is like reading a novel.

Probably the best single introduction to Marx is Marx

himself, especially *Capital,* Vol. I. A new edition published by Random House (Vintage, New York, 1977)* is excellent. If this "takes," the next step is the short (not the long) *Grundrisse* (ed. David McLellan, Harper Torchbook, New York, 1971).* A reader by Robert Tucker (W.W. Norton, New York, 1978) would be a good next choice. Thereafter, perhaps Paul M. Sweezy, *The Theory of Capitalist Development* (Monthly Review Press);* and after that there is a vast, sprawling literature to which no concise guide is possible. With apologies for again putting myself forward, let me mention my *Marxism, For And Against* (W. W. Norton, New York, 1983).

There is no volume on the Victorians themselves. The reader might wish to look at Alfred Marshall's *Principles of Economics* (Macmillan, New York, 1948). It is ponderous but not difficult; the obstacle is the amount of patience, not the amount of knowledge, needed. Keynes, by the way, has a nice biographical bit on both Marshall and Edgeworth in his aforementioned *Essays in Biography*.

The underworld makes for more enjoyable reading. Henry George is out of date, but his *Progress and Poverty* (Doubleday, New York, 1926) retains an emotional appeal and is written in a rich—often overrich—journalistic style. Hobson is more serious and more absorbing. *Imperialism* (G. Allen & Unwin, London, 1938) is still to the point and enormously interesting, more so than Lenin's famous pamphlet by the same name.

Veblen himself makes magnificent reading, if you take to his style. Not everyone does, but aficionados go about quoting his gems. *The Theory of the Leisure Class** (Modern Library, New York, 1934) is his best-known work, but I would suggest *The Portable Veblen* (Viking Press, New York, 1950), with a brilliant introduction by Max Lerner, which projects the man himself and his basic ideas with great clarity. The book itself covers a wide variety of Veblen's work. For Veblen's thought I would highly recommend a penetrating study by Jack Diggins, *The Bard of Savagery* (Seabury Press, New York, 1978). The times themselves are both trenchantly and rollickingly illustrated in a superb book by Matthew

Josephson, *The Robber Barons** (Harcourt, Brace, New York, 1934).

There are two major biographies of Keynes: the comprehensive but somewhat pompous *Life of John Maynard Keynes* by Roy Harrod (Harcourt, Brace, New York, 1951) and the brilliant *John Maynard Keynes* by Lord Robert Skidelsky (Viking, New York, 1986), of which only the first two of three scheduled volumes are out. Or one can meet the man himself directly through his sparkling and lucid prose, and for this the *Economic Consequences of the Peace* (Harcourt, Brace, New York, 1920) and *Essays in Persuasion* (Harcourt, Brace, New York, 1951) are wonderful introductions to both Keynes's style and thought.

When we move to the question of Whither Capitalism and Whither Economics? I must still put Joseph Schumpeter's *Capitalism, Socialism and Democracy* (Harper, New York, 1947) high on the list. For a view that takes off from Schumpeter's, an interested reader might wish to look into my own *Nature and Logic of Capitalism.** Meanwhile, for Schumpeter's life there is no substitute for Robert Loring Allen's *Opening Doors*, 2 vols., (New Brunswick, N.J., Transactions Publishers, 1991).

A parting word relates to the final chapter. There we consider questions about the nature of economics itself, a question that rapidly runs into technical considerations. For the interested reader, however, I suggest the works below— none "easy," all important. Deborah Redman's *Economics and the Philosophy of Science* (Oxford, New York, 1991) is a masterful presentation of the gradual rapprochement between economics and the philosophy of science, a must for the historically minded. Philip Mirowski, *More Heat than Light* (Cambridge University Press, New York, 1989) is a provocative, contentious, and eminently worthwhile critical view of "economics as social science." *Truth versus Precision in Economics*, by Thomas Mayer (Edw. Elgar, U.K., 1993) is one of the very best, most evenhanded, and yet strongest critiques of the subject exactly decribed by its title.

Last, only because it is difficult to obtain, is a fascinating overview of how contemporary economics came to follow its historic path, and of a different route it might have, and may yet, pursue. The author is the Norwegian economist Erik S. Reinert (who writes beautiful English). I would suggest those seeking more information as to the availability of his work write to the University of Oslo, Center for Development and the Environment, P.O. Box 1116-Blindern, N-0317, Oslo, Norway. Reinert has written many interesting booklets and papers on and around this theme but I would inquire first about his booklet "The Role of the State." You will not regret going to the bother.

Notes*

I: INTRODUCTION

P. 14 "The ideas of economists . . .": John Maynard Keynes, *The General Theory of Employment, Interest, and Money* (New York: Harcourt, Brace & World, 1964), p. 383.

II: THE ECONOMIC REVOLUTION

P. 19 Elizabeth Marshall Thomas, *The Harmless People* (New York: Vintage, 1958), p. 50.

"In ancient Egypt . . .": Adam Smith, *An Inquiry into the Nature and Causes of the Wealth of Nations* (New York: Modern Library, 1937), p. 62.

P. 21–22 France, 1305: Henri Pirenne, *Economic and Social History of Medieval Europe* (New York: Harcourt, Brace: n.d.), pp. 102–103.

divan, syrup: Pirenne, ibid., p. 145.

P. 22 "Owed ten gulden . . .": Miriam Beard, *A History of the Business Man* (New York: Macmillan, 1938), p. 83.

Saint Gothard pass: Pirenne, op. cit., p. 35, n. 1; Beard, op. cit., p. 83.

Andreas Ryff: Beard, op. cit., p. 83.

tolls and measures: Eli Hecksher, *Mercantilism* (London: George Allen & Unwin, 1935), Vol. I, pp. 57, 118.

Boston, 1639: John Winthrop, *Winthrop's Journal* (New York: Charles Scribner's Sons, 1908), Vol. 1, pp. 315–317.

* With renewed thanks to Dr. Jaspal Chatha.

P. 23   The Merchant Adventurers Company: W. E. Lingelbach, *The Merchant Adventurers of England* (New York: Longmans, Green, 1902), pp. 47–52; also Sylvia Thrupp, *The Merchant Class of Medieval London* (Chicago: University of Chicago Press, 1948), pp. 165, 169.

fabrics of Dijon and Selangey . . . pilloried instead: Hecksher, op. cit. pp. 160, 164.

P. 24   Sir William Petty . . . "to drink": *The Economic Writings of Sir William Petty*, C. H. Hull, ed. (New York: Augustus Kelley, 1963), p. 274.

P. 25   the Fuggers: Lewis Mumford, *The Condition of Man* (New York: Harcourt, Brace & World, 1944), p. 168.

P. 26   Saint Godric: Henri Pirenne, *Medieval Cities* (Princeton, N.J.: Princeton University Press, 1925), pp. 120–121.

P. 26   Tablets of Tell-el-Amama: W. M. Flinders Petrie, *Syria and Egypt* (London: Methuen, 1898), Ch. 2, esp. pp. 44–48.

P. 27   Maoris: Raymond Firth, *Primitive Economics of the New Zealand Maoris* (New York: E. P. Dutton, 1929), p. 340.

P. 29   wonderworkshop: Sir William Ashley, *An Introduction to English Economic History and Theory*. 4th ed. (London: Longmans, Green, 1925), pp. 229–237.

P. 30   France, 1666: Hecksher, op. cit., p. 171.

P. 31   England, stocking frame: Paul Mantoux, *The Industrial Revolution in the XVIII Century* (New York: Harcourt, Brace, 1927), p. 196.

is met with measures . . . calico wares: Hecksher, op. cit., p. 173.

"Paupers are everywhere!": Karl Marx, *Capital* (New York: International Publishers, 1967), Vol. I, p. 721.

John Hales: Mantoux, op cit., p. 159.

P. 32   3, 500 killed: ibid.

Duchess of Sutherland: Marx, op. cit., pp. 729–730.

"Houses of Terror": Mantoux: op. cit., p. 278.

P. 34   Columbus: John Boyd Thacher, *Christopher Columbus* (New York and London: G. P. Putnam's Sons, 1903), Vol. II, p. 645.

P. 35   With the share received as a stockholder: John Maynard Keynes, *A Treatise on Money* (London: Macmillan, 1953), Vol. II, pp. 156–157.

P. 37   "Every man . . . Circle of Commerce:" Hecksher, op. cit., p. 301.

John Law: Beard, op. cit., pp. 416–419.

P. 38   Aristotle: *Aristotle's Politics*, trans. Benjamin Jowett (New York: Modern Library, 1943), p. 58.

P. 39   Hobbes, "nasty, poore . . .", *Leviathan*, Oxford University Press, 1967, pp. 41, 97

P. 40   Mun's *English Treasure . . .*", see R. Heilbroner, *Teachings from the Worldly Philosophy*. W.W. Norton, N.Y., pp. 24–28.

"To make the Society Happy . . .": Bernard Mandeville, *The Fable of the Bees* (Oxford: Clarendon Press, 1966), pp. 287, P. 288.

III. The Wonderful World of Adam Smith

P. 42   foremost philosophers of his age: biographical details from John Rae, *Life of Adam Smith* (1895) with an introduction by Jacob Viner (New York: Augustus Kelley, 1965); Dugald Stewart, *Biographical Memoir of Adam Smith* (1793) (New York: Augustus Kelley, 1966); William Scott, *Adam Smith as Student and Professor* (Glasgow; Jackson, Son & Co., 1937).

P. 43   Suppose, for example . . . mines of Cornwall: Elie Halevy, *England in 1815* (New York: Peter Smith, 1949), pp. 259–265.

P. 44   Companies of Ancient Britons: Halevy, ibid., p. 242.

Lombe . . . Daniel Defoe: Paul Mantoux, op. cit., p. 199, n. 1.

child labor: Halevy, op. cit., pp. 279–280.

P. 45   "I am a beau . . .": James Bonar, *Library of Adam Smith* (London: Macmillan, 1894), pp. viii-ix.

P. 47   "a man endowed with every great talent . . .": Percy Fitzgerald, *Charles Townshend: Wit and Statesman* (London: R. Bentley, 1866), pp. 359–360.

P. 48   Townshend's fickleness: ibid., p. 334.

P. 49   Quesnay . . . circulation of blood: Ronald Meek, *The Economics of Physiocracy* (Cambridge, Mass.: Harvard University Press, 1963). p. 375, n. 2.

Mirabeau the elder: quoted in Adam Smith, *The Wealth of Nations* (New York: Modern Library, 1937), p. 643; hereafter cited as *Wealth*.

P. 50   Smith-Johnson altercation: Rae, op. cit., p. 156.

P. 51   "the outpouring . . . whole epoch": Max Lerner, Introduction to *Wealth*.

P. 52   "nation of shopkeepers": Smith, *Wealth*, p. 578.

"By nature . . . greyhound": ibid., p. 16.

East India Company: ibid., p. 605.

P. 54   "invisible hand": ibid., p. 423.

"private interests and passions of men": ibid., pp. 594–595.

"system of perfect liberty": ibid., p. 651.

P. 55   "It is . . . our dinner": ibid., p. 14.

P. 59   Sir John Byng: Beard, op. cit., p. 493.

P. 60   In 1720 . . . million and a half: from Gregory King, *Two Tracts* (1696) (Baltimore: Johns Hopkins Press, 1936), p. 31.

"prudence . . . folly": Bernard Mandeville, *The Fable of the Bees* (Oxford: Clarendon Press, 1929), Vol. I, p. 194.

P. 60–61   "No society . . . poor and miserable": Smith, *Wealth*, p. 79.

P. 61   the pin factory: ibid., pp. 4–5.

P. 62–63   "Observe the accommodation . . . naked savages": ibid., pp. 11–12.

P. 63   Law of Accumulation; Adolph Lowe, "The Classical Theory of Economic Growth," *Social Research*, Summer 1954, pp. 132–141.

Arkwright: Mantoux, op. cit., p. 238.

Samuel Walker: ibid., p. 311.

"This won't do . . .": ibid., p. 386.

P. 64 "like him who perverts . . .": Smith, *Wealth,* p. 322.

P. 65 "the demand for men . . .": ibid., p. 80.

"It is not uncommon . . .": ibid., p. 79; "in the very long run": ibid., pp. 94–95.

P. 67 200-year limit; *Wealth,* p. 394.

P. 68 "mean rapacity": ibid., p. 460.

"Consumption . . . the sole end": ibid., p. 625.

"the understandings . . . prevent it": ibid., pp. 734–735.

P. 69 "People of the same trade . . .": ibid., p. 128.

P. 73 "With the greater part . . .": ibid., p. 172.

"If any of the provinces . . .": ibid., p. 900.

"For to what purpose . . .": Adam Smith, *The Theory of Moral Sentiments* (1759), in R. Heilbroner, *The Essential Adam Smith* (New York: W. W. Norton, 1986), P. 78.

P. 74 Pitt's remark: Rae, op. cit., p. 405.

IV: THE GLOOMY PRESENTIMENTS OF PARSON MALTHUS AND DAVID RICARDO

P. 75 Drawing on records: King, op. cit., p. 18.

P. 76 "In all probability . . .": ibid., p. 24.

"The decay of population . . .": Wesley Mitchell, *Types of Economic Theory* (New York: Augustus Kelley, 1967), Vol. I, p. 47.

Pitt's bill: James Bonar, *Malthus and His Work.* 2nd ed., (1924) (New York: Augustus Kelley, 1967), pp. 6, 30. The quote from Paley comes from his *Principles of Moral and Political Philosophy* (London: R. Fauler, 1790), Vol. II, p. 347.

P. 77 "there will be no war . . .": Bonar, *Malthus and His Work,* p. 15.

P. 79 56 percent of invested capital . . . ten years later: Halevy, op. cit., p. 229.

P. 80 Reevesby estate: ibid., pp. 227–228.

But by 1813 . . . 14 shillings per bushel: Mitchell, op. cit., p.279.

P. 81 Alexander Baring's remark: ibid., pp. 279–280.

P. 82 "The interest of the landlords . . .": David Ricardo, *Works and Correspondence,* ed. Piero Sraffa (Cambridge University Press, 1965), Vol. IV, p. 21.

Ricardo's fortune: ibid., Vol. X, pp. 95–106.

P. 83 "From the first . . . refutations": Bonar, *Malthus and His Work,* pp. 1, 2.

"early attachments": Thomas Robert Malthus, (first) *Essay on Population* (1798) (New York: Macmillan, 1966), p. 65.

"at Nature's mighty feast . . .": quoted in Bonar, *Malthus and His Work,* p. 305. The quotation appears only in the second edition of the (first) *Essay.* It was subsequently withdrawn.

P. 84   "the express object of Mr. Malthus's writing . . ." William Godwin, *Of Population* (1820) (New York: Augustus Kelley, 1964), p. 616.

"I have no hope . . . my own voice": Ricardo, op. cit., Vol. XIII, p. 21.

That voice . . . "another planet": Mitchell, op. cit., Vol. I, pp. 306–307.

P. 85   "They hunted together": quoted in John Maynard Keynes, *Essays in Biography* (London: Macmillan, 1937), p. 134.

P. 86   "The subdued jests . . .": Harriet Martineau, *Autobiography*, Maria Weston Chapman, ed. (Boston: James R. Osgood, 1877), p. 247.

"lakes of Killarney": ibid., p. 248.

P. 87   For Edgeworth see article by J. P. Croshaw, *The New Palgrave Dictionary of Economics,* (New York, MacMillan, 1987), Vol. II, p. 99.

Maria Edgeworth . . . coxcomb: Ricardo, op. cit., Vol. X, p. 171.

"The talent for obtaining wealth . . .": ibid., p. 6.

"If, therefore, dealing . . .": ibid., pp. 73–74.

P. 87–88   "unless it is wrong . . .": ibid., Vol. VI, p. 229.

P. 88   "This is . . . old subject": ibid., p. 233.

"And now, my dear Malthus . . .": ibid., Vol. IX, p. 382.

Malthus's opinion of Ricardo: Keynes, *Essays in Biography*, p. 134.

"Thus a new kind of balance . . .": Joseph Townshend, *A Dissertation on the Poor Laws* (1786) (London: Ridgways, 1817), p. 45.

P. 90   "Taking the population of the world": Malthus, (first) *Essay*, pp. 25, 26.

P. 90   "melancholy hue": ibid., p. iv.

"Famine . . . food of the world": ibid., pp. 139, 140.

P. 91   "Spreading like scabrous growths . . .": Robert Heilbroner, in Just Faaland, ed., *Population and the World Economy* (Oxford: Basil Blackwell, 1982), p. 237.

P. 92   "And the effort has begun to pay off": pp. 93–94, Population projections, *U.S. Statistical Abstract,* Dept. of Commerce, 1997; U.S. Table 3, World Table 13317

P. 94   Paley: Mitchell, op. cit., p. 47.

Coleridge summed up the doleful outlook: Keynes, *Essays,* p. 111.

P. 98   "Rents, " said Malthus: Ricardo, op. cit., Vol. II, p. 222.

P. 100   "Mr. Malthus never appears to remember . . .": ibid., p. 449.

P. 101   "Many a merchant . . .": ibid., pp. 98–99.

"True, but a brother merchant . . .": ibid., pp. 376–377.

"I have so very high an opinion . . .": ibid., p. 12.

V: THE DREAMS OF THE UTOPIAN SOCIALISTS

P. 106   As early as 1779: Mantoux, op. cit., pp. 411–413.

by 1811 . . . Luddites: J. L. and Barbara Hammond, *The Skilled Labourer* (London: Longmans, Green, 1920), pp. 257–301.

P. 109   For Owen's life see *The Life of Robert Owen written by him-*

self (London: Chas. Knight & Co., 1971); Frank Podmore, *Robert Owen: A Biography* (New York: D. Appleton, 1924); G. D. H. Cole, *The Life of Robert Owen* (Hamden, Conn.: Archon, 1966).

"I put on my hat . . .": Owen, *A Life*, p. 27.

P. 112   For Ricardo's views see *Works and Correspondence*, Vol. V, pp. 30, 467.

One editorialist wrote: Podmore, op. cit., p. 240.

William Cobbet, *Cobbett's Political Works* (London: n.d.), p. 230.

P. 115   "Robert Owen is not a man . . .": quoted in Alexander Gray, *The Socialist Tradition* (London: Longmans, Green, 1946), p. 202.

P. 116   "When the child . . . circumstances": Robert Dale Owen, *Threading My Way: An Autobiography* (New York: Augustus Kelley, 1967), pp. 57, 58.

Saint-Simon: see Gray, op. cit., pp. 136–138, and Frank Manuel, *The New World of Henri Saint-Simon* (Cambridge, Mass.: Harvard University Press, 1956).

"Arise . . . do today": Manuel, op. cit., p. 13.

P. 118   "Since the world began . . .": ibid., p. 40.

P. 119   "Monsieur: be my saviour . . .": ibid., p. 112.

"Remember . . . impassioned!" Gray, op. cit., p. 138.

P. 120   "We suppose" . . . thirty thousand people in all: ibid., pp. 151–152.

P. 121   Charles Fourier: ibid., pp. 156–196.

P. 126   John Stuart Mill: see Mill's *Autobiography* in *Collected Works of John Stuart Mill* (Toronto: University of Toronto Press, 1981), Vol. I.

P. 127   "I never composed . . .": ibid., pp. 17, 19.

"lest the habit of work . . .": ibid., p. 39.

P. 128   "Whoever, either . . . three": ibid., p. 265.

"The things once there . . .": ibid., Vol. II, pp. 199, 200.

P. 130   "If the choice . . .": ibid., p. 207.

P. 131   "I confess . . .": ibid., Vol. III, p. 754.

"That the energies of mankind . . .": ibid.

"The question is whether . . .": ibid., Vol. II, p. 209.

P. 134   "I beg that . . .": ibid., Vol. XVI, p. 1146.

"Surely no one . . .": ibid., Vol. 1., p. 226.

VI: THE INEXORABLE SYSTEM OF KARL MARX

P. 136   "A spectre . . .": Karl Marx and Friedrich Engels, "The Manifesto of the Communist Party, " *Collected Works* (Moscow: Progress Publishers, 1976), Vol. VI, p. 481.

a year of terror: see Priscilla Robertson, *Revolutions of 1848: A Social History* (Princeton, N.J.: Princeton Univ. Press, 1948).

"The Communists disdain . . .": ibid., p. 519.

P. 137   "really people in our gentle walk . . .": I cannot find the source but am advised by Mr. Fred Whitehead that it is probably Heine's introduction to *Lutetia* (1854).

P. 140 Marx and Engels biographical data: see Edmund Wilson, *To the Finland Station* (New York: Farrar, Strauss & Giroux, 1940, 1972); Franz Mehring, *Karl Marx* (Ann Arbor, Mich.: University of Michigan Press, 1962); David McLellan, *Karl Marx: His Life and Thought* (New York: Harper & Row, 1973).

P. 141 "in mahogany . . .": Wilson, op. cit., p. 157.

P. 142 "And yet there is a great deal . . .": ibid., p. 163.

"a veritable earthly god": Elie Halevy, *Imperialism and the Rise of Labour* (London Ernest Benn, 1951), p. 18.

P. 144 "The materialist conception . . .": F. Engels, *Anti-Dühring* (New York: International Publishers, 1970), p. 292.

P. 145 "Men make their own history . . .": "The Eighteenth Brumaire of Louis Napoleon, in Marx, *Works*, Vol. II, p. 103.

"The hand-mill . . .": "The Poverty of Philosophy, " ibid., Vol. VI, p. 166.

P. 148 "The development of modern industry . . .": ibid., p. 496.

P. 149 Lenchen: see Yvonne Kapp, *Eleanor Marx* (London: Lawrence and Wishart, 1972), Vol. 1, Appendix I, pp. 289–297.

"Our dear mother . . .": David McLellan, *Karl Marx: Interviews and Recollections* (Totowa, N.J.: Barnes and Noble, 1981), p. 165.

P. 150 "You must your war-articles . . .": Wilson, op. cit., p. 365.

"I hope the bourgeoisie . . .": ibid.

"My wife is ill . . ." Marx, *Works*, Vol. XXXIX, p. 181.

P. 151 "swinging his stick . . ." Kapp, op. cit., p. 112.

"I am not a Marxist": McLellan, *Karl Marx: His Life and Thought,* p. 443.

"The philosophers hitherto . . .": "Theses on Feuerbach, " in Marx, *Works,* Vol. V, p. 8.

P. 152 anti-Semitism: see Paul Padover, *Karl Marx: An Intimate Biography* (New York: McGraw-Hill, 1978), p. 166–170.

"Ignorance has never . . .": McLellan, supra cit., pp. 156–157.

P. 153 Proudhon's letter: ibid., p. 159.

P. 154 "The history of capitalisim . . .": *The Communist International, 1919–1943.* Jane Degras, ed. (London: Oxford University Press, 1961), p. 475.

P. 155 "vampire thirst . . .": ibid., p. 245.

"dripping from head to foot . . .": Marx, *Capital* (Moscow: Progress Publishers, 1954), p. 712.

P. 160 "Along with . . . are expropriated": ibid., p. 715.

P. 167–168 unemployment and poverty: see Thomas Palley, *Journal of Post-Keynesian Economics,* Spring 1998, p. 338, Table 1; p. 343, Table 8.

P. 168 "just as Darwin discovered . . .": Padover, op. cit., p. 591.

VII: THE VICTORIAN WORLD AND THE UNDERWORLD OF
ECONOMICS

P. 171   Sir Robert Giffen, *Economic Inquiries and Studies* (London:
George Bell & Sons), Vol. I, 1909, p. 394.

working hours: see Sir John Clapham, *An Economic History of
Modern Britain, 1850–1886* (Cambridge: Cambridge University Press,
1963), pp. 448–449. The citation in the text does not follow Clapham
exactly.

"The English proletariat . . .": Marx, *Works,* Vol. XL, p. 344.

P. 173   "Shall I answer briefly . . .": from Keynes, *Essays,* p. 273.

P. 175   "Considerations so abstract . . .": F. Y. Edgeworth, *Mathematical Psychics* (1881) (New York: Augustus Kelley, 1961), p. 128.

von Thünen: J. A. Schumpeter, *History of Economic Analysis*
(New York: Oxford University Press, 1954), p. 467.

P. 176   Jevons's quotes: W. Stanley Jevons, *The Theory of Political
Economy* (London: Macmillan, 1879), pp. vii, 3.

P. 178   for Bastiat's life see Charles Gide and Charles Rist, *A History
of Economic Doctrines* (London: George A. Harrap, 1915); *International Encyclopedia of Social Sciences,* 1968; and *Encyclopaedia Britannica,* 11th ed., 1910. See also essay by de Fontenay in *Oeuvres
Complètes de Frédéric Bastiat* (Paris, 1855), Vol. I.

"Negative Railway": Bastiat, *Economic Sophisms* (New York: G. P.
Putnam, 1922), pp. 101–102.

P. 179   military adventures: Bastiat, *Oeuvres Complètes,* pp. 26, 27.

Molinari: Gide and Rist, op. cit., p. 329n. The text citation differs
slightly.

P. 179–180   Petition of the Manufacturers . . . : ibid., pp. 60–65.

P. 181   "Everyone wants to live . . .": freely adapted from Bastiat, *Selected Essays in Political Economy* (Princeton, N.J.: Van Nostrand,
1964), p. 111.

"Pass a law to this effect . . .": ibid., p. 135.

P. 182   "Thank God I am not dead . . .": Bastiat, *Oeuvres Complètes,*
pp. 205, 206.

"Truth, truth . . .": ibid., p. xxxii.

"About politics . . . in a fog": in Mitchell, op. cit., Vol. II, p. 30.

P. 182–183   "Political Economy . . . injustice": *Complete Works of
Henry George* (National Single Tax League, 1900), Vol. I, p. 557.

P. 183   "Words fail the thought!": ibid., p. 549.

Henry George biographical details: Henry George, Jr., *Life of
Henry George,* in ibid., Vols. IX, X.

P. 184   "I walked along . . .": ibid., Vol. IX, p. 149.

P. 185   "The name of political economy . . .": ibid., pp. 277–278.

"In daylight . . . like a child": ibid., pp. 311–312.

P. 186   "Take now . . . an almshouse": ibid., Vol. I, pp. 291, 292.

P. 187   "raise wages . . . nobler heights": ibid., p. 188.

P. 189   A reviewer in *Argonaut:* C. A. Barker, *Henry George* (New York: Oxford University Press, 1955), p. 318; see Henry George Scrapbook, no. 24; New York Public Library, p. 7.

A friend asked him: I cannot locate this source.

"I will not insult . . .": Stephen B. Cord, *Henry George: Dreamer or Realist?* (Philadelphia: University of Pennsylvania Press, 1965), p. 39.

P. 190   "The Anglo-Saxon race . . .": J. A. Hobson, *Imperialism.* 2nd ed. (Ann Arbor, Mich.: University of Michigan Press, 1965), p. 160.

"France is needed by humanity": ibid.

Pobyedonostsev; the Kaiser: ibid.

P. 191   "a vast system of outdoor relief . . .": ibid., p. 51.

"these wretched colonies . . .": R. Palme Dutt, *Britain's Crisis of Empire* (New York: International Publishers, 1950), p. 18.

"Yes, the English are mentioned . . .": J. A. Hobson, quoted in *Confessions of an Economic Heretic* (London: George Allen & Unwin), 1938, p. 59.

Sir Charles Crossthwaite: Hobson, *Imperialism*, p. 50.

P. 192   "the middle stratum . . .": Hobson, *Confessions*, p. 15.

P. 193   "My intercourse with him . . .": ibid., p. 30.

"as equivalent in rationality . . .": ibid, p. 30.

P. 194   "timidest of God's creatures": ibid., p. 62.

"I was in the East End . . .": Dutt, op. cit., p. 22.

P. 197   "the endeavor of the great controllers . . .": Hobson, *Imperialism,* p. 85.

P. 198   "Imperialism, the highest phase . . .": *The Communist International, 1919–1943,* ed. Jane Degrad (London: Oxford University Press, 1960), pp. 480–481.

P. 199   "All the advantages . . .": Dutt, op. cit., p. 18.

P. 200   English overseas investment: see Halevy, *Imperialism and the Rise of Labour,* pp. 13–14; also Eric Hobsbawm, *Industry and Empire* (New York: Pantheon, 1968), p. 125

P. 205   Fay's anecdote: *Memorials of Alfred Marshall,* ed. A. C. Pigou (London: Macmillan, 1925), pp. 74, 75.

P. 207   "a whole Copernican system . . .": Keynes, *Essays in Biography,* p. 223.

P. 208   "the blades of a pair of scissors": Alfred Marshall, *Principles of Economics,* 9th variorum ed. (London: Macmillan, 1961), p. 348.

P. 209   "chivalry," ibid, p. 719.

"clerk with £100," p. 19.

"Political Economy," p. 43.

VIII: THE SAVAGE SOCIETY OF THORSTEIN VEBLEN

P. 214   Vanderbilt letter: Matthew Josephson, *The Robber Barons* (New York: Harcourt, Brace, 1934), p. 15.

P. 215   "What do I care about the law?": ibid.

P. 216   Rogers-Rockefeller transaction: ibid., p. 398.

P. 217   A. B. Stickney: ibid., 312.

"I owe the public nothing": ibid., p. 441.

P. 218   "A very strange man, Thorstein Veblen": biographical data from Joseph Dorfman, *Thorstein Veblen and His America* (New York: Viking, 1947).

P. 220   Veblen on religion: "Salesmanship and the Churches, " in *The Portable Veblen,* ed. Max Lerner (New York, 1950), p. 504.

"an advertisement . . . of ferocity": Thorstein Veblen, *The Theory of the Leisure Class* (New York: Modern Library, 1934), p. 265.

P. 222   "From my earliest recollection . . .": Dorfman, op. cit., p. 12–13

P. 224   "He was lucky enough . . .": op. cit., p. 56.

P. 225   On Laughlin's death: Dorfman, op. cit., p. 517.

P. 226   "When I entered the room . . .": ibid., p. 118.

"In a low creaking tone . . .": ibid., 249.

P. 227   "Why, it was creepy . . .": ibid., p. 316.

P. 228   "It fluttered the dovecotes . . .": ibid., p. 194.

P. 229   "A certain king of France . . .": Veblen, *Theory of the Leisure Class*, p. 43.

"We all feel, sincerely . . .": ibid., p. 156.

P. 231   "The discipline of savage life . . .": "Christian Morals," in *The Portable Veblen,* p. 489.

P. 232   "In order to stand well . . .": Veblen, *Theory of the Leisure Class*, p. 30.

P. 234   "The book, I am creditably told . . .": Dorfman, op. cit., p. 220.

P. 236   "The iron rails have broken . . .": Josephson, op. cit., p. 136n.

P. 237   "the lines are located in good country . . .": ibid., p. 245.

P. 238   "Doubtless this form of words . . .": "The Captain of Industry" from *Absentee Ownership and Business Enterprise,* in *The Portable Veblen,* p. 385n.

P. 239   "throws out anthropomorphic habits . . .": Thorstein Veblen, *The Theory of Business Enterprise* (New York: Scribner's, 1932), p. 310

P. 240   "There is nothing in the situation . . .": Thorstein Veblen, *The Engineers and the Price System* (New York: Harcourt, Brace, 1963), p. 151.

P. 241   "the tapeworm's relations to his host . . .": "The Case of Germany, " in *The Portable Veblen,* p. 555.

P. 242–243   "Veblenism was shining in full brilliance . . .": Dorfman, op. cit., p. 492.

P. 243   "He took a hatchet . . .": ibid., p. 456.

P. 244   Veblen's will: ibid., p. 504.

"the high gloss . . .": Veblen, *Theory of the Leisure Class,* pp. 131–132.

"The vulgar suggestion of thrift . . .": ibid., p. 134.

The irrepressible Mencken: Dorfman, op. cit., p. 423.

P. 246   "A gang of Aleutian islanders . . .": Thorstein Veblen, *The*

Place of Science in Modern Civilization (New York: Capricorn Press, 1918), p. 193

His pupil, Wesley Clair Mitchell: Dorfman, op. cit., p. 505.

IX: THE HERESIES OF JOHN MAYNARD KEYNES

P. 248   Veblen's investment: Dorfman, op. cit., pp. 485–486.

P. 249   John J. Raskob . . . "He will be rich": Frederick Allen, *Only Yesterday* (New York: Bantam Books, 1931), p. 345.

P. 252   Bertrand Russell: Roy Harrod, *The Life of John Maynard Keynes* (New York: Augustus Kelley, 1969), p. 135.

P. 253   Keynes biographical details from Harrod, ibid., and Robert Skidelsky, *John Maynard Keynes* (New York: Viking, 1986).

P. 254   "It was the usual stuff . . .": Harrod, op. cit., p. 26.

P. 255   "I want to manage a railway . . .": Skidelsky, op. cit., p. xxiii.

"I evidently knew more . . .": Harrod, op. cit., p. 121.

P. 257   "There was an urgent need . . .": ibid., p. 203.

Keynes contributed more: ibid., p. 206.

"I dislike being in the country . . .": ibid., p. 364.

P. 258   "It must be weeks . . .": ibid., p. 249.

Clemenceau "had only one illusion . . .": John Maynard Keynes, *The Economic Consequences of the Peace* (New York: Harcourt, Brace, 1920), p. 32.

Wilson "looked wiser when seated": ibid., p. 40.

P. 259   "The Council of Four . . .": ibid., pp. 226–227.

"The danger confronting us . . .": ibid., p. 228.

P. 260   Keynes as investor: Harrod, op. cit., pp. 297, 298.

Keynes as Bursar: ibid., p. 388.

P. 261   "But at first, of course . . .": ibid., p. 20.

P. 262   Planck and economics: ibid., p. 137.

P. 263   "These periodic collapses . . .": cited in John Maynard Keynes, *Essays in Biography,* New York: W. W. Norton, 1963, p. 273, 277.

Population projections: *U.S. Statistical Abstract,* 1997, U.S., p. 9, Table 3; World, p. 828, Table 1331.

P. 264   "What is prudence . . .": Smith, *Wealth,* p. 424.

P. 268   "It has been usual to think . . .": John Maynard Keynes, *A Treatise on Money,* Vol. II, pp. 148, 149.

P. 269   "To understand *my* state of mind . . .": Harrod, op. cit., p. 462.

P. 273   "Ancient Egypt . . .": John Maynard Keynes, *The General Theory of Employment, Interest, and Money* p. 131.

P. 275   "If the Treasury . . .": ibid., p. 129.

New York Times, June 10, 1934.

P. 278   "It is better that a man should tyrannize . . .": Keynes, *General Theory,* p. 374.

P. 278–279   "I should . . . the devil": Harrod, op. cit., p. 436.

P. 279   "How can I accept the [Communistic] doctrine": Charles

Hession, *John Maynard Keynes* (New York: Macmillan, 1984), p. 224.

P. 280 "Einstein has actually done . . .": I cannot rediscover the source.

P. 281 "Surely it is impossible . . . Three Cheers": Harrod, op. cit., pp. 477, 488.

P. 282 "Lenin is said to . . .": Keynes, *Economic Consequences,* p. 235.

P. 283 This evening, I participated . . .": Harrod, op. cit., p. 577.

Keynes's final speech: ibid., p. 584.

P. 284 "No such luck": ibid., p. 617.

economists should be humble: John Maynard Keynes, "Economic Possibilities for Our Grandchildren," in *Essays in Persuasion* (New York: W. W. Norton, 1963), p. 373.

P. 285 Sir Harry Goschen: op. cit., p. 222.

"The study of economics . . .": Keynes, *Essays in Biography,* pp. 140–141.

P. 286 Blinder, R. Heilbroner and W. Milberg, *The Crisis of Vision in Modern Economic Thought* (New York, Cambridge University Press, 1995), p. 46.

X: THE CONTRADICTIONS OF JOSEPH SCHUMPETER

P. 290 "Don't mourn for me . . .": Keynes, *Economic Possibilities for Our Grandchildren,* p. 367.

P. 292 ". . . a century is a 'short run' ": Joseph A. Schumpeter, *Capitalism, Socialism and Democracy* (New York: Harper & Bros., 1942, 1947), p. 163.

"Can capitalism survive? . . .": ibid., p. 61.

For biographical details see Arthur Smithies, "Memorial," *American Economic Review,* 1950, pp. 628–645; Gottfried Haberler, "Joseph Alois Schumpeter," *Quarterly Journal of Economics,* August 1950, pp. 333–384; Christian Seidl, "Joseph Alois Schumpeter: Character, Life and Particulars of the Graz Period, " in *Lectures on Schumpeterian Economics,* Christian Seidl, ed. (Berlin: Springer Verlag, 1984), pp. 187–205; Seymour Harris, ed., *Schumpeter: Social Scientist* (Cambridge, Mass.: Harvard University Press, 1951).

"never a beginner": Haberler, op. cit., p. 340.

P. 293 "All knowledge and habit . . .": J. A. Schumpeter, *The Theory of Economic Development* (Cambridge, Mass.: Harvard University Press, 1949), p. 84.

P. 296 "We shall understand . . .": ibid., pp. 89–90.

P. 297 "First there is the dream . . .": ibid., pp. 93–94.

P. 298 "If somebody wants to commit suicide . . .": Haberler, op. cit., p. 345.

P. 298 "Annie," Robert Loring Allen, *Opening Doors* (New Brunswick, N.J., Transactions Publishers, 1991), p. 193.

P. 300   "But the sociological drift . . .": J. A. Schumpeter, *Business Cycles* (New York: McGraw-Hill, 1939), Vol. II, p. 1050.

"one of the most brilliant men . . ." and "the less said . . .": "Review of Keynes's *General Theory*," *Journal of the American Statistical Association*, December 1936.

P. 301   "The evolution of the bourgeois style . . .": Schumpeter, *Capitalism, Socialism and Democracy*, p. 126.

P. 302   conquest of the air: ibid., p. 117.

"Perennial gale . . .": ibid., pp. 84, 87.

"Capitalism creates a critical frame of mind . . .": ibid., p. 143.

P. 303   "tendency toward another civilization . . .": ibid., p. 163.

"Can socialism work?": ibid., p. 167.

Marx—a conservative: ibid., p. 58.

monopolies increase influence of better brains: ibid., p. 101.

capitalist nations less aggressive: ibid., pp. 128–129.

P. 306   "We can assume that every healthy man . . .": Schumpeter, *Theory of Economic Development*, p. 81, n. 2.

P. 307   About a quarter of the population: ibid.

the true elite: ibid.

"The upper strata . . .": Schumpeter, *Capitalism, Socialism and Democracy*, p. 156.

P. 308   "Here is a class . . .": ibid., p. 204.

flesh out a larger "vision": J. A. Schumpeter, *History of Economic Analysis* (New York: Oxford University Press, 1954), p. 41.

"Analytic work embodies . . .": ibid., p. 42.

P. 309   Marshall's view of consumer goods, *Principles,* p. 64.

aristocracy of talent: see discussion by Smithies, op. cit., 634–637.

P. 310   one scholar has suggested: Seidl, op. cit., p. 197, n. 55.

XI: THE END OF THE WORLDLY PHILOSOPHY?

P. 314   Mankiw, *Principles of Economics* (Ft. Worth, Tex.: Dryden Press, 1997), p. 18.

Stiglitz, *Economics* 2nd ed. (New York: W.W. Norton, 1996).

P. 317   Marshall, "human nature" *Principles*, p. 32.

P. 320   Comparative management compensation, *The State of Working America,* 1998–1999, Economic Policy Institute (New York, Cornell University Press, 1999), p. 213; upward mobility of the poor, *Business Week,* Feb. 26, 1996, p. 90.

Index

345

About the Author

ROBERT L. HEILBRONER has been studying the great economists ever since he was introduced to them in Harvard University in 1936. He was graduated summa cum laude and Phi Beta Kappa and went on to practice economics in government and business and then to complete his graduate studies at the New School for Social Research. *The Worldly Philosophers*, his first book, achieved an immediate success with its publication in 1953 and has been translated into three dozen languages and become a standard introduction to economics in scores of colleges and universities. Most recently, *Twenty-First Century Capitalism* and *Visions of the Future* have also reached a wide public, both academic and general. Dr. Heilbroner, Norman Thomas Professor of Economics at the New School, has lectured before many business, government, and university audiences, and has received numerous honors including election as vice president of the American Economic Association and nomination as Scholar of the Year by the New York State Council of the Humanities. He is married and lives in New York City.